PERSPECTIVES

PERSPECTIVES • HUGH DOWNS

Turner Publishing, Inc.

Atlanta

Library of Congress Cataloging-in-Publication Data
Downs, Hugh.
Perspectives/by Hugh Downs.—1st ed.
p. cm.
ISBN: 1-57036-219-X
I. Title.
AC8.D759   1995
081—dc20   95-1432
CIP

Published by Turner Publishing, Inc.
A Subsidiary of Turner Broadcasting System, Inc.
1050 Techwood Drive, N.W.
Atlanta, Georgia 30318

Distributed by Andrews and McMeel
A Universal Press Syndicate Company
4900 Main Street
Kansas City, Missouri 64112

First Edition
10 9 8 7 6 5 4 3 2 1

Printed in the U.S.A.

PERSPECTIVES

C ONTENTS

Introduction

HUGH DOWNS is a very special person. I think people sense that just by watching him on television and listening to him on radio—that there is something very deep yet very approachable in him, a bit like someone we know whose accomplishments far exceed our own but whose person is always accessible to us.

He has been entertaining and informing Americans for more than fifty years. According to the *Guinness Book of Records*, he has appeared more hours on television than any other personality anywhere in the world. He is currently the cohost of the top-rated ABC News broadcast 20/20.

Hugh Downs is a genuine intellect, having read all 132 volumes of *The Great Books of the Western World* (he vowed to do it in seven years, although it took him thirteen). He is a scientist and a member of the President's Circle of the National Academy of Sciences and the Institute of Medicine. He cochairs the Research and Education Committee of the Geriatrics Advisory Board of the Mount Sinai Medical Center. He is Chairman of the Board of Governors of the National Space Society, and he has served as a member of the National Aeronautics and Space Administration (NASA) Advisory Council. He is Chairman of the Board of the United States Committee for UNICEF and a Trustee of the Menninger Foundation.

That's just the official list. Hugh Downs is also an avid explorer of both air and water "oceans." He is a pilot and a sailor and a SCUBA diver. Hugh Downs is a gentle man of great passion who loves to listen and to learn. He truly keeps an open mind. His warmth is genuine. He is honest and sincere. And I think that is what we all sense when he smiles at us on the picture tube or through the radio speaker.

I met Hugh when I was named producer of *Perspective*, a weekly public affairs broadcast on the ABC Information Radio Network. I quickly realized that Hugh's ten-minute essays were unique and so very special that they should not be consigned forever to the ether of space; they should be preserved and savored over time.

It did not take me long to envision this book—a collection of the warmest and most fascinating of Hugh's stories in logical progression, starting with some personal recollections and progressing through history, the arts, human nature, and the future. It is thought-provoking reading, the perfect antidote to the cares and tensions of the day. I hope you enjoy the pages ahead, that you are delighted and stimulated by these essays from a man who cares passionately about us, our world, and our times.

Rob Sunde
Stamford, Connecticut
January 1995

RECOLLECTIONS

Fifty Years of Broadcasting

IT'S HARD FOR ME TO BELIEVE that more than a half century has gone by since I first started broadcasting. May 1939 was a strange month. Every week a headline of heavy import. At its beginning, baseball's Lou Gehrig ended his record streak of consecutive games for the N.Y. Yankees— 2,130 of them. Of course, shortly afterward, Gehrig was forced out of baseball by the muscle-wasting disease that now bears his name. The next week, on May 7, Spain quit the League of Nations, its civil war over and its dictator, Franco, firmly in power.

Another week and Ruby Stevens Fay married Spangler Arlington Brugh. Why did this make headline news? Because their screen names were Barbara Stanwyck and Robert Taylor. It was devastating news to young single men and women.

Advance now one more week to May 22. On this date Italy and Germany signed a ten-year "Pact of Steel" binding them with the declared objective of reorganizing Europe, which meant, of course, conquering Europe. Czechoslovakia had collapsed two months earlier, and the Nazis now occupied Prague.

On the 29th, the last Monday in May, the local radio station in Lima, Ohio, hired me to go on its airwaves. I'd like to claim that it was because they felt the world was in such a mess they ought to do something about it, but truth is, they were a super low-budget operation and could not afford anyone with any experience. Since I had no experience whatsoever, I was perfectly qualified. This may have been a monumental blunder on their part, but it was a great thing for me. I started my career as a broadcaster, and I did learn fast.

This all came about rather strangely. When 1939 came in, I was seventeen. I had graduated from high school in 1938 and, on a speech contest scholarship, had managed one year of college, but there was no prospect for more higher education unless I worked my way through. And so, with summer coming on, I began looking for a job.

It was Depression times, and job hunting was an exercise in futility. People were being laid off and were trying to get on the dole or trying to find anything with the WPA—these were people with job skills. At every place I applied, there was mixed humor and incredulity that I could be dumb enough to think a job might be available.

One day, after pounding the pavement, I stopped at a milk depot, where milk in gallon jugs was available at a discount rate. Carrying my gallon of milk, I walked past the bank building, which housed the studios and offices of the local radio station, WLOK. On a whim I stopped in and inquired of the redheaded receptionist behind the desk what it took to become a radio announcer. Without really looking at me, she said they had auditions on Friday. It was not Friday, so I picked up my milk jug and started to walk out. At that moment, the program director, Howard Donahoe, appeared in a doorway and said he would listen to me now. I set the milk jug back down and followed him into a small studio, where he gave me a piece of commercial copy—an ad for a paint store—seated me at a table with a gooseneck ribbon-velocity microphone hanging over it, and told me to read into the mike when the red light over the door went on.

When the red light came on, I read the one-minute commercial message, trying as much as I could to sound like the professionals I heard daily on the airwaves—men like Paul Sullivan, Peter Grant, Lowell Thomas. When I finished, the red light went off, and I sat there, somewhat stunned that I had had the audacity to think that I could ever be a professional broadcaster. After awhile, the studio door opened and the program director came back in. "That was very bad," he said, "It was terrible. But great oaks from little acorns grow."

He gave me some pointers that, at the time, I didn't quite realize were very valuable pointers. He told me to pay little attention to how I sounded, and a lot of attention to what I was saying—and then he offered me a job, part-time at first and in a few weeks full-time. Part-time, it paid $7.50 a week; full-time was a full $12.50.

The dollar was worth a lot more back then, but even so, this was not a get-rich-quick scheme. I went home and told my father about it, and he said, "I want you to continue looking for a job for a week, and if you can't find a job, then go with the radio station." I guess radio was new enough back then that my father couldn't imagine it as "work."

I've always thought, as far as my father was concerned, that I never did find a job. But those early experiences I had in broadcasting are worth more to me than all the time I have spent with the networks. I wouldn't trade them for anything. It was at this little 100-watt station in Ohio that I was introduced to the rudiments of narrating, interviewing, newscasting, special-events coverage, anchoring, disc-jockeying, emceeing, commentary, sports coverage, announcing, reporting, and hosting. I didn't master all that in those early years, but I was assigned to it all. I tried it all, and I was able to explore where, exactly, I might fit in this broad scheme of broadcasting.

At first it was an "ugly duckling" situation. You know the story, about the swan's egg that somehow found its way into a duck's nest. When the little cygnet hatched, it was ungainly and awkward, and wasn't like a duck at all, although it kept trying to be one. The cygnet was considered by the ducks to be an ugly duckling.

Most of the broadcasters I knew at the time were quite different from me. They had special talents or skills I didn't have. Many of them were singers or actors or had some other performing experience. I have to say, I noticed this with other colleagues even after my early days in radio. Steve Allen, for example, is a massively talented man. He is a musician, a composer, a pianist, and a comedian—and all that is in addition to being a gifted broadcast host. Merv Griffin was a famous singer before he ever hosted a talk show and even went on to become a powerful business mogul.

I always thought of myself as an oddball because I didn't know how to do anything but broadcast. And even at that, it wasn't difficult in auditions for clients to find someone better looking or someone with a louder, crisper voice. The result is, that out of about four hundred auditions, tryouts that I participated in, I won two. And one of those was a fluke.

The Aldrich Family, a prime-time situation comedy, which was usually broadcast out of New York to the network, came to Chicago once for some reason. The regular series announcer, Dwight Wiest, couldn't come with it, so they held auditions, and NBC staff announcers from the Central Division were invited to try out. Because of a communications glitch, no one showed up but me. The date that had been posted on the bulletin board was off by a day, but the local producer had mentioned it to me earlier and told me when it was to take place, so I was the only one to show up. In the control room, when I finally arrived (I had taken a train in from Wilmette on my day off), the producer, out of embarrassment for the poor showing, said to the New York agency man, "Boy, I'm glad he came here. He's a heavy hitter."

The New York guy said, "Who's he?" And the Chicago producer said, "That's Hugh Downs." And he made up some story about how good I was. The agency fellow from New York had no choice really. I was the only one who showed up at the audition, so I won. *The Aldrich Family* went on the air out of the Eighth Street Theater in Chicago with me as the announcer. It was the first time I'd been on network in prime time, and it was a big event. Everything was live in those days. So after the show went through afternoon rehearsals and a dress rehearsal about 6 P.M., it went on the air at 8 P.M. Chicago time, 9 P.M. for the Eastern stations. And then we repeated the whole thing at 11 P.M. for the West Coast stations. Big-ticket shows like this one provided a lot of employment for actors, musicians, and announcers.

Television then was only a dream, a possible one, but still a dream; commercially, it was still impractical. Personally, I couldn't believe that television would ever become as big as radio. My only experience with it had been at the 1939 World's Fair in New York when, as a tourist, I'd been on the little vide-cam unit that RCA had set up there. Like many others who had walked through the display that day, I saw myself on the tiny screen. It was almost a decade before television as a medium began to unfold commercially. Six years after the birth of TV at the New York 1939 World's Fair, I did my first real telecast on WBKB in Chicago. I'll never forget it.

I didn't own a set, and I had never seen a TV broadcast. The whole experience was extremely bizarre. They put several layers of thick Pan-Cake makeup on me, and I do mean caked. I got a real start when I looked at my cadaverous face in the mirror. The makeup artist assured me that I needed every bit of this facial paint or I wouldn't "look right." I figured they knew what they were doing.

I walked into the studio. It seemed pitch black, but more surprisingly, it must have been about 34°F in there. I couldn't believe it. I was shaking from the cold. I complained to a stagehand about how cold it was, but he just adjusted his gloves and grunted at me.

I sat down at the desk and arranged my papers, cleared my throat, and tried to prepare for the unknown. A second later I discovered why it was so cold. Four large banks of gigantic incandescent bulbs came on like the inside of a huge pottery kiln. My eyes immediately shut to small squints, and the floor manager came right up to me and gave me my cue. I could hardly read. In twenty seconds it was warm. Then it got hot. I began to sweat buckets under the torrent of lumens and the blaze of megacandle power. The makeup job suddenly began to break loose from my skin and migrate in pieces independently across my face; it must have looked like a bunch of miniature continents driven by tectonic-plate movement. Sweat poured down my back and into my shoes. At that moment, squinting into those banks of primitive artificial suns, I thanked God that I was completely wet—mainly because I sensed a very real danger that my seersucker suit might burst into flames. Television has certainly come a long way.

When I finished this ordeal (this was in the fall of 1945), I asked if there was a way I could see a television broadcast. I was told they would be doing another one in forty-five minutes, and I was welcome to stay and watch it in the lobby of the Balaban and Katz Theater. So I did. I watched my first television program after I had broadcast my first program.

I had no idea that this new medium would one day become the tail that would wag the dog—or that television would treat me much better than radio had. I still think that radio is, in many ways, more interesting than TV. Television performs a marvelous service for viewers, but radio can do things for listeners that television can't do for viewers, especially when it comes to imagination. And, if you happen to be on the other side of the mike, radio is a lot more comfortable.

What will the next fifty years bring? In addition to Dick Tracy-type wrist radios with "main frame" power, personal phone communicators, and mass communications broadcast fare, there will probably be inexpensive HDTV (high-definition TV)—perhaps even disposable sets that can be unfolded, play for five or six hours, and then discarded and recycled. There is always the potential for a better-educated electorate, too.

I've already started my second half century of broadcasting. When I finish the next fifty years, I hope you'll tune in and help me celebrate— if you're not too old.

Stage Fright

AFTER MORE THAN A HALF CENTURY of broadcasting, I've grown accustomed to speaking in front of large audiences. I honestly can say that I'm actually comfortable doing it. But this was not always true. In fact, for years, at the beginning of my career, I suffered horribly from both stage fright and mike fright. The very idea of standing alone in front of large groups of people, or of addressing a vast radio audience through a bulbous contraption wrapped in wire mesh would make my knees weak, turn my blood to ice water, and provide me with the unmistakable feeling that I was making a slow descent into the infernal realms.

There were horrors and there was stark terror. This may be hard to believe, but when I started in the business, announcers deliberately tried to distract one another while on the air, to break them up; some actually employed forms of terrorism.

Imagine, if you will, that you are standing in front of a live microphone clutching your script in your sweaty little palms and that you are about to read a live news broadcast. Sweat is dripping down the back of your continuously wobbling knees, and you try to take a few deep breaths to relax. Your eyes are fixed on the director in the control booth. Suddenly, the director's hand comes down, and you begin reading the news to millions of Americans glued to their radios. Now comes the terror. Slowly, quietly, a colleague of yours (probably one who calls himself a friend) walks out of the shadows and saunters up to your microphone, takes out a fat Zippo lighter, and calmly ignites the bottom corner of the script you are reading. Suddenly, you have a handful of burning, smoking papers. I'm not kidding; people really did this.

The trick was to finish reading the news in as calm a voice as possible before the script disappeared from your hands in smoke. The other part of the trick was to escape with only a first- or, at the worst, a second-degree burn.

Of course, if you had any spunk at all, you would not submit to such treatment without a fight. You'd try to put out the fire as quickly as possible and, at the same time, continue reading calmly so that nobody out there in radioland caught on that something was desperately wrong back in the studio. I have to admit that prerecording (the way most programming is done today, on tape) has blunted some of the most penetrating edges of broadcasting and left us with an all too predictable, even manicured, medium. In the old days, all of radio really was on fire with excitement, and sometimes it was literally on fire.

The audience undoubtedly sensed this tension, too. Even if they couldn't smell the smoke, they could smell true fear wafting out over the air waves. Mike fright and stage fright claimed the professional lives of radio performers as readily as jade daggers claimed the real lives of sacrificial victims in Mayan temples. In show business terms, performers still "die" on stage but rarely because they say anything or do anything horribly untoward. Tape allows producers, and even lawyers, to review performances in advance, thereby preventing any spectacular gaffes or spontaneous combustions that are known to have happened in the past.

I wonder, though, what was so frightening to me when people were not burning my script? What was so threatening about an unarmed but live microphone? A microphone, assuming that it has proper electrical connections and is in good repair, presents no physical danger, but to a neophyte it sure can bring on an unspecified dread, an anticipation that you are about to be visited by some nameless disaster. It is the anxiety and the apprehension that strangles, and therefore it's only the mind that generates stage fright. There is nothing (nothing concrete, that is) to be afraid of, nothing outside the mind.

The interesting thing about stage fright or mike fright is that most performers and reporters suffer from it to some degree. You certainly do not have to be a professional broadcaster or actor to suffer from stage fright. In a very real sense, it doesn't make a lot of difference if you feel faint in front of twelve million people, twelve thousand people, or twelve people. The symptoms are the same, the fear is just as real, and the cause can be traced back just as easily to one's imagination and the illusion of impending doom.

Some people are paralyzed by these feelings even during the most innocent of events, such as a dinner party or a business meeting. Even getting on an elevator with two other people can be uncomfortable for some folks.

Being afraid of small groups may be an odd reaction in a species that regards gregarious behavior as highly as we humans do. Cooperation and sharing information have helped human beings succeed in the world where other species have failed. But, despite our special refinement—our evolutionary mechanism of sociability—many human beings drop to their knees in fear when required to perform in front of, or just mingle with, even small groups of people.

Jeanne Martinet is the author of a book titled *The Art of Mingling*. Martinet's book is specifically designed to instruct people who recoil from public encounters and provide these wilting souls with verbal ammunition, mental courage, and special instruments of social engagement with which they may emerge triumphant from both dinner parties and elevators alike. It's amazing that such an instruction manual is needed, but here it is.

Whether or not this little book will leave an indelible mark on human society, the techniques Martinet suggests we use to combat fears of mingling are interesting ones. Virtually every remedy she proposes is based on manipulating the imagination. If you are afraid of a large group of people or a small group, you can successfully imagine things to be different and sail through the experience unscathed.

Pretend, we are told, that everyone in the room, except you, is naked. If this were true, if everyone at a party but you were not wearing clothes, then you would be in a particular position of authority over them. In fact, they'd look pretty silly next to you. This simple imaginative device has a very real power to impart social confidence in those who lack it. But there is more.

"Pretend that you are invisible," Martinet says. This imaginative technique, she points out, is based on the very real truth that nobody at a party is paying attention to you anyway. People are generally self-absorbed. Even the most anxious, the most paranoid of attendees needn't worry that others are examining them because they probably aren't. Most people at parties worry about themselves, not about others. So if you imagine that you are invisible, you can gain a little breathing space and prepare for the moment when, through conscious will, you become visible once again.

Another suggestion is to turn invisibility on its head and to imagine that you are not yourself but someone else, someone famous or charismatic, someone worth emulating who would be admirable at a party. Martinet has a special fondness for imaging herself as Bette Davis as she appeared in the movie *All About Eve*. At this point, this book, which is really about how to mingle successfully at parties, crosses an important line and confronts acting and performance directly.

Playing the role played by Bette Davis permits Martinet to wave cigarettes as if they were magic scepters and to wear clothing with a high level of social proficiency. She becomes alluring. Nonsmokers might want to imagine themselves as nonsmoking heroes or heroines, and they can very easily. The point, however, is that a make-believe persona allows us to move in ways that the everyday persona does not.

We might dismiss these imaginative suggestions as whimsy and question the wisdom of relying on social crutches that depend on fantasy. But pretension goes a long way toward affecting the truth. Pretension may in fact be a foundation of truth. To pretend that something is true is more than just claiming something that is false is true. Pretend comes from the Latin *praetendere*, which means to assert. So by pretending something, we also assert something, and we positively put forward something real.

A poor student who pretends to be a smart student sometimes can not only convince others that he or she is smart, such students usually become smarter. We tend to live up to the things we assert. The principle is like tropical fish that grow to a size appropriate to the capacity of the tank in which they live. In the same way, we humans will sink down to, or rise up to, standards we set for ourselves. Don't forget that a bullet fired from a rifle goes where it is aimed.

Aiming is also pretending. A marksman first pretends that a bullet will hit the bull's-eye, and then, if the aim is sound, the bullet actually does hit the bull's-eye. When the bullet fires, what was once merely a pretension becomes a mark of accuracy. The same thing goes for these simple delusions at dinner parties. Imagine that you are a skilled raconteur and graceful socializer and eventually you will become one.

It may be that all human fear—even the worst ones, such as the fear of death or lethal torment or pain itself—operates along the same principles as stage fright, mike fright, and a fear of mingling in public. We may need nothing more to conquer such horrors than fertile imaginations and inner resolve.

Of course, some fears are different. Some fears cannot be overcome by any known power in the universe. One of them is having–some-one–set–your–radio–script–on–fire–and–trying–to–finish–reading–it –before–it–goes–up–in–smoke.

Summer

WHY IS IT THAT SUMMER BELONGS TO CHILDREN? Even grown-ups who relish summer find it mixed with more joyous memories than the other three seasons put together.

Spring is a season that doesn't come into its own until you are an adolescent: it is a season of awakening, and it isn't until some sap of adulthood begins to rise and to flow that a person can get a handle on what spring is all about. To a little kid, spring is a time of a lot of mud and being nagged about raincoats and overshoes and schoolwork and cold remedies.

Autumn requires even more maturity to appreciate. The bittersweet quality of fall is an acquired taste, and you don't acquire it until you are old enough to have learned that beauty is not all instant gratification. To a young child, fall means an end to summer play, a time to be sent back to school and face pressures that had been put on hold for the endless season of summer—the season of heat and freedom, of "field and water and weed."

It takes the poet in us to appreciate autumn. And children, as someone once said, are never poets because they are too busy being poems. Part of the innocence we lose growing up is that freedom from counting down to the end of pleasure. A child rarely thinks on a summer evening: "It's now 7:45, and that means I have only fifteen minutes until my mother calls me in." He rarely thinks: "It's now the 23rd of August, and that means I have less than two weeks of vacation before school starts again."

I remember when I was little my mother would call my brothers and me and announce the news that school would start the next day, and we would be shattered. No inkling that summer was all over. Till it was. Perhaps the compensation for the devastating nature of her announcement was that our unawareness of time gave summer a flavor of eternity. It was never going to end. The mood, right up to the end, was one of endless play. Part of the price of growing up is the realization that a day has 24 hours, a year 365 days, and a long human life about 35,000 days. And when you've spent 20,000 of them, you'll be 54 years old and know that you have very likely used up more than half of your life. If you don't become neurotic about this, chances are you will become philosophic about it. Then you will begin to appreciate autumn.

But summer is open for instant appreciation. The first dandelion, the first butterfly, the uncapped fire hydrant, the swimming hole, the fireworks of the Fourth, and the taste of potato salad at the family picnic all provide an immediate sense of wonder.

I remember that as a child I never understood why people complained about the heat. I was, in fact, unaware that there were degrees of heat and that some of them could be distressing. Summer was hot, winter was cold, and that was all there was to it. Playing hard in high heat and high humidity sometimes made us red in the face, which would cause one of my aunts to say, "My land, why don't you just sit down for awhile? You're going to get overheated." Then she'd ask my father if we could all go someplace in the car, only the way it was worded back then was would my father "take us for a ride in the machine?"

And if he did this—in our 1930 Dodge—we'd go not only with the windows down, but with the windshield cranked open about four inches above the dash, and my brothers and I would sit with our faces in the wind at that opening. We sped along at, maybe, 40 mph down a two-lane, concrete highway to the outskirts of Lima, where there was an ice-cream parlor with marble-top tables and wire-back chairs, and the marble felt cool even when the room was warm.

One of the things I miss in this age of air-conditioning (although I would not give up air-conditioning to get it back) is the drone of an electric fan. There was a black electric fan in our house, with about an eighth-horsepower motor running it, that could throw out hot air with enough velocity to cool you off if you got right in front of it. And if you went to sleep in front of it, you could get neuralgic pain or, all the older people believed, catch a great head cold.

Often, as a summer day waned, we'd sit out on the porch (God, what happened to porches? They evolved, I guess, into patios and verandas, and the porch swing became a glider). In this now-distant era, I remember my family sitting out on the porch on the swing or on wicker rockers or canvas camp chairs, eating Jell-O and angel food cake (if the relations were visiting). We often listened to the radio there—*Chandu the Magician* and *Fibber McGee and Molly* and *Jack Benny* and *One Man's Family*. Sometimes our memories of these times may condense a few key incidents out of many evenings and many circumstances. I suppose all the memories are there, logged into the brain, and, although not immediately retrievable, are probably available under hypnosis, even the trivial and dull ones.

One sharp memory I have of such a summer evening involved a guest's car that was in our driveway, apparently parked without the emergency brake pulled up all the way. In the middle of a pleasant conversation, I saw my father leap up, wild-eyed, and in two strides vault over both the porch railing and a box-hedge and land, running, on our soft green lawn. My only thought at that moment was that his mind had snapped. (In those days we believed that people could "go crazy" with that kind of suddenness.) And then I saw our guest's empty car backing down our winding driveway toward the highway. It was gathering speed, but my father gained on it and got inside in time to apply the brakes and save the day.

Then, I was impressed by the physical prowess this action demonstrated. Of course, when I now reflect that at the time Dad was only thirty-one years old, it wasn't that big a deal. But I was not used to seeing him spring into action like that, and it deepened my perception of his heroism. I wanted to be able to do that. But nobody in the years since has parked a car in my driveway and left the brake off, so I've never had the opportunity.

That lawn, over which my father made his record sprint, was my job for the summer. I had to mow it, and grass grows fast in the summer. I would plug away at it—or peck away at it—and, with some prodding, would finish the far side just about the time the near side had grown back enough to need remowing. And we're not talking about a John Deere or Toro power mower here, either. This was done with an old reel mower with cast-iron wheels that had to be pushed with all your might. It was designed by a torture specialist, and one of his genius ideas was to attach the wooden handle to the tongue with a hexagonal bolt head right at the operator's midriff. That way, whenever the blades of the reel mechanism picked up a large twig and jammed, the machine would come to an abrupt halt, ramming the hexagonal bolt head into the operator's stomach and giving his navel a stone-bruise.

This happened, on average, every minute-and-a-half. But what time does for nostalgia! We can dross out the unpleasant elements and remember stone-bruised bellies as part of the Good Old Days. I can still hear in my mind (and would like to hear again with my ears) the sound of that old reel-type grass-cutting machine and the sound of those cast-iron wheels coming off the grass onto a piece of cement sidewalk. Like the summer thunder rolling across the Midwestern prairies, it's a sound that, for me, has receded into distant memories.

At the time, the lawn seemed to cover ten acres. I doubt it was a full acre. Although the task was neverending (maybe that's why summer seemed to spin on forever), lawn mowing did not occupy a very big percentage of my thoughts. In fact, I managed to enjoy summer far more than I realized I was enjoying it.

Is that really possible? Can we enjoy something and not fully realize that we are enjoying it? I've come to believe that it's entirely possible.

When was the last time you felt so good you thought you might burst? Those feelings belong to summer and childhood. But both summer and childhood are so immersed in good feelings that we take them for granted. It's only later, at other seasons and at older ages, that we can look back and know not just the extent, but the varied ways in which we enjoyed those times.

Two Happys

A GOOD MARRIAGE IS SUPPOSED TO BE A "HAPPY" MARRIAGE, but I've always thought that happy is a slightly misleading word. Some people think that happiness implies only good things without any bad. That's true, of course, but happiness can imply more than just good things. There is a second happiness that includes both good things and bad. This deeper happiness, or what I like to call "great happiness," implies that a thread of pain weaves its way through the pleasure to create a more mature fabric—a fabric fit to cloak the wise. Since some bad things are inevitable, this acceptance is a kind of wisdom.

Lesser happiness is one-dimensional because it is made up exclusively of pleasure. Great happiness, however, can encompass other feelings, including some painful ones. This curious phenomenon of the two happinesses lies at the root of the mystery of marriage, a subject I have been thinking about lately after attending the wedding of my nephew Jeff and a woman named Gwen. Their marriage made me think, in general, about how the real joy of marriage isn't the lesser happiness of simple pleasure; it's the mystery of a great happiness that weaves many things, good and bad, together.

Combining good and bad like this doesn't cancel them out, nor does it blend them into some unrecognizable mush: it tempers a deeper, more profound happiness. It's a little bit like combining tin with copper. Both are soft metals, but when mixed together they make bronze, which is much stronger than either. Successful couples seem to do something similar when they incorporate the inevitable unpleasant aspects of life as integral parts of their lives. Most brides and grooms are given this kind of advice when they get married. They are warned that life is dynamic and will swing from pleasure to pain and back again. Life guarantees such swings. Successful couples learn to weave unavoidable unpleasantness into the greater tapestry of their marriage.

During the service for my nephew and his bride, the minister announced that all of the married couples in attendance would be renewing their vows privately as they heard the bride and groom publicly proclaim theirs. This struck me because my wife and I had already, intuitively, sensed such a renewal. We had already felt that the words being spoken to our nephew and his bride were directed at us. Other couples later said they felt the same way and had been holding hands.

The service covered all the usual warnings about staying together in sickness and in health and when richer or poorer, but even though I'd heard the words many times, the words seemed as fresh that day as when I heard them at my own wedding decades ago—a good thing, too, because marriage requires constant renewal.

Some couples actually will perform a second marriage service (we did once), but that's not necessary. All couples really need to do to renew their faith in one another is to communicate. Ideally, marriage should be renewed every day by getting to know one another.

It may seem corny to say "I love you" (and for some men it seems to sticks in their throats), but it doesn't hurt. I've seen marriages that didn't get renewed. They didn't last either. I've had friends whose marriages suffered terrible troubles and then dissolved. As an outsider I could never know whether the split was an improvement for them or not (maybe that's something only the parties involved ever really know for sure), but I believe that a lack of communication ultimately destroyed these marriages. The formula was always the same: somebody had a problem, and somebody else could never understand. No one communicated.

No marriage is exempt from problems, and communication may be the only way to resolve them. In fact, if marriage can be considered miraculous at all, then communication is proof of that miracle. If taken in stages, the miracle is actually pretty easy to carry off. The first stage is to just listen.

Making time to listen to your mate is as important to a marriage as a blank canvas is to a painting. Not even Rembrandt could paint a painting if he didn't have a blank space on which to paint. Listening provides the same thing in marriage. Both partners need an attentive silence upon which they may create their flourish of the marriage. Anyone unfamiliar with this process can always begin with four simple words: "How was your day?" Once you've asked this question, sit back and start paying attention to the miracles that will follow.

Listening is not a passive activity. A good listener works as hard as the person talking. When the speaker is finished speaking (and everyone finishes if they are given enough time), then the listener can speak. Communication sounds simple, but looking at the number of failed marriages that litter the landscape, communication must be more difficult in practice than it sounds in theory. Communication is a skill, after all, and, like anything, requires a lot of practice to make it work well.

But the good part about communication is that if a couple, even a couple of dullards, practices it every day, they will surely communicate better. It only takes a little quiet time each day, without newspapers, radios or televisions, for two people to get good at understanding one another. Making time is making a miracle.

Communication links two minds together and is the first knot with which life's poignancy can be woven into a tapestry. Couples who communicate well can reinterpret the adversity that befalls them. During the marriage ceremony, a bride and groom are expected to communicate to one another: I so-and-so take thee . . . et cetera. Unfortunately, many couples seem to forget that the whole idea of marriage is nothing but lifelong communication. They are supposed to keep talking—and keep listening.

The daily gift of silence to one's spouse is no small matter. The act of giving is itself intimately intertwined with sanctity. The word sacrifice, for example, means to make something sacred, in other words, make something extremely important. Sacrifice also implies giving something up. A good marriage involves giving up something of value to the other person, but the gift should be offered in the sense of sacrifice. We can give up talking for silence, or television for a walk; we can give up any number of things to provide something that a spouse may value or appreciate.

Sacrifice means more than loss. The loss—something that ordinarily might be considered a deprivation—is transformed by sacrifice into a type of gain, and gain is something good. A keen sense of the importance of giving up certain things can contribute to an overall sense of "great happiness," the deeper happiness that weaves a strand of something bad with something good.

An ordinary married couple gains a certain authority when the partners show such faith in each other. This authority is so powerful that marriage ceremonies in a variety of traditions often suggest the coronation of royalty, for centuries the highest form of authority on earth. The simple act of faith in another human being, by marriage, predates any religion and may even be the archetype of religion. In a sense, the married couple imitates the workings of the universe itself, since many married couples have the power and authority to create whole new universes on their own: their children.

Throughout much of Asia, and for many centuries, the uttermost representation of God was neither that of a man nor of a woman alone, but of a married couple described as father-mother and depicted in divine conjugation. In the West, brides and grooms were sometimes crowned with wreaths of flowers (sometimes with actual crowns of gold or silver) in an effort to suggest their divine authority. Some wedding ceremonies conclude with a procession that circumambulates the wedding ground the way monarchs used to circumambulate the territories over which they ruled.

Religious ceremony goes to great lengths to make a bride and groom feel sacred. But ritual, at best, can only be an outer expression of an inner process. In the end, after the wedding is over and the guests have gone home, the bride and groom are left to perpetuate that sanctity by themselves. That's not easy. And that's why every day demands some effort to renew a marriage. Every day must have some small sacrifice.

Considering that most married couples see themselves less as divine royalty ruling the universe and more as sweating members of humanity's proletariat, the most important sacrifice one spouse can make to the other (aside from the gift of silence) is to relinquish the inevitable rage at life. There is no communication if there is anger. Defusing anger is hard. Even recognizing anger can be difficult.

Angry people can honestly believe they are resolving a problem without realizing that anger is a problem itself. Anger is a disturbance and an impediment to problem solving. Recognizing anger is a tremendous step toward sacrificing the anger, in other words, toward giving it up and turning it into something useful—toward weaving it into the tapestry of the marriage.

Even profound turmoil like anger can be sacrificed and made into something good. After fifty years of marriage, I believe this is true. Marriage is more than just being happy; it can provide a special type of happiness, a "great happiness," one that weaves unpleasant things, like worries, into amiable ones, like pleasure, to form the warp and the weft of a sturdy fabric.

Great literature demonstrates the importance of this strange alliance of good and bad. A good story must have some element of bad woven into it or it is not much of a story at all. Stories described as "touching" imply that they touch some poignancy—something disturbing or painful—and people cherish touching stories over bland ones.

I hope my nephew Jeff and his bride, Gwen, are finding this deeper kind of happiness, the "great happiness" that can sacrifice adversity and turn it into something good. They appear to be doing so. In fact, in this age of devalued values, I hope more married couples might stumble onto the mystery of the two kinds of happiness. Both of them are available.

Underwater World

IF YOU ARE ALREADY A DIVER, or if you have snorkeled on the surface with a mask, or maybe just stared through a glass-bottom boat once—if you've done any of these things, then you have seen the underwater world and you know that it's endlessly fascinating. I often think that many people who would like to explore the ocean floor by diving (but who are nervous about their air supply or sharks or elements unknown) shut themselves out of an enormously rewarding activity that could open up to them if they could just muster the tiniest self-push forward.

First of all, let me say there is nothing abnormal about being a little afraid of plunging into an environment in which you can't breathe. But that fear can be overcome in most cases, and it's easier and safer than you think.

Scuba diving has become very big in the last fifty years. It has been a hobby of mine for over thirty of those fifty years, and at one time, for a brief period, I taught diving. While I am certified (which amounts to being licensed) as a diver, I am not certified at present to teach, but I did in the '50s because standardized certification didn't exist when I started diving or when I taught it. The equipment sold today is much more sophisticated, much more dependable and safer than the gear you could get when I started.

It was only twenty years before the time I started diving that the whole idea of scuba became a reality. The letters s-c-u-b-a stand for "self-contained underwater breathing apparatus." There had been an apparatus for breathing underwater for nearly a century before that, but it was not self-contained. The first attempts at diving (without having to hold one's breath) involved putting a bucket over the head of the diver. This usually resulted in the diver passing out underwater because it was not understood that inhaling and exhaling turned the oxygen in the bucket into carbon dioxide. Asphyxiation takes place rather swiftly if you are rebreathing the same small amount of air.

So divers quickly learned that if they wanted to survive underwater, they needed fresh air to breathe. The bucket became a helmet, and an air hose connected to pumps on the surface (or on the deck of a ship) pumped fresh air under pressure down to the submerged swimmer. The spent air was released harmlessly into the sea. A diver could stay down as long as fresh air was pumped into the helmet.

Obviously, long air hoses and gas-operated compressors are not "self-contained." Self containment of one's air supply remained the Holy Grail of divers for many years. But how could this be achieved? They couldn't go back to the bucket and rebreathe old air, since that was lethal. How could they get rid of the long hoses and the surface pumps and swim freely like fish and move with the sovereignty of great ocean-going mammals?

Two methods were developed, one open and one closed. The closed method allowed the diver to rebreathe the same air after the carbon dioxide was removed. Rebreathers used filters to do this. Closed rebreathers are complicated and considerably less reliable than the open-circuit approach. The open approach simply compresses an hour's worth of fresh air into a tank, which the diver carries on his or her back. The used-up air, the carbon dioxide, is easily exhaled back into the sea in a trail of bubbles. But figuring out how to breathe compressed air was a trick in itself.

Air pressure at sea level is about 14 pounds per square inch. A rigid metal scuba tank can hold air at between 2,500 and 3,000 pounds per square inch. This supply can last for many breaths, but there's a problem. How do you get the air out of the tank at the correct pressure? You could build a step-down valve to reduce the pressure from 3,000 to 14 pounds, and that would be fine at sea level, but water pressure increases as you go deeper. At thirty-two feet down in seawater the pressure doubles to 28 pounds per square inch. No human being has strong enough chest muscles to work against that kind of pressure. You'd never get a breath. So the regulator had to be adjusted at each new depth. It had to step down tank pressure to a breathable pressure equal to the depth. It seemed

ridiculous to burden a diver with such complicated technical adjust-
ments for every few feet descended —— somehow the device had to do
this on its own.

Jacques Cousteau solved the problem: he invented the demand regulator, which senses the sea pressure at any depth and gives the diver, on
demand, the exact amount of pressure needed to compensate. The
inside and outside pressure is continuously compensated. If a diver is 64
feet down, the outside sea pressure is about 42 pounds per square inch.
When the diver demands a breath and starts to inhale, the air comes out
of the tank at the correct pressure of 42 pounds, and she breathes as easily and as naturally as if she were at surface. At 64 feet down, a full breath
of air contains three times the amount of oxygen as a breath taken at sea
level. Breathing this kind of compacted, concentrated air can actually
last longer than a sea-level breath—you don't feel the need to breathe
as often.

That's the good news. The bad news is that the breath at 42 pounds
of pressure also brings three times as much nitrogen, the other, and most
common, gas in air. If absorbed into the blood, this nitrogen will bub-
ble out as froth when the diver returns to the surface. This dangerous
condition is what they call "the bends." If these bubbles come out in the
brain or the spine, they can dry brain and nerve tissue and produce
stroke-like effects.

While the bends is a serious condition, it can be avoided completely
by not exceeding certain limits of bottom time. If you simply follow recommended diving tables, you can safely avoid this condition. You can
dive in shallow depths for hours with no danger at all. But the deeper
you go, the shorter your safe bottom time becomes. Even if you do
exceed the time limits, you can still avoid the bends by decompressing
slowly, either by rising gradually and stopping for the prescribed length
of time about every twelve feet or so, or by resurfacing and going into a
decompression chamber.

Diving, when done properly, can be safer than many sports not associated with danger. In fact, I've always believed that diving is easier than

swimming, although I wouldn't recommend it for nonswimmers. If you take up diving, learn how to swim first. But consider this: when you are swimming in water over your head, you have to keep your head out of the water at least part of the time in order to breathe. With scuba diving, you don't. You can sink to the bottom and go to sleep if you want. Your air supply is firmly clenched between your teeth.

There's a good group called the Moray Wheels, which comprises handicapped divers, some of whom are wheelchair bound. But when they are underwater, they swim as well as fish and nonhandicapped divers. Diving is superb for anyone who has problems with joints or limbs and who needs to get away from gravity for awhile.

After more than thirty years of diving, there are still surprises for me in adventurous situations, in unfamiliar life, or in using new equipment or technology. Of course, that's what keeps the sport fresh for me, as fresh as when I first submerged in a swimming pool to learn it.

Seventeen years ago I did a night dive off the Great Barrier Reef in Australia. We went down about seventy feet with a powerful light, and a variety of fish came up to us to stare for awhile. Many years later, at a meeting of the Ocean Trust Foundation in San Salvador, a night dive was organized. Eleven of us on the board were divers. The organizers asked how many of us had done night dives, and about five of us raised our hands. Among the five were Dr. John McClosker, curator of the Steinhardt Aquarium in San Francisco, and Dr. Sylvia Earle, an oceanographer who holds depth records in different kinds of diving. I didn't realize at first what they had in mind.

When I learned what they were seriously proposing, I was incredulous. Get this: on a moonless, overcast night, they wanted to descend to a depth of 125 feet without lights. I could hardly believe it, but I was intrigued and felt that I had to try it. After the dive boat arrived at the edge of the ocean shelf about two miles offshore and anchored in sixty feet of water, the captain extinguished all on-board lights, including the running lights. At that moment I learned what dark was.

As we slipped into that inky water, one by one, I decided I'd climb down the anchor chain to the bottom, and if I didn't like what was happening, I'd climb back up (never letting go of that chain) and get back on deck. About halfway down, my eyes dilated wider to compensate for the darkness, and I saw that tiny phosphorescent creatures in the water glowed when agitated. Soon I could see the ghostly outlines of other divers as they moved near me.

I let go of the anchor chain and stayed near one of the divers, who turned out to be Sylvia. We all moved toward the edge and, on reaching it, went down another sixty-five feet. By then my eyes were so used to the dark that I could see a whole busy world on the cliff wall we floated near: little fish with phosphorescent lights under their eyes going about like little Chevrolets, spotting things to eat and then grabbing them and darting away.

Dr. McClosker had plastic bags with him. He managed to retrieve two specimens of a species that he knew existed in the Mediterranean and that he had suspected were also in the Caribbean. His find made *The New York Times* the next day. After about a half hour of this midnight minuet, where only the life forms glowed, we all surfaced and could see the dark shadow of the dive boat interrupting the string of distant shore lights.

I've always been respectful and slightly fearful of the sea, but running against this attitude is the strangely comfortable feeling that I belong where I am when I'm diving. There may be an atavistic sense of where we came from eons ago. It has been pointed out that when life came out of the sea and onto the land, it brought some of the sea with it—not only water, but salt. The salinity of our blood is about the same as that of the sea. It is red only because the corpuscles that carry oxygen also contain iron oxide, the metal compound responsible for rust. We are, as one anthropologist has said, "bags of sea water." We weep and sweat and bleed salt—so we've never really gotten that far away from our initial, ocean home.

Now that we have the technical capability of returning to the sea in free diving by taking along our precious air supply in a scuba tank, it is perhaps natural that we have a right to feel at home—day or night—in the deep ocean.

Harleys and Open Roads

MY FATHER'S GENERATION saw travel accelerate from one-horsepower horses to rocket ships with literally millions of horsepower. Not one to be left behind, my father was once the proud owner of a 1914 Harley-Davidson motorcycle. My father passed away a few years ago, and his bike was gone the better part of a century before that. Somehow I sense a rebirth of both of them in the new fashion of motorcycling we see today.

My old man's Harley could eat up real estate like nothing else, which in 1914 was saying quite a lot. There couldn't have been more than a few miles of paved highways in 1914, and motorcycles, like all vehicles back then, had to be capable of what (today) we call "off-road" travel. Part of the charm of riding a motorcycle in the wee hours of the twentieth century was the remarkable practice of accelerating rapidly just before a large chuck-hole and spanning its yawning maw in a single bound. My father was particularly fond of recounting those moments of limited flight.

As I got older I began to see that the association of motorcycle operation and flight was more than coincidence. There seemed to be a metaphor at work that linked the open road with the inner flight of spiritual edification. The invention of the motorcycle neatly fit this metaphor by providing a powerful icon of celestial sovereignty. My father was one of the very first human beings to recognize this. He never described motorcycle riding in religious terms, but he was nonetheless one of humanity's earliest devotees of the motorized pilgrimage.

I can't for the life of me remember who said it or when, but someone once said Americans revere motor vehicles as gods. Every year we sacrifice close to fifty thousand human beings to these gods upon an altar made of millions of miles of asphalt. I've passed many of these sacrifices and watched the flickering red ring of ritual flares illuminate somber highway priests performing the triage of the ill-fated. Seeing so many accidents made me wonder: how in the world did we wind up with roads and such bloodthirsty gods anyway?

The ancient Romans didn't invent roads. The Romans improved paving technology and laid straighter roads, but roads are much older than ancient Rome. When Julius Caesar struck north in his attempt to conquer the British Isles, he probably used roads that were already in existence because his march was supposed to have been accomplished in a matter of days. Even Julius Caesar couldn't have built a road from Italy to the coast of northern France in a few days. We can be fairly sure a road existed; we can be even more sure that it was unpaved. In that respect, I guess, my father's ditch-jumping Harley-Davidson roamed a world that closely resembled the unpaved roads of pre-Roman days—a humbling bit of historical continuity.

Most likely, the whole idea of roads goes back to hunting paths, which probably developed from the natural tracks made by animals as they moved through the bush. Even in distant prehistoric times, roads represented the promise of wealth and prosperity, because at their end mankind found gaggles of valuables on the hoof. The names of some modern roads, Route 66 and the Al-Can Highway, for example, continue to suggest images of hope and profit.

Henry Drummond, a turn-of-the-century British explorer in Africa, described a natural system of roads that must have been in place from the most ancient times. Drummond wrote, " . . . it may come as a surprise to the unenlightened to learn that probably no explorer in forcing his passage through Africa has ever, for more than a few days at a time, been off some beaten track. . . . Every village is connected with some other village, every tribe with the next tribe, every state with its neighbor, and therefore with all the rest. The explorer's business is simply to select from the network of tracks, keep a general direction, and hold on his way."

Ancient hunters followed game tracks through the bush to reap the rewards waiting for them at the end. Later, during the transition from the Neolithic period to the Bronze Age, roads led to commercial sites like tin, copper, and especially amber mines. Amber, a fossilized tree resin, made an enormous contribution to prehistoric commerce. Amber is beautiful, and it was used as jewelry, but also, when rubbed against cloth or human hair, amber develops the mysterious phenomenon called static electricity.

The ancient Greeks called amber *electrum* because it was associated with their sun god Elector, which is how we wound up with the modern word electricity. The modern Baltic states are home to one of Europe's largest deposits of amber. The roads connecting these fields with the countries of southern Europe have undoubtedly been in existence since prehistoric times.

The Romans prized amber even more highly than the Greeks. One expedition to the Baltic amber mines by Emperor Nero returned with over thirteen thousand pounds of the stuff. One writer tells us this amber was "used extravagantly at the amphitheater for weapons, games, and for the fastening of the cords which separated the front seats from the arena."

The word road is connected with both ride and raid. The only time the word road appears in the Bible, for example, is when David returns from a raid and Achish asks him, "Whither have you made a road today?" Shakespeare also uses road in the sense of an armed raid in *Henry V*, in which he writes, "The Scot who will make road upon us with all advantages." And again, in Coriolanus we read, "So then, the Volsces stand but as at first, ready, when time shall prompt them, to make road upon [us] again."

Maybe this early sense of the word road as a raid explains why we have such mixed feelings about the open road. There is a definite sense of foreboding associated with "the road" that contrasts sharply with the promises of hope, profit, or gain.

When Rudyard Kipling wrote, "He yearned beyond the sky-line, Where the strange roads go down," he struck a note similar to that struck by Marlon Brando a hundred years later in the movie *The Wild One*. Brando's character roared down strange roads on his Triumph (no, it wasn't a Harley) in a restless quest. I remember when I saw that film for the first time in the mid-1950s, the image seemed new and alarming:

motorcycle gangs raiding small towns in America. But the image wasn't new at all, raiding along roads goes all the way back to Neolithic hunters, who used roads to raid both game and each other.

By the nineteen-sixties the Japanese had radically changed the image of motorcycling. The introduction of Hondas, Yamahas, Kawasakis, and Suzukis transformed the outlaw image created by Brando's "Wild One" into the law-abiding image of the bike-riding ordinary citizen. Today's Harley biker could easily be raiding corporations, but hardly small towns. The megabucks biker was typified by multimillionaire magazine mogul Malcolm Forbes, who rode a Harley.

In 1984 all motorcycle manufacturers combined sold 1.3 million machines. In 1988 only about half a million were sold. The reason for the decline is simple: the biggest section of society that buys motorcycles, young men between eighteen and twenty-four, dropped in number dramatically between 1984 and 1988. Interestingly, while overall sales were down, sales at Harley-Davidson actually went up. In a way, I attribute this phenomenon to a rebirth of my father's style of biking.

My father was no outlaw biker. In 1914, when he bought his bike, a Harley-Davidson cost $700. To appreciate this, you should know that a brand-new Ford automobile only cost $400. According to my father, the Harley was engineered better, would last longer, and provided a vastly superior ride. He rode his Harley to classical music concerts performed in distant places like Columbus and Cincinnati, cities many miles from his farm home.

Maybe it was due to the supposed anti-intellectual feelings at the time, but my father said his mother, my grandmother, used to warn him, "Milton, if anyone asks you where you go on that motorcycle, you tell 'em you're seein' a girlfriend. Don't tell 'em you're driving a hundred miles to listen to that classical music stuff." I think if they were both alive today, my father would feel right at home roaring up to a performance of Mahler's Fifth with Malcolm Forbes's distinguished Harley gang. After all, my father pioneered the gentleman-biker image when Malcolm was still selling magazines on the street one at a time.

Harley-Davidson keeps selling motorcycles not just because they make a well-crafted machine, but because Harleys embody a peculiar spiritual reverence Americans have for the open road. Harleys have almost as much value sitting still, where they can be regarded as sculptural icons, as they do tooling down the highway, where they can be appreciated as practical methods of transportation. But there is one important caveat.

Motorcycles, like anything that pretends to the sacred, risk the wrath of the divine as much as its benevolence. Motorcycles can be dangerous, but most of the danger isn't from motorcycling, it's from automobile drivers who don't check their blind spots. Maybe it's because my father rode a bike, but looking out for motorcyclists before I make a sudden turn has always been a natural reflex for me.

The next time you get behind the wheel of a car, remember that there are millions of people who ride motorcycles. I see them now as modern-day expressions of a particularly ancient lineage. What was it Walt Whitman said—"To know the universe itself is a road, as many roads, as roads for travelling souls."

Dreams of Flight

WHEN I WAS NINE YEARS OLD and my brother Paul was seven, we set out to build an aircraft and fly it. We had a small red wagon and had located a plank that reminded us of an airplane wing. With great patience (and a longer attention span than we ever displayed in classrooms), we wired the plank athwart the wagon gunwales and concocted a flight plan. The idea was for one of us to pull the wagon with the other one in it, and if we pulled fast enough, it would leave the ground. Once airborne, we could fly to places like Uncle Harry's and Africa and other points of interest.

The early test flights were inconclusive. I'd say about fifty-fifty. The taxiing was flawless. The craft went where we directed it, and any ground-control unit would have given us high marks. Even the takeoff roll was impressive: straight down the runway gathering speed. Where we fell short was in getting it off the ground. It didn't take us long to figure out that we weren't pulling it fast enough to get airborne. We had an idea that each of us could run about eight miles an hour, and our airplane may have required twice that speed to lift off. So, if each of us could run eight miles an hour and we both pulled the wagon, that should give us sixteen miles an hour, and that ought to do the trick. Then, once airborne, we'd both jump in the wagon and could be pilot and copilot.

I'm sure you'll be surprised to learn that we still couldn't get airborne. We didn't give up though. That night our perseverance was rewarded only by an explanation of our failure from our father, who had arrived home from work and watched three of our aborted takeoffs. (We always aborted just before we would have run out of sidewalk and vaulted into Jameson Avenue and its unforgiving traffic.) Dad explained, in quite scientific terms, why our experiment wasn't working and why it was doomed from the start. To this day there is a residue of feeling on my part and, I'm sure, on my brother's, that if Dad had just kept his big mouth shut, we'd have overcome the thin marginal difficulties and gotten our wagon into the air.

Even today, remembering the disappointment, Paul and I can console ourselves with the fact that we were basically right. Several "ifs" point to this: if we had had a whole lot more speed than we could muster, maybe forty times the speed; if we had bothered to install some control surfaces and linkages to manual and pedal controls; if we had constructed an empennage with vertical stabilizer, rudder, and elevator; if our plank wing had been fashioned to have cord and camber and been fitted with ailerons and spoilers; if we had done all these things, our red wagon might have left the ground as a glider. Only then, if we had immediately found thermals or ridge-lift, we might have made it to Uncle Harry's, but probably not Africa. But the point is we were not wrong in principle. It wasn't as though we had built a submarine and expected to fly in it.

Children are resilient, and whatever cold water was thrown on that project did not in any way chill my deep interest in flying. I dreamed it and made further plans, with a dim notion that I'd have to have a firmer connection to reality in the next project.

Human beings vary in their degree of fascination with flight. Some are obsessed with the idea of flying; others are mildly interested to indifferent. And people in a third category have a positive aversion to it. These folks can have a powerful fear of flying, and some of them believe that if God had intended us to fly, we'd have feathers and beaks. Of course, if God had intended us to go to the theater, we'd have better seats.

I am, I must admit, in that first group—I am obsessed with flying. Not with any particular aspect of it. Just flying. I never tire of watching a big jet come in and settle on the runway of an airport. All that weight supported by the air seems miraculous to me. As an airplane pilot, I don't have an impressive number of hours, although I have an assortment of ratings garnered largely from broadcast assignments that allowed me to learn new types of flying. In addition to single-engine land (the standard first license issued to a flyer by the FAA), I went on to multiengine, seaplane (both boat and float), glider and glider tow, and hot-air balloon. I keep proficient and keep my medical certificate current in spite of the fact that right now I don't have an airplane. When I fly planes with engines, I rent them. The same with balloons.

Lately I have been concentrating on gliders, that is, soaring machines. Curiously, my father, who used to fly with me in an old biplane I had, didn't want to fly in my glider because, he said, it was an airplane without an engine. I explained to him that glider speeds are much more forgiving, and if you do pile one up, you don't have a hot engine in your lap or a lot of gasoline, which might catch fire, to contend with—but he still preferred the airplane to the glider.

Ballooning (which, by and large, is a safe sport and is under FAA jurisdiction in this country) is still tinged with a tad of madness. Balloonists carry champagne with them. They have almost no control over where they go—their controls deal only with up and down. In a hot-air balloon you put more heat in the canopy if you want to go up, and you let it cool if you want to come down, but where you wind up at the end of the flight is largely determined by wind direction. This teaches a pilot something about resignation.

Gas balloons are even iffier: you throw out ballast if you want to go up and release some of the helium if you want to come down. Eventually, you run out of one of these. In France, I have seen gas balloonists use hydrogen instead of helium. This seemed pretty unsafe considering that hydrogen is highly flammable. (Hydrogen was what the dirigible Hindenburg was using when it exploded in Lakehurst, New Jersey, just before World War II.) In France the people loading hydrogen from large tanks into this gas balloon were smoking cigarettes! I couldn't believe it. Yes, I could, and I moved out of range of where I thought the debris would land when it all blew up. Fortune smiled on this group that day, and there was much cheering when the ground crew finally let go and the gondola began to rise majestically. It looked like the occupants were on their way around the world in eighty days.

My license for balloon piloting reads "limited to hot-air balloons with airborne heaters." I am not licensed to fly gas balloons. And I am not going to be. But I enjoy hot-air ballooning even though, technically, it is not flying. A balloon does not fly through the air, it floats *with* the air. All those B movies involving balloonists in storms with their scarves flying missed the point of how a balloon works. If you are in a balloon and the wind is moving at five miles an hour, you are going five miles an hour along with it, so the air over the basket is not moving at all relative to the basket. It is as though you are indoors. An airplane has to have motion *through* the air in order for it to stay up, but not a balloon. So the balloon doesn't really fly, it floats.

I don't know how old I was when my first dream of flying occurred. But as long as I can remember, I have had a recurring dream (it recurs less and less frequently now) about a magic ability to run down a flight of stairs or an inclined pathway. At some point during a leap from one stair to another, I decide not to land on that particular spot or particular stair. Instead, I defer alighting and extend my foot to reach a point farther on or a stair farther down. In my dream I can do this indefinitely. I don't have to land at all. I merely decide to land a bit farther along the way. This feat of flight is always accompanied by a feeling of extreme deliciousness—a great liberating feeling of not being earthbound and a revelation, a conviction, that personal flight is possible.

Some anthropologists have suggested that evolution may be at an end as far as human shape and function is concerned. If we were to develop personal flight for reasons of survival, we might spend a hundred thousand generations or more growing a membrane between arm and body, lightening our weight, hollowing our bones, or changing body hair into feathers. But, in a single generation, we put a gasoline engine on a kite at Kitty Hawk and began flying. We don't spend eons improving our visual skills by growing large eyes like a tarsier—we grind lenses to make telescopes and microscopes. Technology seems to have taken over the task of evolution, and we probably will retain our general appearance from now on, altering it slightly perhaps to reduce back and foot troubles, but even that can be done with prostheses or corrective surgery. It's doubtful if our brains will get any bigger. We'll probably just build increasingly powerful machines to do all that thinking for us. But my guess is that we will continue to fly ever faster and higher until we have inhabited and colonized much of the solar system. Eventually, far into the future, we will fly well into this and other galaxies.

Ross and Mars

WE MAY YET SEE, in the not too distant future, American astronauts and Russian cosmonauts travel together to the planet Mars. A study released a while back by American and Russian scientists concluded that a mission to Mars would be much cheaper if the two countries pooled resources than if they attempted the trip independently—in fact, the study says it would cost sixty billion dollars to go to Mars with the Russians instead of six hundred billion if the U.S. were to try it alone. Both countries already own the hardware and possess the know-how to get to Mars. Nothing new needs to be developed. The study said earthlings could have a working outpost on the planet Mars in twenty-one years.

Remember, the scientists who suggested this Martian plan were grown adults. I remember when grown adults would laugh at any suggestion of space travel. Today grown adults are laughing at how cheap a trip to Mars could be. I also remember a time when any American who suggested sharing rocket technology with the Russians would have been investigated and blacklisted.

Not long after the turn of this century, my father, just a boy, went to look at some automobile skid marks. People came from miles around just to look at about four or five feet of rubber skid marks made by a driver who slammed on his brakes. My father said he remembered someone saying the car must have been traveling fifteen miles an hour to create such a wonder. Another person said, "No," because it was a known fact of science that the human body disintegrates at such a speed. Fifteen miles per hour, he said, was a physical impossibility. This involved some ignorance as well as faulty science, since a railroad engineer, Casey Jones, had already achieved ninety miles per hour.

I can only imagine what that man's response would have been if he were told that one day Americans and Russians would climb into a large bullet and shoot themselves to the planet Mars at twenty-five thousand miles an hour. Times change; a lot happens in a hundred years.

About a hundred years before my father went down to look at those skid marks, Russian and American seafarers were jointly exploring the Pacific Northwest with a level of cooperation we might expect on the trip to Mars. Americans and Russians have worked together on many occasions in the past, most of us just don't remember when or how closely.

Americans who remember their high school history might recall that Secretary of State William H. Seward purchased Alaska from Russia in 1867, but few Americans know that Russians also settled in California, nor do many remember names like Joseph O'Cain or Alexander Adreyevich Baranov.

In the early 1800s, Alaska was about as far away from Europe and the U.S., and about as cold and well known, as the planet Mars seems to us today. But relentless explorers from Russia who moved East, and explorers from America who moved West, met in Alaska and struck up fast and profitable friendships. The first time Alexander Baranov and Joseph O'Cain met was around 1800 near the island of Nunchek outside Prince William Sound.

Joseph O'Cain was a Bostonian working as first mate aboard the British schooner *Phoenix* out of Calcutta. The *Phoenix* had broken a mast and was making for well-wooded Nunchek to find a suitable replacement. Alexander Baranov was chief manager of the Russian colonies in Alaska, which sounds like a big deal, but Baranov was nearly starving at the time. Baranov hailed the great East India merchants dressed as an Aleut Indian and paddling a skin-covered canoe known as a *baidarka*.

Captain Hugh Moore and First Mate O'Cain were quite surprised when Baranov revealed his true identity as head of the Russian colonies in Alaska. They were further surprised to discover the terrible hardships suffered by the Russians in Alaska and the dangerous scarcity of their resources. Both men had assumed the Russians were doing well. Unfortunately, the Alaskan adventure had rarely been kind to the Russians, and when they finally sold the territory to Secretary Seward in the 1860s for $5 million, they undoubtedly felt themselves well rid of it.

Baranov explained that the main difficulty he had was transportation and that if foreigners were able to ship his furs for sale in Hong Kong and bring him supplies from outside, he was all for it—even though officially he was not authorized to trade with foreigners. First mate Joseph O'Cain and Chief Manager Alexander Baranov became fast friends, and O'Cain held high hopes for future business.

Their next meeting took place about 1801 on Kodiak Island. This time O'Cain was serving as first mate aboard an American ship, the *Enterprise*. O'Cain suggested to Captain Ezekiel Hubbard that they should go directly to the Russians to trade. This would do two things: one, they could avoid trading with the dangerous Tlingit Indians; and two, by trading in Kodiak instead of down the Alaskan coast, they would gain several weeks advantage in reaching China ahead of their competitors. Baranov was overjoyed with the arms, ammunition, cloth, and molasses disgorged by the *Enterprise*, and he handed over more than two thousand otter pelts in payment. The *Enterprise* sped on to the lucrative markets in Hong Kong and sold Baranov's furs under the American flag.

The next year, 1802, Baranov discovered his most promising settlement on Sitka Island had been wiped out in a Tlingit Indian attack. Out of the 450 Aleuts and Russians who worked there, only forty-two survived. The total number lost that year was six hundred people, some of whom wound up as slaves of the Tlingits. Baranov swore that he would drive the Tlingit out of Sitka and retake his most prized settlement, but how?

The "how" came next year when Joseph O'Cain showed up again, this time as captain of his own ship, appropriately christened the *O'Cain*. Due to his rapport with Baranov, O'Cain gained the backing of the Winship family, a wealthy Boston shipping interest. The Winships bankrolled O'Cain's dream of supplying the Russian colonies and establishing a viable Pacific trading link to China.

The goods O'Cain brought with him from Boston were greatly amplified in Hawaii, where pork, fruit, and coconuts were added. Even the Hawaiian King Kamehameha, who knew all about Baranov's troubles on Sitka, sent his best wishes for a speedy victory over the Tlingit.

Baranov was delighted when O'Cain arrived, but was unable to pay him. He had just shipped over a million rubles worth of pelts to Siberia and had nothing more to trade.

O'Cain, a paragon of Yankee ingenuity, was undaunted. He suggested that Baranov loan him a number of Aleuts and Russians to hunt otter along the California coast. In four months Baranov's share of this rapid foray came to eighty thousand dollars worth of pelts, more than enough to pay O'Cain for the needed supplies. O'Cain sailed off to sell the pelts in Hong Kong, and Baranov took the guns and ammunition to retake Sitka from the Tlingits. The year was 1804 and Thomas Jefferson was serving as America's third president.

The Tlingits were formidable adversaries, and the battle to retake Sitka Island was a pitched and fierce one. Due to the aid supplied by his American friends, and assisted by the fortuitous appearance of a Russian frigate, the *Neva*, that had learned of Baranov's troubles in Hawaii while on a diplomatic mission to Japan, Baranov's forces prevailed. Sitka was retaken and renamed New Archangel.

Despite the military success, the colony at Sitka proved hard to maintain. The otter were becoming scarce, the Tlingit more aggressive, and supplies continued to be a problem. The winter of 1805–06 was devastating. Nikolai Petrovich Rezanov, an imperial chamberlain and high official in the Russian-American Company, arrived that year and found the colonies to be in a "disastrous situation."

Rezanov purchased a ship from (who else?) some Americans and sailed south to San Francisco bay to establish diplomatic relations with the Spanish. This required no small amount of pluck, since all ports in California were closed to foreigners. But Rezanov was well endowed with pluck, élan, and considerable social charm. He not only won over Spanish officialdom, he concluded his trip with a marriage proposal to Concepçion Arguello, the daughter of the commandant of the presidio. Arguello accepted. Rezanov returned to Sitka loaded down with grain and other supplies. He had even gained permission from Spanish authorities for Baranov and his colonists to establish an outpost along "the one unoccupied stretch" of coast just north of San Francisco Bay.

Baranov and his colonists acted swiftly on Rezanov's considerable diplomatic achievements and, in 1812, established an outpost along California's Sonoma coast.

Today many Russian tourists who visit the United States know a great deal about this period of American history, and they head directly for a small town two-hundred miles north of San Francisco called Fort Ross. The word Ross comes from *russ*, present in the word Russia. The Ross Colony was home to Russians, Aleuts, and local Pomo Indians, who farmed, hunted, and attempted to resupply the northern colonies in Alaska. The Russians sold Fort Ross in 1841.

If Russians and Americans do decide to go to Mars together, I can imagine the sight that awaits the crew members as they leave the Earth: the jagged California coast as it turns into Oregon, Washington, British Columbia, and then Alaska. The gentle sweep of the Aleutian Islands as they gracefully arch toward the Kamchatka Peninsula of Siberia might well remind future spacefarers of an earlier cooperation between Russians and Americans. A cooperation in a land nearly as forbidding, certainly as remote, and almost as cold and as barren as the one that awaits them on the planet Mars. In another one hundred years I'd be willing to bet that Mars will seem no more remote to us than Alaska does today.

Horseflesh on the High Plateau

I WAS SITTING IN THE BACK SEAT OF A LARGE, American-made taxi cab the other day, stuck in the interminable traffic jam that immobilizes New York City streets. The cab driver was tapping his thumb on the steering wheel. The other cars around us were motionless, except for the quiet rumbling of their idling motors and the shaking of their metal bodies. Wisps of exhaust fumes spiraled through the dense air, destined to wreak havoc on the atmosphere far above the city.

As I sat in the cab, staring through the thicket of urban masonry and asphalt, I recalled that the average speed of crosstown traffic in New York in the year 1890 was fifteen miles an hour. That was the speed of horse-drawn hacks. The average speed today is about eleven miles an hour.

The oppressive conditions of the traffic jam increased as the full weight of this comparison dawned on me. My internal combustion crosstown cab ride was taking more time than the same ride took a hundred years ago—by horse. It also cost more money. But worse, the cab I was sitting in was surrounded by hundreds of other automobiles, each equipped with, variously, four-, six-, eight-, and twelve-cylinder engines that produced from a dozen to several hundred horsepower each, and relentlessly banged away gallons of toxic gasoline fumes every second.

Even at an idle, going nowhere, these engines managed to simultaneously waste an irreplaceable natural resource, taken from deep within the earth, and harm the environment above. Horse travel assumed a sudden urgency—a nostalgic imperative.

At this point I completely lost my grip on the cab ride and slipped, shamelessly, into a profound reverie regarding humanity's loss of the horse. Lamenting our loss of the horse is no mere daydream; it is a perfectly normal condition, and I believe many of us succumb to it regularly. And it's easy to understand why.

Horses were the primary means of transportation, work, and play for more than five thousand years. They were used in war, in agriculture, in sport, and amusement. Horses entered human myth and religion and roam our literature as powerful symbols of many things in many cultures. A trifling five or six decades of automobile and airplane traffic could hardly be expected to wipe out the memories of five thousand years of thundering hooves. We may not ride them every day, but horses are still very much a part of us.

The United States was perhaps the last theater in which large populations of people migrated on horseback. The American cowpuncher and range rider, the buffalo hunter and the mountain man lived the last of an equestrian tradition that extended across Europe and the Middle East and onto the great plains of central and far eastern Asia. This tradition extends back in time and counts the centuries like layers of an onion. The relatively recent romance with the cowboy age omits the thousands of years of horse culture that led up to it.

Ironically, fossils of the *eohippus*, the "dawn horse" ancestor of the modern horse, appear in strata laid down more than fifty million years ago in the Mississippi Valley. Mysteriously, this early horse and its more mature progeny disappeared from North America. The horse did not reappear on the American landscape until Europeans reintroduced it during the Age of Exploration.

About five thousand years ago, somewhere in the vast, uncharted steppes of central Asia, members of a nomadic warrior tribe known as the Scythians wrangled and broke wild stallions and tamed them into saddle mounts. Stallions proved to be so difficult to tame, however, that early Scythian horsemen hit upon the idea, and the practice, of gelding them—castrating them at an early age.

That wasn't the only ingenious idea that Scythians had regarding horses. They invented the saddle and stirrups. They also invented trousers. Trousers were designed specifically to match saddle and stirrups. Bone, wood, and antler bits—some segmented in two parts like a modern snaffle bit—were used to control a horse from its mouth from before 1000 B.C. And remember, the Scythians roamed the largest expanse of prairie land on earth, ranging from Mongolia and Siberia in the East to the Caucuses and the Crimea in the West.

In 1924 a Russian anthropologist named Sergei Rudenko discovered a number of Scythian tombs in the Altai mountains, where the borders of China, Mongolia, and the old Soviet Union meet. The tombs contained Scythian kings, who had been placed in deep trenches and then covered with crisscrossed logs that were topped with soil. The first rains penetrated the logs and promptly froze solid, placing the contents in a deep freeze. This allowed the bodies interred to travel through time virtually undisturbed and undecayed. The bodies of these kings and courtiers and their horses were buried around 500 B.C., but when Rudenko exhumed them in the 1920s, they were strikingly well preserved. The skin, intact and elastic, appeared fresh.

Saddles were trimmed in beaten gold. The horses that had pulled the royal Scythian chariots were also fitted with a curious and unique device: face masks made of stiff felt. These strange face masks for horses were not only covered in intricate curlicue designs, they had felt antlers that made the horses look like elk that had arrived from some dizzying world of fantasy.

Taming horses spread across the planet. The Chinese genius for invention contributed the two most popular ways to harness a horse. The trace harness, which places a strap across the breast bone and another over the shoulders, was in use in China certainly by the fourth century B.C. The collar harness, which uses a thick, padded ring that fits around the shoulder and breast bone, was in use by the third century B.C. Before these Chinese inventions arrived in Europe, European horses were hitched to wheeled vehicles with throat-and-girth harnesses that choked the horse and made pulling loads inefficient.

It was only in our century that the saddle pony gave way to the motorcycle and the coupé, that buckboards became pickups and Conestoga wagons turned into station wagons. It's true that even today, mostly in the West, cowboys and cowgirls ride herd on dapples and roans and palominos and bays. Americans continue to flock to real rodeos and make-believe western movies. But despite these real vestiges of a glorious past, America's horse culture is nearly gone. These rodeos and Western movies are more a measure of what's been lost than evidence of what we have left.

But this is not the case in remote areas of China near where ancient Scythians broke horses to ride. Last summer on a large plain called Litang in western Szechuan province, for example, several thousand horsemen and their families gathered for a yearly rodeo. Prior to the beginning of this century, Litang and its environs belonged to Khams (pronounced calm), the eastern province of old Tibet. The Litang rodeo is something to behold, or so claims my peripatetic son, who visited there. Thousands of Tibetan warriors clad in fiery silk brocade cloaks were armed to the teeth with cap-and-ball muskets, bows and arrows, and traditional Tibetan short-swords, which were jammed in their belts.

The Tibetans have developed a short, stout pony with an enormous lung capacity. (Litang sits at about 12,500 feet above sea level.) Many of the bridles and halters had intricately worked cheek-pieces of gilded filigree or silvered cloisonné. Large felt bands around the horses' necks supported bells. Many of the horses this year at Litang wore simple felt masks with appliqué symbols reminiscent of those ancient, but more elaborate, Scythian steeds who appeared caparisoned as elk.

The Tibetan riders tied their stirrups together under the bellies of the horses so they could lean over and touch the ground. This extreme lean permitted them, at a full gallop I might add, to pick up prizes of packs of cigarettes that were tied to ceremonial scarves and placed on the ground. Makeshift bows and arrows were used (also at full gallop) to knock down small targets of balanced pieces of wood. They also raced in speed events.

Off in the distance the Litang monastery sat on the side of the hill as if it were scudding on a cloud across the sky in a Ming dynasty painting. My son says the life of the old-time cowboy and bronc buster appears very much alive in—of all places—the Chinese wild west. Intricate

Chinese and Tibetan saddle blankets covered these sturdy little mounts. So small were some of the horses that they were actually dwarfed by their riders. But there was no doubt among the thousands in attendance that these were brave little ponies indeed.

The rolling thunderclap of the hooves across the flat plain of Litang was enough to make the hackles on the back of your neck stand straight up in a thrilling bristle. And the sight of dozens of divots of topsoil flung high into the air by angry chargers recalled riders of distant ages who bore down upon satrapies and walled townships and sacked them. Some of the older riders in modern Litang had fathers who did exactly such things back in the 1920s and '30s when Chinese warlords commanded light cavalry and maneuvered them across the highlands of Tibet.

A horn honked behind me and my distant reverie evaporated like tailpipe exhaust on a wintry day. I landed with full force in the back of my taxi cab, which was still stuck in traffic and still in New York City. The driver was still tapping his thumb against the steering wheel, and the cars around us were still vibrating at idle—still burning fuel. And I wondered deeply, whatever possessed us to get rid of the horse?

CHAPTER TWO

PHENOMENA

The South Pole

THE SOUTH POLE IS A POLE, a bamboo pole. In 1982, I moved it to a new location: that point on earth from which it is impossible to go farther south—the Pole itself. I went there not to discover it (several people got there ahead of me, Amundsen and Scott in 1911 and Admiral Byrd twenty-some years later); my trip was a more personal odyssey, and it also was work. The broadcast material I gathered was gratifying, but the discoveries I made were personally thrilling.

If you keep moving straight south from any place in the world, you will, of course, arrive at the South Pole. For political reasons, the practical route for U.S. citizens is through New Zealand. It's considerably more complicated to go through South America or South Africa. The distance alone from New York to the Pole is impressive: The southern-most tip of New Zealand, a country even more "down under" than Australia, is still father away from the South Pole than Paris is from the North Pole.

So, after twenty hours of commercial jet travel from New York—across this continent to the West Coast, then to Hawaii, and finally New Zealand—it is necessary to go farther south on U.S. Navy or Air Force planes for another six hours to McMurdo Station on the edge of Antarctica, and then it's three more hours to the pole. On broadcast assignments, I have been among circumpolar peoples in the north—in northern Siberia and among the Eskimos of northern Canada and Alaska—but the southern end of the world has always been more intriguing to me because there are no circumpolar peoples there—no southern Eskimos, no southern Laps, no nobody. But there's plenty of land.

Antarctica is bigger than the United States and Mexico combined and is almost totally covered with ice. Any human being who has lived there has done so only within the last century and has represented the only living things to penetrate the interior, where there are no plants, no animals, no birds, no insects, no germs. If you put out a piece of wood or meat, it will not rot. It will shrivel some in the dry air, but it will never rot.

The South Pole itself is located on a continental plateau on top of a cap of freshwater ice two miles thick. The temperatures are colder than -100°F in winter, with strong winds and drifting snows—a most inhospitable place. Still, in the winter, when it is dark for six months—the sun never coming above the horizon—people will live at the tiny U.S. station located there. They will have enough fuel and food to survive until the sun comes up next spring and planes fly again between Pole Station and McMurdo on the edge of the continent. And they will eat well, as I did when I visited the station and shared their fare.

It was midsummer when I was there, a balmy -26°F, and I had the opportunity to participate in a refined measurement of the geographic pole's actual position. During the year, due to the constant movement of the ice, the mark was found to be off by ten meters, a little over thirty feet. Using satellites and the corresponding ground receiving stations, plus other surveying equipment, it is now possible to locate the pole position within about twenty inches. In early December 1982, scientists determined the precise location and put a surveyor's pin in the snow. Under their direction, at 2304 GMT (6:04 P.M. Eastern Standard Time) on December 10, I pulled the South Pole out of its January position and carried it a little over thirty feet to plant it where it belongs.

I asked to do this when I heard it had to be moved. This privilege was enormously important to me, even though entirely symbolic. I was merely a lackey, after all, carrying and replanting the pole under the direction of Dr. Loreen Utz, the scientist who supervised and checked the calculations.

I've been asked why this was so important to me, to do the actual moving. The only answer I have is the one mountain climbers give when asked why they climb a certain mountain. They answer with the cliché "Because it was there." To the question why did I move the pole, I have to say, "Because it was there—and it belongs over here."

After putting the Pole where it belongs, I walked around it, crossing all the meridians of the world and all the time zones, literally going around the world in twenty-four steps. I walked a tiny circle at true latitude S89° 59.995'. All the longitudinal meridians of the world converged through it to the pole—which, by the way, is a fifteen-foot bamboo rod with a green flag attached to the top. When I looked at the wider circle of my distant horizon, I realized that even that horizon was puny compared to the immensity of the whole continent. Antarctica is covered with seven and a half million cubic miles of ice that moves like Silly Putty, glacial rivers and shelving that eventually spill into the Weddell and Ross seas. In some places this plasticized ice pours, in slow motion, over dolorite sills in gigantic ice-falls. The ice at the top can take weeks to work its way down to glacier level at the bottom.

I stood at the base of one of these stupendous ice-falls once and watched the plateau sheet move its tonnage in ultra-slow motion and in greater volume than Niagara or Victoria Falls, silent, gleaming white, breathtaking. I remember trying (and failing) to establish some relationship between myself and this awesome cataract. I could not speak. A wave of emotion caught me and brought me to a new perspective. I came to regard what I saw as something put there for my benefit and instruction. The temptation to think of this natural wonder as having some purpose may spring from the arrogance of assuming that all natural wonder has been arranged for people—for their pleasure, for their testing, for whatever. But in the presence of this particular wonder, I appreciated myself as a brief flicker of vital warmth, full of pathetic vanity. I silently asked myself, "For whom was this arranged? Why does this beauty exist so far from almost all human eyes?"

I would not likely return to this place again, I thought, to wonder at its overwhelming presence. There would probably be neither opportunity nor time. And I realized that it will be pouring its shining torrent of immensely slow ice over that mountain range long after my great-great-grandchildren have aged and died.

From within the depth of this liberating humility came the realization that it was all right just to be there at that moment—that it was reward enough to stand in such a place and be reduced to zero, forced to give up all my self-importance. My reward was the security of knowing that God still seemed to be on the job and would probably remain in that position for a considerable amount of time to come.

When I could talk again, I did a short taped essay for 20/20, which immediately returned me to the small-scale and self-important unreality that we all need to reinforce our sanity.

Scientists of various disciplines are discovering many useful things in Antarctica about the history and probable future of the world's climate (Antarctica is the "engine-room" of the world's weather). They are also learning whether we may see another ice age, or if we are still moving away from the last one. Core samples of ice from far beneath the cap contain ancient air bubbles that reveal the composition of the earth's atmosphere thousands of years ago and let us know whether carbon dioxide is building up or being depleted.

Antarctic fish manufacture a sort of antifreeze in their blood and tissue, which one day may be synthesized in quantity to end crop failure from frost damage. Tests for virus killers and epidemic disease control are also being conducted way down under. In fact, the list of potential payoffs from Antarctic research seems endless.

I left Antarctica on the fifteenth of December, having sojourned on a giant continent that has no country. By treaty, no nation has sovereign territory there. The logistic and scientific cooperation among the treaty nations has been a resounding success for twenty-five years. It has been a model of how the whole world might cooperate one day.

Seeing a Century in a Single Second

HOW LONG SOMETHING TAKES depends a lot on how much attention we devote to it. Sometimes waiting for a bus for only twenty minutes can seem like ten years, and at other times cutting a birthday cake can suddenly make us realize that a whole decade has gone by unnoticed. Time, at least our sense of time, seems like a creative act of human imagination.

Saint Augustine seemed to agree. He felt that time had more to do with the soul than with the outside world. "What, then, is time?" asked Augustine. "If no one asks me, I know what it is. [But] if I wish to explain it to him who asks, I do not know." Few people can explain exactly what time is.

It is even more difficult to grasp distant events in history and understand their relative position in time, their positions in relation to time's most inexplicable moment—what we call "now." Saint Augustine was the bishop of a North African city called Hippo in the year 396. But how long ago was that really? The year 396 is to us only "a long time ago." It will seem longer or shorter to different people, depending on their imagination. How much harder it is to imagine all of time, that is, the entire history of the universe.

In fact, I have discovered that so few people are able to grasp the entire history of the universe in proper scale that I felt moved to supply the following modest (but much needed) intellectual prosthesis. Here is a time scale of a history of the universe based on a simple formula: let one second equal one century. You'll be surprised how useful this is.

If one second equals one hundred years, then one second ago would be the start of the nineteenth century's "Gay Nineties." Two seconds ago places us just after 1776, the year the United States of America became a sovereign nation. Three seconds ago pushes us back to the age of the buccaneers and pirates. A mere ten seconds ago takes us to the beginning of this millennium, during the time of the Norse explorers to the New World and the Norman conquest of England. Saint Augustine would have lived about fourteen seconds ago, according to our one-second-to-one-century time scale.

The dawn of the Christian era would be only twenty seconds ago. Thirty seconds ago brings us, roughly, to the Trojan War and the Dorian invasion of the Peloponnesus. Reading a history of these events can sometimes seem as if they happened at the dawn of time. But when we think of them as happening only thirty seconds ago, the Trojan War and the Dorian invasion of the Peloponnesus seem very close. If we double that thirty seconds to a full minute, in other words, a full sixty centuries ago, we come to the very beginning of the ancient Egyptian kingdoms and dynasties—all of that human history took place in one short minute, according to our time scale.

If we double that minute to two minutes, we are pushed all the way back to about 12,000 B.C. Humanity was in the New Stone Age and nearly two thousand years away from developing the agricultural revolution. A strange menagerie of animals began to disappear then: the saber-toothed tiger, the camel-leopard, the dire-wolf, the woolly mammoth, and more. By three minutes ago we arrive at about 18,000 B.C.— twenty thousand years ago—when human beings were at the tail end of the Old Stone Age.

By this time we can see that humankind is a frighteningly brief event compared to really old things, like the earth or the universe itself. But let's continue with this scale and get really frightened—let's go back a full ten minutes. Ten minutes ago puts us sixty thousand years in the past. This time might predate our entire species, *Homo sapiens sapiens*, which is typified by Cro–Magnon man. Our species might have begun earlier, but, when we're only talking about ten minutes, it doesn't seem to matter much.

Twice ten minutes, twenty minutes ago, takes us 120,000 years in the past, to a time that Neanderthal man roamed the earth with perhaps other hominids who were not truly human.

Pushing back a full hour, we arrive at about 360,000 years ago, a time when human beings were distinct from other primates but probably did not have use of fire or language. We might assume that change was very gradual beyond this point. Two hours, three hours, or four hours ago reveals prehuman primates in pretty much the same condition as those six, seven, and eight hours ago.

If we jump back twelve hours, little more than four million years ago but only half a day in our time scale, we arrive at about the time of Lucy, the famous four-foot-tall hominid discovered in the Rift Valley. Lucy is a likely candidate for the first human, or at least, one of the first. But even Lucy is only half a day back in history, if we follow our one-second-equals-one-century rule.

Yesterday, one full day ago, would take us back nearly fifteen million years. We would see profound changes taking place among early mammals that now are extinct. Three days ago shows the ancestors of certain aquatic mammals crawling around on land, slowly transforming from primitive otterlike animals into animals that resembled seals and finally—as they completed their return to the sea—into dolphins and whales. (Although it must have been about forty million years ago, or four and a half days by our reckoning, that whale ancestry was still based on land.) Also about this time we might expect to find a common ancestor for both mankind and the great apes.

It would take a full week, again calculating each second as a century, to arrive at the time of the dinosaurs, sometime around sixty-eight million years ago. Actually, the last of the dinosaurs probably died around sixty-six million years ago (roughly a week ago). Two weeks ago uncovers the beginning of the dinosaurs and places us before the time of any mammals, even primitive ones. If you stop and think about this, you might appreciate just how long dinosaurs lasted. More than two weeks at our one-second-to-a-century time scale is an impressively long time. Compare the dinosaurs' stay of more than two weeks to the measly few minutes of all of humanity, and you can get a pretty good idea of the meaning of the word important.

Now if we leap back more than a month, we arrive at the time of the Devonian shark and the primitive cockroach and a few ants. The planet was covered with carboniferous forests that, as they decayed, would one day—only a month later by our reckoning—become petroleum.

PERSPECTIVES • HUGH DOWNS

Twelve months ago, a full year ago, there was no life on this planet at all. The earth was still cooling and only beginning to form a hard crust. A year ago on our time scale takes us back about three and a half billion years in actual time. The sun and the planets of our solar system were formed only about a year and a half ago—each celestial body a great glob of gas that collapsed on itself gravitationally and took more than a billion years to cool. The sun, of course, is of sufficient size to sustain thermonuclear fires (of the fusion variety) and will not cool off for another five billion years.

Finishing our time journey of one-second-equal-to-one-century, we arrive at what is assumed to be the beginning of time, somewhere between four and five years ago on our scale, to a time called $T=0$— the Big Bang. The Big Bang theory is still the most widely accepted by modern physicists. It describes the universe as beginning in an explosion from absolutely nothing and expanding like an inflating balloon to what we see today.

The most distant objects in space certainly seem to be receding from us at great speed, as if the whole universe were expanding. The logical beginning for this inflationary phenomenon would be a single point in the distant past where all time and space were compacted into an extremely dense event. Before that single event there must have been nothing at all (if there was a before).

Physicist Alan Guth from the Massachusetts Institute of Technology speculates that shortly after the Big Bang (and I mean very shortly after, like ten to the minus thirty-fifth of a second after) the universe rapidly expanded for a period that lasted about ten to the minus thirty-second of a second. During this unimaginably short flash, the entire universe inflated by a multiple of ten to the twenty-fifth power. In other words, it got *huge*. This single "inflationary expansion," Guth says, was responsible for most of the matter and energy that we see today.

Einstein's simple formula of $E=MC^2$ stipulates that energy and matter are equivalent. Guth speculates that all matter could have been created with a mere twenty pounds of starting matter. As the inflationary expansion took place, the energy expended would account for the rest. In fact, the original twenty pounds of matter needn't have been present at all if the expansion exploded with sufficient energy. The energy expended during the expansion would create the matter. If there is energy, then there must be matter. Remember, they are equal. As Guth says, "The universe could be the ultimate free lunch."

If we use our time scale of one-second-to-one-century, the free lunch began about four or five years ago, a particularly humbling fact when we consider that all human history from the beginning of ancient Egypt only took a single minute.

The Ladies Room and the Laboratory

HAVE YOU EVER NOTICEd how some men subconsciously seem to overlook women? This is a psychological myopia, not physical shortsightedness. No surgery or drug or lens will ever correct it. It can only be corrected with a sudden flash of insight, the realization that women are important, the sudden realization that the assumption of male dominance is wrong-headed. Let me give you an example of how it can lead to wrong scientific conclusions.

A few years ago scientists discovered that small, daily doses of aspirin reduced the risk of heart disease. Aspirin acts as an anticoagulant and therefore reduces the chance of clot formation. Blood clots can get stuck in heart valves or block vital pathways in the brain, but tiny amounts of aspirin keeps the blood fluid and slippery. Good news. Then someone noticed something. The test trials for this important study were conducted exclusively on men. The study provided no hard evidence that aspirin performs as well, worse, or better in women. It seemed like an oversight.

Dr. Elizabeth Karlin, a professor at the University of Wisconsin medical school, says the oversight is not limited to the aspirin study. A whole raft of therapies now being given to both men and women were originally only tested on men. Everything from AIDS studies to cholesterol-management programs (both drugs and diets) to antidepressant medicines were originally tested on men and provide no data on women. The physiological differences between men and women are great enough to cause concern. Many American women are now wondering if they haven't been overlooked by medical research.

A few years ago the General Accounting Office (an investigative branch of Congress) accused the National Institutes of Health of conducting medical research that overlooked the important differences between men and women. Some people were surprised at the magnitude of oversight, but others, like historians of science, were not surprised at all. Women have been overlooked by science since the time Aristotle announced that women had more teeth than men. All Aristotle had to do was ask his wife to open her mouth and count her teeth, but somehow he overlooked that simple experiment.

Modern science was born as much from oversight as it was from insight. The essence of science is an ability to discriminate one thing from another precisely. When you concentrate on one thing, you ignore something else. Discriminating between the sexes has had a profound influence on the growth of science, from its most ancient roots in Greece right up to today. The reason sex influenced science at all is due to the way human beings go about knowing things.

People know things because of a subtle relationship between the mind and nature. Knowledge can be described as the result of a subject and an object joining together. Dr. Evelyn Fox Keller, a physicist who also writes about the philosophy of science, says, "Knowledge is a form of consummation, just as sex is a form of knowledge. . . . Both are propelled by desire. Sexual union remains the most compelling and most primal instance of the act of knowing."

The great philosophies and sciences of the past were invariably described using metaphors that reflected the sexual customs of the culture that produced them. Like many women writers today, Dr. Keller provides several examples of how sex and science mingle. Consider first, she suggests, the ideal transcendent philosophy of Plato.

In *Symposium*, Plato states flatly that knowledge is achieved through Eros—Eros being the Greek word for sex. He considered the material body a burden that had to be transcended. Sex offered an opportunity to perform just such a transcendence. Plato says, "When a man, starting from this sensible world and making his way upward by a right feeling of love . . . begins to catch sight of that [eternal] beauty, he is very near his goal." Notice that Plato does not say, "when a man or woman" or "he or she," he says, "man" and "he" on purpose. Plato considered women hopelessly bound to the material world because of their role in procreation.

Women were denied access to the rarest of Plato's experiences, not because Plato was guilty of some individual oversight, but rather because Plato was the product of fifth-century Greek culture. Plato's ideal love was homosexual, for that was the custom in ancient Greece, and the dynamics of homosexual love became the model upon which Plato built his theories of knowledge.

Plato's lovers were not themselves considered to be the object of love; the real object of love was an inner image of the lover, an ideal. So when Plato turned his attention to the material world, he perceived all objects as forms indicating ideals (exactly the same relationship he describes between male lovers). Plato's philosophies are ethical, rationalistic methods to achieve a harmonious society. They became the bedrock of modern Western thought.

Just like the ancient Greeks, Renaissance Europeans created new ways of understanding, using sexual metaphors that reflected their sexual customs. In 1620, Sir Francis Bacon published *Novum Organum*, or the "new instrument." The new instrument was really a new intellectual tool known as the Baconian method, a precursor to the scientific method of investigation. Bacon insisted that science should be a methodical, disciplined examination limited exclusively to fact and direct observation. Scientific investigators could no longer cite Galen, Aristotle, or even the Bible as authorities without first demonstrating actual experiment.

Before Bacon came along, knowledge was believed to provide wisdom, or even meditative insight. But Bacon showed that scientific investigations can also provide people with power, specifically, power over nature. He described it as the same power that a seventeenth-century husband could exert over his wife. Bacon imagined the mind as a husband and nature as a bride. He suggests, "Let us establish a chaste and lawful marriage between Mind and Nature . . . a chaste, holy, and legal wedlock." This proposed marriage of mind and nature (Bacon's metaphor for knowledge) reflected the unequal condition of the sexes in seventeenth-century Britain. Bacon says, "I am come . . . leading to you Nature with all her children to bind her to your service and make her your slave." Or again, Bacon says his techniques do not "merely exert a gentle guidance over nature's course; they have the power to conquer and subdue her." (This has led to a lot of mischief we are just now beginning to recognize and pay for.)

Bacon's sexual metaphor for gaining scientific knowledge was a good description of the way men treated women back then. Martin Luther's *Vindication of Married Life*, for example, advises husbands to maintain power over their wives because, "The regiment and dominion belong to the man as head and master of the house." Luther and Bacon were only confirming what the Bible taught and what many people already believed: that men should dominate women.

Heretical sects like the Rosicrucians and certain alchemical schools rejected the lower status of women. These groups, who made significant contributions of their own to mathematics, physics, and chemistry, believed that knowledge was an equal union of the mind and nature. Alchemists understood men and women as two equal halves. Paracelsus wrote, "A man without a woman is not whole, only with a woman is he whole . . . both are of earth and form together one whole." In a way, Paracelsus foreshadowed the equality sought by modern women. Had his science been more effective, perhaps his egalitarian ideas about the sexes might have come down to us with greater force.

Three to four hundred years ago scientists had one foot planted in objective reasoning and the other one rooted in magic and superstition. Bacon, for example, believed warts could be cured by rubbing them with pork fat and then hanging the fat in a south-facing window. Remember, modern science is the direct descendant of minds like this. Science has removed most of the superfluous embellishments it inherited from the past, but it hasn't removed all of them. Especially not the pernicious myopia some men have when they try to grasp the place of women in the greater scheme of things. This myopia is not just limited to drug testing.

My daughter-in-law is a physician, and she provided me with several examples of male myopia in the medical world. She showed up for a job interview once and her prospective employer said he needed "three doctors and a woman." He meant a woman doctor—an incredible but almost predictable oversight. She also told me that staff dressing rooms attached to the operating theater at a major hospital where she once worked were marked "Doctors" and "Women." She arrived one day to assist in the surgery of one of her patients and, naturally, walked through the door marked "Doctors." Amazingly, the half-dressed surgeons and anesthesiologists—skilled anatomists to a man—began covering themselves in embarrassment.

There is a popular myth that the objective, the rational, and science itself, are somehow intrinsically male preserves. This myth also perpetuates the belief that the sensitive, the emotional, and nature itself, are somehow all female ("Mother Nature," for example). Even our reference to "hard" facts as opposed to "soft" facts reflects this sexual bias. Not only is this myth completely wrong, it could be doing harm because it represents women as less important than men.

For example, breast cancer has nearly doubled among women since 1960, and it now kills forty-four thousand women every year. But in 1989, the National Institutes of Health spent only $77 million to fight breast cancer and to find out why it is spreading so quickly. That's about the same amount of money the government spent for a few days' activity in the Persian Gulf .

There is reason to believe that, as our definitions of the roles of men and women change, our science and philosophies will change, too. Imagine, the mysteries of quantum phenomena, the secrets of black holes, and the enigma of time could very well be understood in new ways because of the way men and women relate to one another. It may not happen anytime soon. Let's make sure we stay pointed in the right direction.

Gold

SCIENTISTS STUDYING THE ATMOSPHERE in Antarctica have discovered an extraordinary thing in a continent full of extraordinary things. Antarctica's only active volcano, Mount Erebus, is shooting pure gold into the atmosphere every time it erupts.

Mount Erebus does not produce very much gold. There are no twenty-four-carat lava flows condensing into the sea, no airborne ingots crashing to earth, not even a rain of nuggets. Instead, Mount Erebus gently perfumes the ash of its eruptions with microscopic crystals of gold, a kind of twenty-four-carat aerosol. This is not enough to call bullion, but it is pure gold.

The scientists who discovered gold in the volcanic exhaust of Mount Erebus had gone to Antarctica to study the hole in the ozone. As with so many scientific discoveries, discovering gold was serendipitous. Accident or not, the scientists expect that their discovery will be extremely valuable because no other volcano contains gold in its ash. Following the path of gasses emitted from this Antarctic peak will now be all the easier as the microscopic gold crystals can be seen as the "signature" of Mount Erebus.

I think there's a lesson here because only scientists would attach such a high value to such miniscule amounts of gold. There is nowhere near enough gold in Mount Erebus to interest people who work in the precious metals market, for example. A gold trader would value the discovery according to the fair market value, which in this case is practically nil. Mount Erebus may be spewing gold, but we can all rest assured that the price of gold will remain unaffected and will not be devalued in any way. And yet, scientists hail the discovery as practically invaluable.

Instead of fair market value, scientists value the microscopic gold crystals for their considerable symbolic worth. They know that whenever these crystal are detected in clouds or haze, they can confirm the presence of emissions from this particular volcano and can then accurately track their progress. This is important because scientists suspect volcanic emissions may play a part in ozone deterioration.

There is a surprising similarity between the symbolic value a scientist attaches to clouds of microscopic gold coming out of a volcano and the value the rest of humanity has attached to gold since its discovery. Gold occupies a privileged place for us, and much of gold's value stems from what it symbolizes to people. Gold has an invisible attraction; what it represents seems to be as important as what it is physically. And gold has several interesting physical properties, not the least of which is that it is incorruptible, a bona fide miracle by any standard.

Copper coins fished from the sea, if they've been there long enough, become brittle cakelike masses that break apart easily in the hands. Silver stains and turns pitch black. But even after a thousand years in the drink, gold coins will look as bright as the day they were minted.

Gold is able to ward off the ravages of time—a trick most of us deteriorating humans would love to learn how to do. Gold has traditionally been regarded as immortal because it doesn't deteriorate, and it rapidly became a symbol of perfection to millions of people who aspired to the rarefied heights of incorruptibility.

When medieval alchemists talked about transmuting base metals into gold, they weren't trying to get rich quick by turning lead into a more saleable commodity. They were talking about transmuting a base human mind into something divine, something that couldn't die, something that was, metaphorically, like gold.

But even people who are motivated by more mundane interests— common greed, for example—value gold as if it were, at the very least, economically immortal. People who are motivated by nothing more than sheer personal gain know that because of its physical properties, gold won't change in value as quickly as other forms of wealth. Paper money will rot in a wet basement in a matter of weeks. Equity in a house can be ruined if the house is destroyed by fire, earthquake, or storm. Purely abstract wealth is particularly vulnerable to decay; wealth in bank accounts or shares in a corporation can become worthless if the bank folds or the company collapses or the stock market plunges.

Gold may vary greatly in price (in what it is worth relative to other things), but everyone knows that gold will retain a particular intrinsic value, even if the entire credit system were to collapse. You would have to physically alter the gold to lower its intrinsic value, and that's difficult to do chemically, even if you want to. Someone somewhere will always be prepared to exchange certain things he or she owns for a certain amount of gold. I've always thought that curious. Why do so many people accept gold as fundamentally valuable? Surely, life would go on just fine if gold didn't even exist. The intrinsic value of gold is not of the order of things like food or air—things that are essential to live. So what is it about gold that practically compels people to value it?

One reason is that gold is rare. In fact, it has been estimated that all the gold mined for the last five hundred years (which is probably well over 90 percent of all the gold ever mined), amounts to about fifty thousand tons. Gold is dense, so dense that if you took all fifty thousand tons and made a cube cut of it, the cube would only be fifteen yards on a side. That doesn't seem like very much. One ton of gold isn't very big. One ton of gold, two thousand pounds, shaped into a cube would be only thirteen inches on a side. It's hard to imagine that a cube of gold only thirteen inches wide could not be lifted without a block and tackle or power machinery. This is why gold jewelry is usually not solid. Even chunky all-gold necklaces and bracelets are usually made hollow. Otherwise, they would be uncomfortably heavy to wear. Maybe this heaviness is another reason gold is so passionately valued. There's a lot packed into small spaces. Perhaps heaviness is on a par with rarity.

But the relative rarity of gold cannot account for the near frenzied following it commands. The fact that its rich, deep color and smooth texture delight the senses must also contribute to its value, as must the fact that gold has been readily available to people with only minimal technical ability. If you want to make something useful out of a gold nugget, all you have to do is bang it into shape while it is cold; you don't even have to heat it. Banging is a technical skill that even our earliest ancestors seemed able to master.

Gold dust in rivers or nuggets lying close to the surface were most likely the first sources of gold to be utilized by early people. Uprooting a tree or plowing a furrowed row of soil have both, on occasion, exposed small nuggets of gold.

Actual veins of gold are much rarer, and because they lie deeper in the earth, they are far more difficult to reach and harder still to mine. But panning for gold has been around for many thousands of years. Some cultures used a coarse cloth, a corduroy, to wash river sand that contained gold dust. The heavier gold particles settle between the ribs of the texture where they can be easily picked out with the fingers. Other cultures used sheep skins to accomplish the same end. In fact, sheep skins used to pan for gold was the original meaning of a "golden fleece."

Gold is so malleable that one ounce of it can be beaten into a single, continuous piece of wire fifty miles long. If the same ounce were used to plate wire made from some other substance, say copper or silver, there would be enough gold in one ounce to plate a wire one thousand miles long. The same one-ounce lump could also be pounded into a flat sheet that could cover three hundred square feet. It could be beaten into a film so thin, seven or eight molecules thick, that light would come through it. And, curiously, such light is greenish, not yellow.

Due to its efficient electrical properties and the fact that it will not corrode, gold is used to coat contact points, terminals, printed circuits, and semiconductors in the electric and electronic industries. In many electronic applications there is no substitute for gold. Gold also has the unusual ability to reflect close to 98 percent of incident infrared radiation that falls on it. That's why the face masks on astronauts' space suits are plated with gold. The plating is thin enough to see through and yet reflects practically all the dangerous radiation from the sun. With no atmosphere to filter the sun's rays, astronauts need protective gold-plated visors. Even buildings in warm climates on earth have used gold plating on windows to reduce the amount of air conditioning required.

These unique practical applications may make gold appear irreplaceable, but if gold didn't exist, engineers would undoubtedly find ways to do without it. And none of its practical applications account for the unusual passion people seem to display for this metal.

In the final assay we seem forced to return to the enormous symbolic quality of gold. Gold is bright, but it doesn't scintillate; gold reflects as though it radiates like the sun. Combined with its incorruptibility, gold became a fitting image of transcendence. To possess it suggests to religiously minded people that they, too, might transcend sickness, old age, and death. It's no coincidence that the ancient Greek word for gold is *christos*.

But gold is also considered transcendent by people more concerned with material profit than spiritual profit. Owning it ensures that one's wealth will most likely transcend currency devaluation, market depressions, even an out-and-out collapse of the entire credit system.

In a very real way, gold's invisible influence on the human mind is still very much with us. If it isn't, then how could we possibly explain that the discovery of miniscule amounts of microscopic gold crystals, in an out-of-the-way volcano in far away Antarctica, would make headline news?

CHAPTER THREE

EDUCATION AND THE ARTS

Education: It Never Ends

ANY FARMER WILL TELL YOU that to get good sprouts for next year you have to plan ahead. You must take care if plants are to grow well—you also must invest a lot of hard work and a lot of money. If you don't work at raising those sprouts or spend money on the proper supplies, you will have a bad crop. That's pretty simple.

Children are just like those sprouts, only more valuable and more complex. They require a lot of care and training to prepare them for living in the world and taking charge of the world, and our children are now in serious trouble.

Poor education in America has finally become an international embarrassment. Our students were recently beaten in math studies by every single developed country in the world. So who did we beat? Well, we beat countries like India, Mexico, Afghanistan—yes, we beat the entire third world in math. This is no simple embarrassment. It could end our leadership as a world power. Not planning for education can bring our country to its knees more thoroughly than any weapon launched by a foreign government.

How could the country be brought to its knees? Because education means not only teaching Johnny and Susie how to be doctors and lawyers, education prepares the citizenry to run the country. A blighted crop will rot in the field; any farmer will tell you that. No country can afford backward leadership.

Education has always been, more or less, on the back burner in this country. When early Americans were expanding their manifest destiny—towards Texas, California, and Oregon—there wasn't a lot of time or the wherewithal for schools. Life on the frontier was a pretty busy affair for folks just eking out a living.

Early Americans never really trusted educated people anyway. Education had been the monopoly of a European elite. In Europe either the church or the aristocracy controlled who learned what. The early

Americans had fled the tyranny of those privileged classes. So when we hear that early American frontiersmen used phrases like "Book larnin' ruins your shootin' eye," we know they meant it. Pride in being unschooled was not just simple sour grapes, it was a kind of patriotism. It set Americans apart from the European ruling class.

It's amazing but sadly true that we contemporary Americans have a very real remnant of that spirit. We may not say things like "Book larnin' ruins your shootin' eye," but we still associate book learning with some distant class and not with ourselves. In modern America, education really is open to all of us. When we think education belongs to someone else we fail to understand the meaning of education.

Imagine a woman who goes through college and attains a Ph.D. She marries, loves, and supports her husband, has children, runs a household, and may never actually work in her specialized field. I've heard others say of women like this (and I've heard this more than just once), "What a waste of a college education."

What do those people think an education is? Marriage is a wonderful way to use a Ph.D., no matter what you study to get it. If we go to college and get a degree in electronics, if we go to night school and study automobile repair, or if we learn to speak Chinese we will certainly be more expert in those specific fields, but more importantly, we will be transformed: we will be better people at whatever we do.

It really doesn't make much difference what you study. The reason for any education is not what you learn factually so much as learning how to learn. Sure, you learn how to look up facts, but the real secret power of learning is that you learn how to learn. This skill is tantamount to achieving an open mind.

The word educate comes from the Latin word *educare*, which means to lead, to draw, or to bring. A good education will bring or draw out a better person, a person better equipped to do anything, a better person who is not limited by the specifics that were studied in school.

Western civilization has been studying Greek and Latin (and the cultures related to those languages) for twenty-five centuries. Originally it was useful to know Greek or Latin because people actually spoke those languages and most books were written in them. People don't speak Attic Greek or Roman Latin today (I admit that I had to look up the Latin meaning of educate), and few, if any, books are written in these languages.

But why did the study of languages nobody spoke persist for so long? Because people benefited from the spirit of those languages. Greek and Latin still have as much potential benefit to a modern American who patronizes shopping malls as they did for the ancients who bargained in traditional bazaars.

Let me tell you a story (many of you already know it) about the spirit of education. In the early part of the last century, chemistry was emerging as an exciting frontier of discovery. I can't think of any field more practical than chemistry. Discoveries in chemistry have totally changed our lives precisely through their practical applications. These discoveries were not easily come by. Scientists labored over unknown forces and exuded a great deal of sweat to figure them out.

One of the more notable milestones in chemistry was the discovery of the structure of the benzene ring by August Kekule. Benzene was originally discovered by the English chemist and physicist Michael Faraday in 1825, but it wasn't until 1865 that Kekule described it as a ring. Chemists knew there was such a thing as benzene, but it didn't behave according to known laws. The structure of benzene was perplexing because its atoms, unlike those in other chemicals, aren't laid out in a line.

Historians of science agree that Kekule's original training as an architect enabled him to imagine structure differently than his colleagues— his colleagues, of course, had been trained specifically as chemists or physicists. Well, that's not all so surprising, is it? Principles learned in one field being transferred to another is a fairly common thing. But Kekule's discovery of the benzene ring came about through a much more interesting demonstration of association: Kekule *dreamed* his discovery.

He had a dream one night of a snake biting its tail. This was not simply the product of Kekule's fantasy, it was also part of his education. The image of the snake biting its tail is known as the *ouroboros*, and it has been in the repertoire of human thought since the time of ancient Egyptians. The *ouroboros* is a symbol of matter perpetually consuming and recreating itself. Kekule took this dream and made the historic leap to linked carbon atoms forming the benzene ring.

I doubt if Kekule would have looked for the structure of chemicals in Egyptology while he was awake, and he certainly had every right to dismiss a mere dream as useless in scientific discovery. But Kekule was a person "drawn out" by his education. He could grasp the essence of one thing and then objectively transfer it to another.

The spirit of education is the lack of preconceived ideas. An education means opening the mind without prejudice. Every day we are presented with useful solutions to our problems from unexpected sources, but, sadly, we usually fail to recognize them. Without the benefit of an open mind, drawn out through the process of education, we are fooled.

Discovery itself is not the only important thing. The *ability* to discover is equally important. We have risen from the ignorance of animals through our ability to discover. Animals discover things, too, but our ability to do this has increased while theirs has not. America as a nation has become a superpower because of discovery. Without a strong and healthy education system, our ability to discover is crippled.

Education requires two parties: an inspired educator and an inspired student. I can assure you it is far more difficult to find an inspired educator than an inspired student. A student can do little without the benefit of example.

Teachers are so important to a culture that the status of a teacher in a society is a good measure of the degree of civilization of that society. When I was busy looking up *educate* in Latin, I also looked up the word *teacher*. The Latin word for teacher is *doctor*. While it may be true that in America medical doctors are respected (and rewarded), an English teacher who may also be a doctor usually isn't. Well, life tends to reward efforts of the flesh over those of the spirit.

It may not be necessary for doctors committed to teaching school to drive Rolls-Royces and Mercedes Benzes like many of their medical counterparts. But teachers should be rewarded and respected, or our children will not achieve the open minds they so desperately need. Teachers are real doctors, and they need our support.

A recent poll among our dedicated teachers showed 51 percent had thought about quitting at least once. Among those who actually did leave, a full 83 percent doubted they ever would return. Sixty-four percent were surprised just how low the professional prestige of a teacher turned out to be, once they actually went to work. No wonder our schools are falling apart and are understaffed and plagued with disciplinary problems. We cannot expect such schools to produce scholars in the same league as the Europeans or Japanese.

To raise our standards we will have to do three things. We will have to put significant amounts of money into education—that's obvious. We also will have to start thinking differently about teachers, professors, and educators to attract the superior talent we need. And most important of all, we need to educate ourselves. All of us should continue our education. We should read more books, increase our vocabularies, and be interested in anything and everything—we need to work at opening our minds. We can't hand over the responsibility of educating our children to the doctors we hire to teach schools—the most fertile ground, for any young sprout, is the ground it puts its roots into at home.

Teaching and Learning

EARLY IN LIFE I GOT THE IDEA that I could teach myself all the facts and skills I would ever need. This idea blossomed into arrogance as soon as I could read (which I was taught how to do, of course, by teachers). But I was convinced that with reasonable effort and access to an occasional small store of research, I could master even the most esoteric disciplines of craft and wisdom without any intervening tutoring agent.

Two events led me to this idea. When I was five, I wanted to ride a bicycle. I had ridden tricycles and owned one, and I came to scorn it because little kids could ride tricycles and they easily remained upright when not in motion. But there was something magical about two wheels that stayed up and did not fall over. The older children somehow had the knack. I grew to want it desperately.

Attempts to train me on a neighbor girl's Schwinn proved futile. Older children would run alongside, holding me up and working at cross purposes until speed or attention span would cause them to drop away and let me go on alone to an immediate and inevitable crash. These pileups hurt me and scared me, but they only fanned the flames of desire. I felt I had to conquer this vehicle.

Then one day (my little tutors having despaired and gone on to other things) I tried it by myself. I had discovered that I need not sit up on the too-high seat, but could stand on the pedals, since a girl's bicycle didn't have a top bar. I jumped into position after getting the bike in motion, expecting a swifter and more spectacular smashup than when my ground crew launched me. But to my surprise, it all fell into place in a second. I turned into my falling and corrected it! I pedaled. I glided. I stayed upright. I even controlled the machine and gave it direction—all by myself. I traversed an incredible fifteen yards or so before coming to a full stop and a dignified keel-over—a sort of in-place crash. The elation that accompanied this success was so intense that I never knew if the fall was painful. I was euphoric. If I'd come down on a forest of javelins I'd never have known it. I was invulnerable, immortal, in my ecstasy.

There have been high points in my adult life: the first time I soloed a single-engine airplane; a night dive off San Salvador in 125 feet of water; a landfall after sailing 3,300 miles of ocean in a small boat, guided by a sextant and the sun and stars; some moments driving racing cars and motorcycles (where the triumph consisted mainly of staying alive). But from a feeling standpoint, nothing has approached the ecstatic blast of that miraculous ride across a whole, big backyard on that full-size two-wheeler. And since success had come about when I went it alone, I couldn't shake the idea that no credit whatsoever was due those who had tried to teach me and had failed. Education only worked when I taught myself.

A second incident reinforced my concept of self-sufficiency and the arrogant idea that I could be both teacher and pupil in all things. I was nine years old. We had an old Underwood typewriter in the house. It fascinated me, and I wanted to put my own words into type. Type gave the words a dignity they never had in longhand. I operated the machine, staring at the keyboard and whacking at the keys with the trigger finger of each hand (a method, I later learned, that was referred to as the hunt-and-peck technique, employed by all self-respecting reporters). I also learned there was a system called "touch" typing, but believed it to be utilized only by secretaries. Then, one year in the '30s, the champion typist of the state of Ohio was a one-armed man. He obviously used the touch system and must have used it supremely well. I was determined to learn it.

I pestered my father into finding a book on touch typing, which he brought home one night. I plunged into it with such zeal, teaching myself, that in a short time I could type faster than I could think (which was no particular record as far as typing is concerned). I could also type anything without looking at the keyboard. Knowing that people went to schools for this kind of training, I felt that the function of the teacher was merely to keep students on track or to goad them into practicing.

I want to look now at this early theory of mine on self-teaching from two opposite viewpoints. First of all, it is nonsense that teachers are unnecessary; it is nonsense that one can learn everything there is to be learned without, in certain instances, specific kinds of in-person guidance. We can memorize dates without a teacher, but some skills simply cannot be acquired from books. Discrediting my playmates' efforts to teach me how to ride a bike is probably unfair to them, inept as they may have been as instructors. Some aspects of those tutored rides, although wobbly and confusing, contributed an undeniable kinesthetic transmission of balance and, I now believe, prepared me for my first successful attempt.

Teachers are also indispensable as backup systems when skills that could result in fatal mistakes if done incorrectly must be practiced. In landing an airplane, for example, a flight instructor safely guides a student around many possible disasters. There are the inevitable exceptions, of course—rare exceptions. The late General Benjamin Foulois in 1911 was commanded by the U.S. Army to "assemble a flying machine and teach yourself to fly." He did. He also lived into his eighties. But General Foulois was a pioneer, something subsequent pilots can never be.

I'm glad I realized when I was young that my theory about teaching myself was arrogant, because the discovery shed light on the nature of self-motivation. I learned that teachers are important. Obviously, some teachers may unwittingly stand in the way of self-motivation, but I learned that, with or without a teacher, if you are taught, you learn yourself. Perhaps there is a double error in such an ungrammatical phrase, something like, "I'll learn you to do-such and-such." But in the end you only learn yourself. Nobody else can "learn" you.

Since those early years I have made use of many teachers and instructors, and I'm grateful to many of them for the things I could not possibly have accomplished without them. But the basis of what little stove of skills and knowledge I have acquired is my psychological conviction that whatever I am expected to learn, I must learn myself. It simply can't be "learned" into me.

You can teach yourself a lot without teachers, since you're the one who has to learn. But even when teachers are indispensable, the real learning is still done by the student.

Perhaps because of the syllable *fill* in fulfillment, we tend to think of *fulfillment* as filling up a vessel. This can be misleading. A human being is really more of a flow system than a keg. I like to think of a human as a firehose. If a person is caked on the outside, or corroded on the inside, or kinked or cramped so that only a trickle of life gets through, then that person is blighted and unfulfilled. But people who remain open and unrestricted and relatively unselfconscious find no impediments to their flow of life and experience a torrent of living. These are the types of people we can unreservedly call "fulfilled."

I have always wondered through what mechanism self-help literature gains leverage on motivation and—even if it does, if it is effective—then how do these books work to get people to be self-motivated? It seems anomalous. And yet there must be a reason why self-help books and articles sell in such quantity. (And there seems to be an endless list of books from *The Power of Positive Thinking* and *How to Win Friends and Influence People*, to *Winning Through Intimidation* and *How to be Your Own Best Friend*.) There must be some link between inspirational reading and self-motivation. Whether it produces any permanent results on a meaningful statistical scale might be hard to ascertain. But for the same reason that even good teachers cannot do the learning for their students, inspirational reading material cannot self-motivate in the subjective sense: self-motivation simply cannot come from outside.

Self-fulfillment likewise may be a kind of "other-directedness." To gather in what is worthwhile about life, one has to put out energy. Instead of getting out what you put in, you get in what you put out. The idea is not as complicated as it seems, and it's just corny enough to be true.

Kid Lit

YOU MIGHT THINK THAT CHILDREN, with all their noise, obstreperous behavior, and short attention spans, would be the most obvious people on earth. You might think it would be hard not to notice young people. Well, individual adults, especially parents, have no trouble at all recognizing children, but society (that subtle psychological network operating inside adults) is not all that quick to recognize the existence of children. Surprisingly, societies either discover children or they do not discover children. How can we tell?

There's one easy way. Children who live in societies that have "discovered children" enjoy a literature written especially for them. Children's literature develops, and can only develop, in societies that recognize children as children and not as miniature adults or as protocitizens or as family automata who happen to be short in stature.

The idea of a generation gap, for example, is relatively new. The idea only developed within the last several hundred years or so. But without a gap to distinguish children from adults, the labels *child* and *adult* merely refer to different measurements of height and not to groups that have different and specific needs.

Look at the way children were portrayed in ancient literature. The child Astyanax, mythological young son of Hector and Andromache, was flung from a high parapet to the ground during the siege of Troy as if he were merely, as one scholar describes the scene, a "stage prop." In the famous Greek play about the witchlike woman named Medea, Medea's children also achieve little more dramatic stature than that of rag dolls.

Ancient Greek playwrights who departed from this pattern and included dramatic treatments of children that suggested, however embryonically, a more developed sense of humanity were sometimes scorned. Euripides's more rounded portrayal of children in his play *Alcestis* earned him a biting diatribe from Aristophanes. I suppose this would be like Neil Simon suddenly finding fault with the work of Andrew Lloyd Weber. "Cats, Andrew? You're going to populate a musical play with nothing but cats?" Something like that.

We may also be appalled that the ancients would have such little regard for children. But they did. And adults continued to disregard children in striking ways for a very long time. As late as the sixteenth century we find that the famous essayist Michel de Montaigne believed that children had "neither mental activities nor recognizable body shape."

This remarkably demeaning opinion of children is all the more remarkable when we remember that Montaigne was a particularly liberated thinker for his time and pioneered certain humanistic convictions that help shed light in the dank recesses of a stultifying and backward church. But Montaigne was not exempt from the prejudices of adulthood.

Soon after Montaigne, in 1658, we notice a major turning point in attitudes toward children. A particularly innovative educator and religious leader named John Amos Comenius brought out an illustrated textbook of Latin designed specially for children. By the next year, 1659, Comenius's *Orbis Sensualium Pictus* was translated into English under the title *The Visible World in Pictures*. *Orbis* was the first picture book ever made specifically with young readers in mind. Its publication is remembered by historians as a milestone, a moment when mature society began to realize that children are not just pint-size adults with memory deficits, they are children. John Amos Comenius realized that children were complete people in their own right and that they have special needs. This seems so obvious to us today.

But children did not really begin to enjoy the special recognition we accord them today for nearly one hundred years after Comenius. With thinkers like Rousseau and Locke, and with the dawning of the Age of Enlightenment, children rode the wave of special recognition being granted to women and other groups that had been previously disenfranchised. Children began to be seen as a group all their own. Nothing underlined this distinction more emphatically than the need for, and the actual development of, books written especially for children.

Groups gain authority when they have their own literature. *Literature* is literally the written word. To possess the written word is to possess writing, and writing is more than mere record scratching. Writing is the graphic key with which we unlock a symbolic imagination; writing grows like feathered wings from the mind and allows us to soar in spirit. Writing is very important. Without it we are rendered illiterate. When children gained this awesome power, the resulting literature reflected their unique world view.

Children rarely author books themselves, although some have. Instead, children's books are usually written by adults. Writing children's books is not easy. In fact, the younger the audience, the more difficult the task. But what gems we have in this field—Beatrix Potter and Lewis Carroll, A. A. Milne and E. B. White. Their original tales, sometimes accompanied by original illustrations, are masterpieces that can be enjoyed by people of any age.

There is a certain vision unique to children, a vision not necessarily crafted by adults, that is perpetuated in nursery rhymes and nonsensical poems. We also find this vision in insulting verse and incantations, in lamentations, and in stories about unusual people or animals. This nursery tradition tends to be fairly old because parents repeat to their children the rhymes they heard when they were children, and so on. Often adults have little or nothing to do with the manufacture of such rhymes. Children have passed them down through the centuries. So we might hear on a modern street in London:

> *Blessed be the memory*
> *Of good old Thomas Sutton,*
> *Who gave us lodging, learning,*
> *As well as beef and mutton.*

Thomas Sutton, the founder of Charter House in England, was born in 1532 and died in 1611. Children chant old riddles, too. See if you can guess this one:

> *As I was going over London Bridge*
> *I met with a Westminster scholar.*
> *He pulled off his cap an' drew off his glove,*
> *And wished me a very good morrow.*
> *What was his name?*

The answer, if you did not catch it, is Andrew, from "He pulled off his cap *an' drew* off his glove." A marvelous collection of such wit was published under the name *I Saw Esau: The Schoolchild's Pocket Book. I Saw Esau* is a compendium of children's verse edited by Iona and Peter Opie and illustrated by Maurice Sendak.

> *I saw Esau kissing Kate,*
> *The fact is we all three saw:*
> *For I saw him,*
> *And he saw me,*
> *And she saw I saw Esau.*

I Saw Esau is a beautiful book to hold and read. It is no ordinary children's book. The rhymes inside are true grit and sometimes reflect a brutal reality, like this jump-rope ditty:

> *Mother, Mother, I am ill!*
> *Send for the doctor! Yes I will.*
> *Doctor, Doctor, shall I die?*
> *Yes, my child, and so shall I.*
> *When I die pray tell to me,*
> *How many coaches will there be?*
> *One, two, three, four . . .*

When the counting stops, the girl skipping rope determines how many funeral hearses will parade through the streets carrying her bier. A gruesome thought to ponder, perhaps, but, at least, it's an inevitable event.

Children also have a near magical way of relating to nature. And we find several interesting incantations addressed to animals. For example sea gulls are recognized as portents of the elements: "Sea gull, sea gull, sit on the sand, It's never good weather when you're inland." Makes you wonder how children know such things. They must be very observant.

They know crows are threatening birds, because crows steal things and screech at little flightless mammals like children. So crows can be dealt with severely: "Crow, Crow, get out of my sight, Or else I'll have your liver and light." Plainly too bad for the crow. But other things children say seem plainly absurd:

> *One fine day in the middle of the night*
> *Two dead men got up to fight.*
> *A blind man came to see fair play,*
> *A dumb man came to shout hurray.*

Apparently, we are told by the editors, this last verse is "one of the oldest forms of nonsense." In 1480, a professional minstrel recorded a similar verse in a notebook, which may now be seen in the Bodleian Library at Oxford University:

> *I saw three headless [men] playing at ball,*
> *A handless man served them all,*
> *While three mouthless [men] sang and howled,*
> *Three legless [men] drove them away.*

Childhood is years of testing and trying out both possible and impossible experiments. Based on the results of their experiments, children stake out the limits of their own reality. Different children extend their limits in different directions and establish boundaries at varying distances according to individual style, ability, and courage. The absurd suggests the question "how?" How could headless men play ball or handless men serve them all? Answers to such questions establish the boundaries of our reality.

Why on earth, if life is good as we are told, do we have so much bad mixed in with it? It seems a contradiction. Adults resolve this contradiction in one of two ways: either they become inured to it and are dull, or they teeter on the brink of madness and slide through life with little control. Either way awareness seems to be compromised. But children ask these basic questions about life for the first time, not for a wearied umpteenth time.

Children can explore nonsense seriously and mount courageous battles against their fears. They commune with nature and believe in spells, and they can stop their enemies with rhymes. These acts are little wonders.

Only a few hundred years ago, society didn't even recognize children as a separate and distinct group (some societies still don't). In the Middle Ages, children were seen as servile runts, not really ready for anything. But children are quite ready, indeed, for what they do best: they are precious resources of spontaneity. If you wish to expand your reading a bit and perhaps pick up a few tips about life, crack a book written for children and read what's inside. The world that lies between those covers is a world you probably lost a very long time ago.

Critics

CRITICIZING IS NOT THE SAME as critiquing. Criticism can mean two very different things: *criticizing* implies a deliberate denigration of something, and *critiquing* can mean a thoughtful judgment on the quality of a work of art (and that may include practically any effort: literature, drama, or radio and television broadcasts, whatever).

Critics attempt to bring a careful and reasoned consideration to their craft. They apply a standard of reference to the work being judged, and they shape an opinion about its merit. Critics then announce their opinion in some published form. This interesting exercise is done all the time and not only by people who make their living doing it—the dreaded professional "critics"—but also by the rest of us. We see a movie, for example, and then compare it to other movies of its type and to our own experiences in life.

We might prefer that the movie had been directed differently or acted differently or even filmed in a different way. We may also recognize in movies uncannily accurate reproductions of our own true life experiences. Then we announce this opinion to others: "I wouldn't waste my time going to this movie," or, "Don't miss it. It's the best thing I've seen in a decade," or maybe something in between. At that moment we, too, are critics.

Criticism faces an intriguing challenge these days because there are so many excellent products to consider. The challenge is that we can lose what I call an "appreciation range" by applying too high a standard to the things we judge. Today, largely due to an amazing array of technical advances, we have access to the very best in nearly everything: the best stage performances, the best recordings, the best in print, even the best movies, now available on video. As a result, we run the risk of losing an important frame of reference for our powers of discrimination. We have become so used to excellence that we risk refusing to settle for less than the top half-percent. We can narrow our capacity to appreciate what other artists do—artists who may not be performing in the top half-percent, but who make interesting contributions nonetheless.

We might neglect appreciating how much an artist has improved. We might fail to appreciate an artist's perseverance or simply fail to judge him or her within the specific arena in which that artist works. Such failings can breed disappointment for us, the audience, because we might discard some efforts simply because they fall short of what we imagine is perfection.

In the little town in Ohio where my mother grew up, there was one theater. In it vaudeville, operetta, and recitals took place along with concerts, plays, and full-blown operas. Every couple of months my mother would see something that was probably, justifiably, third rate, at least by the standards of the day. Every couple of years a good production would be staged—a play, an opera—and this she would find mighty impressive. Then, about once a decade she would go to New York and see a performance at the Metropolitan Opera, a performance that would be predictably overwhelming. My mother had a broader base for judging and for appreciating art than we do.

Some of us will not tolerate anything but the very top talent. Anybody with thirteen dollars can buy a compact disc and hear Itzak Perlman play a violin concerto. We are not likely to buy to a recording by someone who is labeled second-rate. But without the contrast of other artists to throw Perlman into relief, we risk not understanding just how superior he really is. The so-called lesser artists may be way up there in talent and dedication anyway. By not appreciating them, we miss out on important work, and in the bargain, we fail to appreciate the true greatness of a master like Perlman.

Consider a scale of 0 to 10, and suppose that 10 represents perfection. Ten is really an empty category, because no art is ever really a ten; ten is an ideal. Let's say 9 represents the very best, the undisputed top—*My Fair Lady*, for example, or Laurence Olivier, or Hank Aaron. Nine, we might say, is undisputed excellence.

Eight is very good, satisfying, maybe thrilling, even though we have experienced on rare occasions something a notch above this. Seven is good, solidly good. Six is OK, maybe worth a trip or a look. Five is so-so, the definition of mediocrity. The work may appeal to you, if you happen to like the genre, but your life will not be blighted if you miss it. Four is poor, save your money. Three can be called pathetic, really not good. Two is bad. One is god-awful. And zero is perfectly horrible.

Now, a word about the last three categories: two, one, and zero. When a product is really bad, it begins to inspire a peculiar fascination—the audience can actually wonder how the work could possibly have come out so bad. There have been a few movies like this, movies that are so truly dreadful that they inspire wonder: "They're pulling our legs, right?" or, "How could they possibly have produced something so awful, even if they tried?"

One film that came out several years back, called *Plan Nine from Outer Space*, stars Bela Lugosi, and it is bad, bad, bad. Lugosi, of course, had established a reputation for doing horror movies rather well. This one, however, was (in the minds of many moviegoers) so horrible that it immediately gained notoriety as something prodigious in its paucity of talent. The whole film—the editing, the writing, the acting, the very concept of it, everything—was perfect in its ghastliness. On a scale of zero to ten it was certainly a one, and many believe it could qualify for a zero. Some fans actually debate just exactly how bad it is. In fact, *Plan Nine from Outer Space* is so bad that it enjoys perennial success as a cult classic.

It is a curious irony that few achievements that are really artistic or virtuous can ever be considered perfect, since perfection is so widely accepted as an ideal and unattainable in art; there is no 10, not really. But things that are truly awful can reach a sort of perfection in their horribleness. This is amazing. They can be ranked zero and simultaneously be considered a sort of classic. I hope this doesn't reflect some hidden characteristic of human nature.

Our reaction to professional critics (the people who are often responsible for influential pronouncements) is significant, whether we read them and are influenced by their opinions or suffer because of their reviews. Many people wonder why critics are so negative. There is a popular notion that critics exude a sour outlook on life. The notion is due to the volumes of scathing reviews that professional critics generate, necessarily, in order to gain notoriety for themselves.

I think there are multiple reasons for scathing reviews. Critics are not hired to praise everything they see or hear or read. Any critic who did that would not last long. They are hired to make an honest attempt to assess merit. This is not easy. Most critics are experienced; they have been exposed to a wider range of examples in their particular specialty (like books or movies) than the general public. It is from this wider exposure that they base their rigorous standard of judgment. They have a refined sense of the trite, the failed attempt, the cheap imitation, the shallow ploy, and they expose such failings with dispatch because that is what they must do. But experience is a double-edged sword that also can turn a critic into a jaded and brittle soul.

The truly jaded and brittle are easily irritated by the "presumption" of artists who swagger their way into the limelight and fall short of the standards that the critic imagines must be upheld. Good critics with considerable experience recognize worth, and, if they are secure in their position (and their reputations), they are capable of lavishing praise where they think it is deserved. But among less-experienced critics or those who are jaded or brittle there is fear that they will appear unsophisticated if they praise too much, even if they have been privately impressed with something they are reviewing.

I saw a cartoon awhile back that showed a critic sitting in front of a TV set laughing his head off, slapping his thigh, and falling on the floor in paroxysms of mirth. In the last frame, seated before his typewriter and sour-faced, he was writing, "The usual tawdry mix of stale jokes, sight-gag clichés, and pathetically off-time delivery."

Like any commercial commodity, kind words are more valuable if they come from a critic who is known to be harsh. When kind words flow from a normally harsh critic, they will be quoted widely in ads, in promotional material, and on book jackets. Such publicity will elevate the critic to celebrity as well as the artist being reviewed. The temptation for critics to create value like this is high and can hardly be ignored. I have come to believe that such forces influence professional critics. Considering that they are only human (although there are those among the reviewed who might question that classification), these forces strike deep.

Do we really need someone else to tell us whether we enjoyed a performance or a book? Are we so insecure, so afraid to make up our own minds, that we need to have our judging done for us by proxy? Apparently so. I understand that if all the reviewers attack something we haven't yet read or seen and especially if all our friends agree with them, then we might save some money and time. But there is also this puzzle: how is it that mixed reviews can destroy a work? That has always seemed difficult to explain. Mixed reviews can kill a work almost as effectively as uniformly bad reviews can.

Regardless of any review, good, bad or mixed, the humanity of the performers comes through in the ways they react to criticism. Predictably, the reaction mirrors the review. A positively glowing review produces an opinion among the reviewed that the reviewer is also a positive and glowing individual. We might even think he or she is intelligent, likeable, and a skilled professional. A negative review, however, can produce among the reviewed feelings that the reviewer is also negative. Actors are believed to be the most sensitive to critical reviews because acting requires that players become their personae. If, in addition to being sensitive to his part, an actor is also vain, then he can become his bad reviews, too, and that must sting severely.

There is a story about the acting team Alfred Lunt and Lynn Fontaine. At the pinnacle of their career, they opened in a play on Broadway, and at breakfast the next morning read a review in a New York paper that tore apart Fontaine. The review read something like this: "Lynn Fontaine, aging and never truly talented, tried her best to bring her role to life, but the attempt was pathetic," and so on, for a very long paragraph. I'm paraphrasing here, but the review went on to describe her husband as: "Alfred Lunt, on the other hand, always a talented man, added glory to his solid reputation by a brilliant performance. In addition to his talent, his appearance is impressive. In spite of a slightly weak chin, he can be considered truly handsome." Fontaine, reduced to tears, looked to Lunt for some comfort or support, and he said, "What the hell does he mean, 'weak chin'?"

To a broadcaster, critics are like ratings: if favorable, we rush to believe they are accurate and important; if negative, we want to dismiss them as inaccurate or unimportant. Somebody once said of the broadcasting business that "You are only as good as your last segment." At times that maxim can seem brutally true.

I'll admit that if a critical review of this particular commentary is forthcoming, I will not be inclined to come forth to read it. I think I'll postpone Judgment Day for some later, more compelling time.

Listen Up

MUSIC HATH CHARMS, THE SAYING GOES, to soothe the savage beast. This may be true, but I'm not sure I'd want to face a charging lion armed with only a flute when I could have a high-caliber rifle. He might not be in the mood for an unaccompanied sonata by Bach. Under the circumstances, I'm sure I couldn't play that well anyway.

There is evidence that music has an effect on some animals under certain circumstances. Cows are said to be more inclined to give milk while listening to soothing music. But we have no way of knowing how cows hear music; their tails certainly don't keep time. The hearing range and sensitivity of most animals seem to accept music the same way our ears do, but what their brains do with the impulses, or what their spirits do with the movements, are unknown.

Musically speaking, humans differ from most other animals in that we establish formal rules to regularize pitch and rhythm. We sense pitch variation and measure tone according to the number of vibrations per second. This is physics. Rhythm and pitch, incidentally, are the same thing. We might beat a drum four times a second or once a second to establish a rhythmic pattern. Four hundred forty beats a second produces a particular tone, middle A.

Nature rarely produces regular rhythms, but sometimes it does. We find them in the very small and very large. Atoms have frequencies that are consistent (in a very high range), and planets and satellites rotate and revolve with exquisite precision in very majestic, slow rhythms, but in between these size extremes nature is spare with rhythmic or tonal regularity. Birds sing rather well, and whales "sing" an undeniably haunting profundo of sorts, but their pitch and rhythmic consistency is nowhere nearly as precise as human instruments (including voice) that are regulated according to mathematical laws.

So why do humans delight in producing tones and rhythms? It's as though we are somehow in tune with the very small and the very large realms of the universe. We weave tonal patterns and produce harmonies that are related to the mathematical foundations of the cosmos. And we do this not for survival or aggrandizement but for fun, to amuse ourselves and, perhaps most meaningfully, to overwhelm ourselves with aesthetic satisfaction.

I can imagine a very long time ago, long before civilization, primitive people sitting by a river bank, watching the rhythmic bobbing of a tree trunk floating by. They sit quietly watching the gentle up and down movement of the log and, at the same time, the constant downstream flow of the river.

Hunters, who needed to observe the movement of animals closely, imitated many animal movements, many of which have certain spontaneous rhythms to them. Early holy men wore the skins of some animals in further imitation. They also recreated the "dance" of these natural, totemic guides. It's possible that the earliest rituals were based on such observations and imitations, which elevated natural movements to disciplined dance.

Blowing through a bone or a shell so that it whistled for the first time must have been an intriguing experience. The ability to make music could easily have been developed and lost countless times before it was really learned, but once learned, such skill made its way rapidly into human ritual.

Bowmen, too, noticed sound—the twanging sound produced by a bowstring. Perhaps by accident, someone noticed that when pressing the bow against a hollow gourd the sound was amplified. Here we have the ancestor of the harp and the various plucked and bowed instruments: the sitar and oud; the guitar, mandolin and lute; the violin, cello, viola, bass, and the hammered clavier dulcimer. All of these make their music through vibrating strings.

Scientific and mathematical facts may explain how we make music, but they don't explain why. Why is music pleasant to us? I grant that not all music is pleasant to all people, but music is obviously pleasant, or we wouldn't produce so much of it and listen to it live or at home in recordings. So why do we blow through tubes and pluck and hammer strings and beat on skins stretched over kettles? Perhaps music binds us to our ancestral roots, those experiences by the river bank, or perhaps it rekindles the destiny of the hunt.

Another possibility is that certain pitch relationships and rhythmic intervals resonate with certain brain patterns in the same way that certain chemicals fit brain receptors. The way nicotine, for example, is said to lock onto the same brain receptors as do endorphins that ease pain and bring on feelings of euphoria. Trying to analyze or quantify feelings we call aesthetic may be a tall order, but we know definitively that music does more than just soothe; it challenges, it evokes moods, it inspires, it moves us. Some people believe it can heal.

Sir Francis Bacon said to King James I, "This variable composition of man's body hath made it as an instrument easy to distemper; and therefore the poets did well to conjoin Music and Medicine in Apollo, because the Office of Medicine is but to tune this curious harp of man's body and to reduce it to harmony." Homer noted that music can prevent anger, sadness, and disquiet, "in addition to promoting health." A growing list of modern medical experts is taking a new look at this potential. Some now believe music does indeed heal or at least contributes to the body's efforts to heal.

The late Howard Rusk, founder of the Rusk Institute of Rehabilitative Medicine, set the tone when he said that music might add a new and vibrant dimension to rehabilitative medicine. He included music as an ingredient in the holistic approach to patient care.

Dr. Matthew Lee edited a book titled *Rehabilitation, Music and Human Well-Being*, in which nearly two dozen medical experts offer different views on why music is valuable in treating disease. Can you imagine going to a doctor for an insurance physical and being told you need a dose of Mozart or a shot of Mendelssohn? Or maybe your particular malady might respond better with a hit of Elvis or a blast of Quincy Jones or the Grateful Dead. The pharmacy could be transformed.

It has been fairly well established that very loud sounds, sounds that continuously batter the eardrum, can cause deafness at an early age. This is not the fault of music, just the levels at which it is sometimes performed. The first time I heard a group called the Who in England, I was impressed with the fact they had 1,000-watt amplifiers driving high-efficiency speakers. The sound was quite powerful. Years later, in Hartford, Connecticut, I watched Bruce Springsteen's people unload and set up towering racks of speakers powered by 750,000 watts! At the concert, I was glad to see the auditorium was made of steel-reinforced concrete. It would otherwise simply have crumbled into rubble under the impact of the sound waves that the E Street Band produced. This was music you could feel in your chest as well as hear with your ears. People who attend many such concerts have reported some hearing impairment.

When I told my brother Wallace about this, he said that he had had a "music" experience even more jolting than 750,000 watts of serious rock. He was at dinner with his family, and they were discussing popular music. His then-thirteen-year-old daughter said to him with a straight face, "Daddy, what kind of music did they listen to when you were alive?" He said it ruined his whole day.

You might not think there's a connection between bread and music, but I stumbled on one with the same kind of serendipitous accident as a bowman twanging his string or an early hominid whistling through a dried bone. One of my hobbies is baking bread. I haven't baked a lot in the last decade because I've been too busy with broadcasting, but back when I baked often, I always listened to music while I kneaded dough, waited for it to rise, put my creations in the oven, and then placed them near an open window to cool. I began to fancy that the quality and nature of the bread was influenced by the kind of music I played. By "played" I refer to records, tapes, and more recently CDs. I work better when I do this.

The connection between the bread and the music became so strong in my mind that if I was trying for a heavier type of loaf, I'd put on some Wagner, and if I wanted bread with a lighter personality, I'd play chamber music or the French impressionists—Ibert, Debussy, and Ravel make good light breads. My wife began to eye me suspiciously, and wondered aloud if I shouldn't be locked up, then she wondered what my secret to baking might be. We joked about the music-bread connection.

I've recently discovered that a Japanese baking firm is quite serious about the effect of music on yeast. It believes there is a connection between the kind of music that goes into the stereo and the kind of bread that comes out of the oven. They aren't kidding. Maybe, subconsciously, I wasn't either. If cows give more milk when they listen to music, why shouldn't those little yeast fellows make the bread rise better when they hear the sonic beauty produced by the Great Masters? The Japanese baking firm claims they do.

On the matter of listening to music, technology may have tapped into a sort of "fountain of youth." In contouring the playback of a recording, it is possible to get an effect more pleasing than hearing the real performance. Years ago an audio engineer I worked with referred to a recorded sound as "better than real." "Wait a minute," I said. "If reality is the criterion, nothing can be 'better than real.'" He then explained to me what he meant. As we get older, certain frequencies (pitches) begin to fade as our eardrums become less responsive—notably, higher frequencies drop. Now, if in the playback of a good recording you can boost the gain on those frequencies that are beginning to sag, you aid hearing in a peculiarly satisfying way. You hear the music as you had once heard it with younger ears. This is what he meant when he asserted that the music was better than real.

Perhaps the new computer technology called "interactive" may allow us to perceive graphic arts in a similar way. As we age, we lose certain visual sensitivities. Computerized enhancements of graphic images, even three-dimensional sculptures, could be tailored by each user to "boost the gain" in needed areas. This technology may allow individuals to enjoy the work in ways they did when they were younger.

My only advice for this experience is to put on some Mahler, or maybe some UB-40, and let the spirit leaven. Listen to the moving timbre as it flows down the great river of life.

Words Break Bones?

WHEN I WAS A CHILD, I remember my mother taking me aside one day and explaining that sticks and stones would break my bones, but names would never hurt me. It seemed like an important lesson at the time. It provided me with protection against the cruel and inevitable insults that children hurl at one another. After my lesson, when I was on the receiving end of a taunting or insulting outburst, I could tell the difference between words and stones. I valued the lesson about sticks and stones and eventually passed it on to my own children, and they, in turn, handed it on to theirs. Sticks and stones will break your bones, but names will never hurt you.

That was lesson number one in social relations: how to defuse insults directed at you. Lesson number two was the golden rule: Treat other people the way you would want them to treat you. Armed with this terse, yet profound set of teachings, I set forth to explore the world; I was reinforced against the broadsides of insult and took pride in my attempts (at least) to not offend anyone else.

Those lessons came quite a while ago. Over the years, the times seem to have magnified and exaggerated the entire spectrum of life, not just school life. Abortion, homosexuality, sexism, ageism, drugs, child abuse, and capital punishment (just to name a few) are not new issues. What is new is that an unprecedented amount of information about these topics suddenly became available to the population. The deluge of details about issues that are inherently confidential (or, like capital punishment, require that a person form intimate convictions) has had the effect of increasing the potency of words.

The recognition of so many new issues seems to have transformed the lesson about words and stones and bones into an analogy. Insults do inflict damage on people after all, mental damage. And mental damage is analogous to breaking bones with stones. Words can hurt. To reduce such damage, society began to change its speech. "He and she" for example, was substituted for just "he," and "humankind" was substituted for "mankind." Many women are sensitive to these modifications, and accommodating their wishes costs nothing. Schools are even teaching old dogmas new tricks by reinterpreting essential tenets of human history, including Aristotle.

Carol Delany, a professor of anthropology at Stanford University, explains, "Of course there's a lot to be praised in Aristotle's work—the whole flowering of philosophy and metaphysics and logic. I wouldn't deny that. On the other hand, Aristotle was definitely sexist—and elitist and racist. For us to just pass over or ignore these inconvenient or very unpleasant assumptions, I think, really does a disservice to students."

A hundred years ago, even fifty, nobody would have had any idea what Delany was talking about. Airplanes and automobiles may have made the world smaller in the last hundred years, but the phenomenal increase of information during that time has actually made the world larger and more complicated. This information explosion magnified the importance of issues that once received little public attention. The magnification, in turn, scattered the population as people took up new, more distant positions on a greatly expanded field of play. The polarization of American opinion has reduced a union into a conflicting fray of bitter ends.

Freshman dorms are now patrolled by resident assistants who have received specific instructions to promote cross-cultural understanding and discussion. The intent is to foster a "politically correct," or PC way of speaking and behaving. One such resident assistant at Stanford, Marcus Mabry, told us, "We organized forums where students discussed gender, race, and sexuality. And most PC folks used a language that reflected shared beliefs: college-aged females are 'women,' not girls; Hispanic students are, to be proper, 'Chicano' or 'Latino,' assuming that someone is straight is 'heterosexist,' and the fear of gays and lesbians is 'homophobia.'"

It's important not to offend people, but exercises in word substitution do not directly affect substance. Despite that, there is a widespread belief that words can alter physical reality. Some doormen now call themselves "access controllers," and some elevator operators are now known as members of the "vertical transportation corps." Of course, they still guard doors and ride in elevators. The U.S. Department of the Interior managed to replace the word "cowboy" (and I swear this is true) with "mobile mountain-range technician."

Obviously, when a paperboy insists that he be called a "media courier" (and one paperboy actually did), we should recognize that changing a name does not necessarily change reality. A California state penitentiary was renamed the California Institution for Women. Convicts were renamed "residents," and guards were renamed "staff," cell blocks became "cottages," and the words "mess hall" were replaced by "village cafeteria." Despite these bits of bunting, which some might consider politically correct speech, the place is still a prison with convicts and guards and a mess hall.

Changing language so that incarceration in a penitentiary is represented as some kind of holiday retreat does nothing to advance the efficacy of the work. In fact, changing names may make it more difficult to recognize deeper problems because everything appears on a merry-go-round of changing identities. People who change their language to reflect an absence of racism or sexism or any -ism will undoubtedly cause less offense, but offending people is not the real problem. The deeper problem, the actual cause of social strife and pain, is behavior based on the racist or the sexist convictions held by whole segments of the population. The course of society is guided more by behavior based on conviction than it is by perceived insult.

Modifying language can immediately reduce offense given, and—in the long run—people who carefully choose their words to avoid offense tend to modify their actions similarly. People who change the way they speak think differently; and thought is the foundation of conviction.

The movement to recognize and accommodate a proliferation of new issues is a well-intentioned movement. College-age females can be called women just as easily as they can be called girls. If Hispanic people prefer Latino, then so be it, but even well-intentioned movements can wiggle off course into irrational territory.

The University of Connecticut reportedly announced a ban on "inappropriately directed laughter" and "conspicuous exclusion of students from conversations." Transgressions of such bans would be nearly impossible to prove. They also assume, in an odd sort of way, that spontaneous attitudes can be miraculously commanded through legislation.

The silliness generated by the so-called politically correct movement is relatively unimportant silliness when we consider the alternatives. Many students arrive at university actually believing that black people are genetically inferior to white people. Others may believe that homosexuality is rare or unnatural behavior. The role of a university is to provide students with guidance through subjects that specifically address such explosive issues. Subjects like biology and history, for example, can shed light by revealing that humans of any color are essentially equal. And history reveals that homosexuality is neither new nor rare. Biology and history aren't the only subjects that reveal these truths, which unfortunately are not self-evident. It takes education to understand them.

Individuals within any particular group can, and do, vary in abilities: intellectual, physical, and moral. But groups of human beings are just groups. Groups are equal. This is not an opinion; nor is it the preserve of people who imagine themselves to be "politically correct." Equality is a demonstrable fact.

The former resident assistant at Stanford, Mabry, wrote in *Newsweek* that, "In many discussions students argued that homosexuality was immoral, or that blacks were less capable than whites. PC students would say, 'Are you insane? You're full of it.' But I never felt it was my mission to tell anyone he couldn't oppose affirmative action or argue that Native Americans were inferior to whites."

And rightly so. Students are supposed to debate issues, all issues, especially controversial issues. Students learn that way. They learn by discussing, debating, and confabulating issues until they feel convinced one way or another. Inevitably, some students graduate with all the prejudices they arrived with completely intact. Ironically, others are bending political correctness to serve what are considered politically incorrect goals. For example, an independent conservative newspaper at Stanford, the *Stanford Review*, boldly prints the words "Politically Incorrect and Proud of It" on its masthead.

Two Harvard graduate students recently warned in *The New York Times* of "the Dangers of Political Correctness," as if *correct* might really mean *incorrect*. The authors wrote, "Call it intellectual intolerance. Call it left-wing McCarthyism," and they called political correctness "a set of liberal ideas considered so basic, so true as to be unquestionable . . ." The authors have a point. Discussion should always remain free and open, but there is also inherent danger in attempting to reverse progress. Consider *Newsweek's* warning that "the content of PC is, in some respects, uncontroversial: who would defend racism?" Unfortunately, many people defend racism every day. Dismissing human equality as left-wing McCarthyism or as a liberal idea is troubling indeed. Overzealous, politically correct students are offensive themselves, no doubt. But freedom and equality are neither liberal nor conservative properties. They are simply American.

My mother, who never heard of political correctness, equipped me with two simple tools that accomplished the same end as political correctness, but with a lot less complication. The first tool is knowing the difference between words and stones and the relative hurt that each can inflict. The second tool is to try never to do anything to anyone else that you wouldn't want them to do to you. These simple tools can be useful to an individual, but if an entire society takes them up, these tools have, and always have had, the potential to refashion social strife into social rapport.

Metaphors Are Doors

SCIENCE HAS FOR DECADES searched in vain for someone who can actually read minds, and for two or more people who can really communicate telepathically. But there is already a way to peek into another person's intellectual and emotional world; we just usually overlook it. The way is through the door of metaphor.

The popular notion of a metaphor is a decorative figure of speech used to enhance what someone has to say. If a politician wants to emphasize the instability of his government, he might describe the situation as "our ship of state founders in a tumultuous bipartisan sea." He could get the same idea across if he just said, "Bickering is not good for the government," but the metaphor does more than just decorate. In addition to conveying this speaker's alarm, the metaphor conjures up an almost-impossible image of a government plunged into the sea; the image suggests that a powerful life-and-death struggle is underway, something far beyond the simple facts the speaker wishes to convey.

Imagine feeling the wind whip through your hair or the biting cold as water slips over the decks. Imagine still the mounting sense of urgency in trying to untangle lines, and reef in sail. Metaphor has the unique ability to take this image of a foundering ship and superimpose it on the image of government.

Some people believe all human knowledge comes from this ability to think of one thing as if it were another. Harvard professor and poet Ivor Richards once said, "Most sentences in free and fluid discourse turn out to be metaphoric." Robert Frost flatly declared, "All thinking is metaphorical."

Aristotle was sufficiently impressed by metaphor to say, "The greatest thing by far is to be master of metaphor. It is the one thing that cannot be learned from others. It is the mark of genius." On the surface metaphors don't seem likely to indicate truths of any kind because metaphors are literally false statements.

Consider these metaphors spoken by a young Italian boy: "But soft, what light through yonder window breaks? It is the east, and Juliet is the sun! Arise, fair sun, and kill the envious moon, who is already sick and pale with grief." We can be relatively certain that neither Romeo, nor his audience, believed Juliet was a large gaseous sphere burning at fifteen-million degrees Kelvin, eight light-minutes away in outer space. Instead, the audience accepts the metaphoric reality Romeo creates about Juliet. If Shakespeare had put a simile in Romeo's mouth instead of a metaphor (the window is *like* the east, and Juliet is *like* the sun), the audience would understand just as well but they would lose the dramatic impact of declaring, metaphorically, that she *is* the sun.

The word *metaphor* comes from the Greek *metapherein*; in which *meta* means over, and *pherein* means to carry. Metaphor implies an ability to transfer, or carry over, one thing to another. Metaphors are called figures of speech because they provoke the listener to imagine—to picture—a single sense in which two different things could be united. Solar qualities like warmth, light, and magnitude are in this case carried over to Juliet. The literal meaning of metaphor, to carry over, can itself be taken figuratively. People choose metaphors that reflect the way they feel. Once the metaphoric meaning is understood, we can understand how a speaker might feel if we look at the literal meaning of the speaker's metaphor.

University of California linguist George Lakoff relates a story about an Iranian student of his who was eager to grasp American English. When this young man discovered the phrase "a solution to your problem," he was convinced he had found a significant clue to the American psyche. In a published report Lakoff tells us the student "thought it was a chemical metaphor in which there was a large vat filled with problems in liquid solution, at times dissolving and at other times becoming solid and precipitating out. He thought this was a very nice metaphor because the problems never really went away they just dissolved at times and at other times reappeared when they became solid. He thought the citizens of America must have a very enlightened view of life; he was shocked to discover that they didn't have this understanding at all."

The interesting thing about this student's misunderstanding is that he took a literal statement metaphorically—which in itself tells us something about the student. Metaphors derive most of their power from the tension between literal and figurative interpretations. Metaphors work because the literal and the figurative meanings are in a kind of perpetual motion.

This peculiar ambivalence of metaphor to be literal one minute and figurative the next has come in quite handy for philosophers; especially when they try to discuss difficult ideas like morality. Friedreich Nietzsche, for example, compared the continuity between literal and figurative meanings found in metaphor with a similar ambivalence found between morality and immorality. We may not admit it, but the concepts of good and evil are rarely as clear cut as we say they are.

Murder, torture, and robbery are usually considered immoral, but the very same acts committed during times of war become, in the minds of some, acts of moral patriotism. Morality and immorality, just like literal and figurative interpretations of metaphors, slip back and forth as the mind sees fit. We can learn a great deal about the way people see the world by paying attention to the literal side of their metaphors.

For example, Lakoff says that some people imagine love as an extension of eating. A man might refer to a certain young lady as a luscious dish that had him drooling, or he might talk about his insatiable sexual appetite that left him sex-starved and hungering for kisses that taste sweeter than wine. A woman might imagine love in religious terms. She might say she adores some man, or maybe she idolizes him. She may put him on a pedestal where she can devote her life to him, or more strongly, she might sacrifice her life. We might well expect to hear this woman sing the praises of her Adonis.

These metaphoric descriptions are not simply cute ways of describing love, they often reflect the speakers' underlying assumptions about sex, marriage, and life in general. Some men, for example, habitually describe women in military terms. Men like this might describe women as bombshells who are dressed to kill. The way they describe love can even be overtly violent. They can refer to relationships as conquests or battles, where ultimately one party will knock the other off their feet.

People like this may also perceive the rest of life as a war. They might face cutthroat competition in the business world or describe success as victory. Anyone who is aware of the literal meanings of the metaphors they use usually also are aware of the underlying emotional attitude that produced them. Unfortunately, most people don't examine their metaphors. There is a very good reason for this.

We are indebted to Henry Watson Fowler for a great many things, not the least of which is his indispensable book, *Fowler's Modern English Usage*. Fowler points out that metaphors are divided between the quick and the dead. Some metaphors (usually ones we've never heard before) are so effective in provoking insight they can be called living, but the other metaphors have been repeated so many times that the metaphoric sense is lost altogether. Fowler calls these dead metaphors.

A sentence like "The judge is sifting the evidence" is so familiar there is no need to imagine a fine screen shaking grain gravel, or facts. We could just as well substitute "sifting" with "examining" and the listener would get the same idea. In this case sifting is a dead metaphor. But Fowler points out that in the sentence "Satan hath desired to have you, that he may sift you as wheat" we have a full-fledged, living metaphor.

Professor Lakoff, the linguist at Berkeley, discovered something particularly revealing about dead metaphors. First of all, most people don't realize they are speaking metaphorically when they use them, but—and this is particularly significant—dead metaphors reveal a speaker's emotional world just as well as living ones do.

Consider a young married couple who, after a few years, begin to have trouble. By listening to the metaphors they use, we can discover that each has radically different assumptions about their marriage. The husband might complain that his wife "hasn't lived up to her end of the bargain," or that "She wasn't respecting my rights," or maybe "She violated our solemn contract."

Clearly, this husband imagines marriage as some kind of binding agreement, a legal bond, perhaps, or a pact. But when we hear his wife say, "We are drifting apart," "We've reached a dead end," or that she's "just spinning my wheels," we get the definite impression that the wife imagines marriage as a journey.

These metaphors are different because the husband and wife simply imagine marriage differently. Any couple lucky enough to recognize that their basic assumptions are different could probably solve more problems if they discussed the spirit of marriage in general than to continue scrapping over little specifics.

Metaphors permit us to peek into someone else's mind almost like telepathy is supposed to do, but finding the door of metaphor is not always obvious—we have to work at it. Virginia Woolf once described a person who worked at understanding things as "a man or woman of thoroughbred intelligence who rides his mind at a gallop across country in pursuit of an idea." Not a bad metaphor to live by.

Mona Lisa and Leonardo da Vinci

LEONARDO DA VINCI'S *MONA LISA*, has played a prominent role in art history during her nearly-five-hundred-year life. In fact, she was exerting a powerful effect on the art community even before she was finished. Recently an incredible discovery launched the *Mona Lisa* onto the crest of a whole new wave of imagination, and some of us may have noticed her enigmatic smile come to life again.

A computer program compared the *Mona Lisa* with the only known self-portrait of Leonardo da Vinci— these two pictures turned out to be mirror duplicates. Incredible as it may seem, it is very likely that the *Mona Lisa* is actually a cleverly disguised Leonardo. I say "very likely" because nothing is 100 percent sure in art, but we certainly have a new and fascinating theory.

This remarkable discovery was made by Lillian Schwartz, a computer analyst in New Jersey. As Schwartz herself told *The New York Times*, "It was this self portrait that, in a series of experimental computer-model juxtapositions at AT&T Bell Laboratories, was aligned with the *Mona Lisa* to produce a congruence so striking as to preclude coincidence."

Leonardo da Vinci believed experience and mathematics were the foundations of science. He experimented with just about everything, and he analyzed his findings mathematically. This was especially true of his paintings and drawings. Every figure followed rigid mathematical proportions. The proportions of his self-portrait and that of the *Mona Lisa* appear to match perfectly. So does everything else: angles, the gaze, the turns in the nose, and especially the bone supporting the face.

The history of the *Mona Lisa* has been as enigmatic as her smile. Leonardo kept this painting with him for many years. No receipts were ever found that record anybody ordering it, and he doesn't seem to have passed it on to the woman depicted. Instead, he sold it to the king of France. It's quite possible that the *Mona Lisa* was a private interest of the painter and not a commission.

The woman's identity has always been in question. There is no proof at all that she is Mona Lisa del Gionconda (there actually was such a person). In fact, there is some evidence that suggests Gionconda was not the model. In addition to her, there are two other women who seem as likely to have sat for the great master, and even other candidates are possibilities, but so far there is no proof.

Even before the computer comparison there had been speculation that the model was possibly a man. This ties in with many people's belief that Leonardo da Vinci was homosexual. And twelve years before Schwartz's discovery, art historian Roy McMullen actually suggested the image might contain a good deal of Leonardo himself. In his book, *Mona Lisa, the Picture and the Myth*, McMullen writes, "In spite of the exposed breast cleavage and the pregnancy theory, it has been seriously argued that the personage is actually a young man in woman's clothing. . . . There is something masculine in the face and . . . in this instance, plenty of context. To begin with, there is Leonardo's very probable homosexuality. Then there is his very evident, lifelong obsession with sexually ambiguous figures," which McMullen goes on to list.

He then continues with his prophetic suggestion: "What about the possibility that Leonardo, consciously or unconsciously . . . projected into the painting an image of himself, transformed by narcissistic memory back into his handsome, beardless young manhood?" That's a pretty good guess, Mr. McMullen.

These sexually tumultuous suggestions could not have come during a more sexually tumultuous era in our history. Questions concerning sexuality are reaching fever pitch from both liberals and conservatives. Attitudes about sex have changed a lot in the past few decades. They are still changing and are headed for much greater change in the very near future. Suddenly, in the middle of this tumult, Leonardo da Vinci reaches across the centuries.

Sexual behavior was permanently changed when effective birth control methods hit the market and safe abortion techniques became a reality. These may be controversial practices, but the change is permanent, and we are going to live with it. And now, in counterpoint to the freedoms of the sexual revolution, there is the deadly captivity of the current AIDS epidemic.

The sexual revolution can be said to have started with Sigmund Freud and not with the Pill. Freud's insights permanently changed the way we perceive sex and behavior. He provided a tool that helps us understand sex, but more importantly, understanding sex helps to dismantle a host of personal problems. Freud's dictum that no neurosis is possible in a normal sexual life is a particularly arresting statement, and one worthy of serious consideration.

Freud once analyzed a short note left by Leonardo that described an early childhood memory, and he became the first person to recognize the importance of a sexual dynamic at work in Leonardo's art. Freud had a field day with this idea because infant memories are tailor-made to fit Freudian theory.

Freud's discovery that even infants have strong sexual feelings was a milestone in medicine. Today that milestone suggests that AIDS education had better start early, long before children are old enough to run the risk of contracting AIDS sexually. Unfortunately, there is still a great deal of resistance to explicit AIDS education. Shame continues to over-shadow discussion and weaken reasoned thought. Since sex is clearly a biological phenomena, it seems strange that we don't think of it the way we think of the cardiovascular system, for example, or hair growth. But soon we may be forced into that kind of objectivity in order to survive.

Painting the *Mona Lisa* very well may have been such an objective exercise, a way for Leonardo to explore his own sexual identity. As a Renaissance man, Leonardo was interested in establishing experimentation as the foundation of science. He may have created the *Mona Lisa* in that spirit, as an objective psychological experiment.

Both Leonardo and his *Mona Lisa* have been ideals for centuries. As the quintessential Renaissance man (weight-lifter, artist, scientist, inventor), Leonardo has been a paragon of maleness, just as the *Mona Lisa* has been a paragon of feminine beauty, a particularly erotic one in fact. In the nineteenth century, art historian Walter Pater went so far as to describe her as the embodiment of eroticism.

If you were to compare the *Mona Lisa* with the erotic images in a *Sports Illustrated* swimsuit issue, you'd probably break out laughing, but in her day she was just as sexy. Even before the painting was finished, the *Mona Lisa* was generating imitations, several of which were nudes. These paintings were variations on a theme. They repeat a classical paradigm, similar to the way Christ or the Buddha are painted over and over—but the specific illumination in this case was decidedly sexual.

By the middle of the sixteenth century, Francis I, the king of France, had come into possession of the *Mona Lisa*. He hung it in his bathhouse at Fontainbleau where, I suppose, he and his friends saw it as a kind of pinup—a profoundly philosophic pinup, but erotic nonetheless. But for all of the ribaldry (and undoubted dalliances) that took place in the royal bathhouse, sex was not necessarily trouble-free and spontaneous in the sixteenth century. Sex always has had a dark and troublesome side, too.

One of Sigmund Freud's students, A. A. Brill, commented that until Freud came along sex had ". . . been kept . . . incarcerated for almost two thousand years. . . . As it had not been permitted to function openly and naturally since the passing of Pagan culture, sex went underground . . . often [causing] confusion by popping up where and when least expected." Brill pointed out that Freud's discovery "established that [sex] was not only astir, but often very meddlesome."

Admittedly, much of the work pioneered by Sigmund Freud has been modified since his death (and some has been proved wrong), but a surprising number of fundamental observations are still well on the mark. Particularly the idea that confused sexual feelings contribute to mental illness. If children are taught appropriate sexual behavior early, there is a good chance of not only cutting down disease and teen pregnancies but perhaps a chance also to create a generation that will guide government, industry, and the military with a more mature and even hand. That is, if this generation lives through the process of dating and finding a mate. Sexually transmitted diseases that were once curable have again become incurable. Antibiotics have no effect on some newer strains of gonorrhea and syphilis. Herpes and chlamydia are both serious and spreading. And on top of these, we are faced with AIDS.

There is no cure for AIDS. Since some symptoms do not appear for up to eleven years, what we have seen so far is a slowly unfolding time bomb. But only a few weeks after exposure to the AIDS virus, the immune system will produce antibodies, and there is a test for those antibodies. People who are antibody positive should be made aware of that, and everyone should fully and explicitly understand the methods of transmission if we are going to stop AIDS.

Some may choose to stop all sexual activity, but for the majority that choice seems unlikely, if not unreasonable. Human nature being what it is, people will continue to engage in sex regardless of the cost. There is an obvious reason for this. The drive to propagate the race is explosively powerful and will not be contained.

You may have seen a condom ad in which a woman says she will do a lot for love but she won't die for it. There's no reason to die for sex, I'll agree, but dying for love may be around for awhile. Romeo and Juliet, and Abelard and Heloise were not peculiar to their eras. This is the enigmatic, double edge of sexuality.

What better representation of this duality than the bittersweet smile of the *Mona Lisa*? What better lesson can we learn from this enormously important Renaissance smile than to understand our own bittersweet sexual feelings?

HEALTH AND MEDICINE

Smell

OUR SENSE OF SMELL is possibly the most influential of all our senses. But we don't notice smell like we do our other senses. Somehow smell lacks theatrical power—the way sight dazzles with scintillating brilliance or sound thrills with peals of thunder or great music. However, smell is not without deep and lasting effect. Science now tells us that smell plays a much more significant role in our lives than we once thought. It may even be responsible for a good deal of thought itself.

Aside from smell's being upstaged by sight and sound, we tend not to notice smell because we have taught ourselves and especially our children to ignore smell—if not to ignore it outright, at least to suppress it. By the age of ten, children have lost some of their earlier abilities to distinguish smells. A similarly dramatic loss in smell acuity happens around the age of eighteen. Evidence seems to indicate that this loss is learned and not physical.

Another reason smell gets such short shrift is the connection made during the last century between washing and health. When bathing became popular, odors, particularly body odors, became repulsive sensations. But before bathing, before dry cleaning or deodorants, the way a person smelled told a story. People in the past "knew" things from the way others smelled the way we might look at someone today and know things about them from the way they appear.

Sniffing another person to find out where they've been or what they've been up to sounds peculiar. It sounds too animal-like to be comfortable. But smell is a peculiarly "animal" sense. The other four senses receive data from the outside. The data have to be processed in a small ovoid gray nuclear mass in the lateral wall of the third ventricle of the brain, in a place called the thalamus. But this is not true of smell.

Smell receives data from the outside, but those data are transmitted directly to reactive sites in the brain without being processed by the thalamus. Both the mechanics and location (the limbic system) of smell suggest a primordial sense. Smell is one of the earliest (if not the earliest) of sensory abilities. Smells can trigger memories in exquisite detail, even compel us to action, in a way that is virtually subconscious, almost automatic. We are rarely alert to the minute amounts of chemicals that are constantly entering our noses and even more rarely aware that they do anything significant, except smell good or bad, if they smell at all.

We associate smell with animals because some animals can smell so extraordinarily well. When an animal breathes, molecules responsible for smell adhere to a specialized membrane stretched over a conchlike bony apparatus in the nose. We "get the message" when the nerve cells in this membrane react to the outside stimulus and send the message directly to the brain.

If you took all these specialized cells from a human being and spread them out contiguously, you would have an area about the size of two ordinary postage stamps. Now for comparison, an average-size dog has enough of these specialized cells to cover a woman's scarf.

The physiological sensitivity that dogs have developed with smell affords them uncanny feats of tracking. Dogs, especially hounds, can accurately trace the path of a person two weeks after the person has actually passed by. Equally spooky demonstrations have been observed in sharks, insects, hedgehogs, mice, rabbits, and eels—all have remarkably well developed senses of smell.

But we shouldn't be too awed or sell ourselves short just because other animals can detect smells with almost supernatural ability, because the sense of smell in humans is surprisingly well developed.

Smell is not only infinite in variety, it is also about ten thousand times more acute than taste, which has only four known variations: salt, sweet, bitter, and sour (although in India "acrid" is considered a fifth taste). For example, we can detect the presence of ethyl mercaptan, an odoriferous substance found in rotting meat, in one part per four hundred million parts of air. That's nothing less than extraordinary and, I daresay, extremely useful.

There is further evidence that we react to individual smells that mark each of us perhaps as unerringly as dogs and other animals do. The reason a bloodhound can track a person two weeks after the person has gone by is because each one of us has a specific and unique smell. These smells are chemical identifiers and seem to be part of an elaborate (and heretofore undetected) method of communication, a communication as significant and precise as speech or writing.

During the last part of the nineteenth century it was discovered that young women living together (and having no contact with men) entered puberty later than women who had contact with men. This discovery was consistent enough that it earned the name the French Boarding House syndrome. The cause was unknown.

Later, in a now-famous 1971 study, it was further discovered that young women living in a dormitory, or those who are simply close friends or roommates, are remarkably prone to synchronized menstrual cycles. Since some of the women in the study never spoke to each other, suspicions rose that there was an external reason for this, perhaps a recognition of certain odors.

What researchers suspected were human pheromones. The word *pheromone* is a compound of two Greek words: *pherein*, which means "to carry" and *horman*, which means "to excite." Pheromones are analogous to hormones—they both alter physiology. But instead of being secreted internally like a hormone, a pheromone is released outside the body and is intended to alter the physiology of another animal. Pheromones are the primary method of communication for many animals when they deal with sex, food, navigation, or danger. For example, if you disturb a nest of wood ants, they will release a pheromone made up of formic acid. As soon as nearby wood ants receive this pheromone they immediately will come to the aid of those in the disturbed nest. Conversely, an injured minnow will release a pheromone that instantly alarms other minnows in the area and sends them fleeing for safety.

Communication by pheromone is precise rather than vague, and compelling rather than suggestive. Since pheromones actually alter the physiology of the recipient animal, the recipient doesn't ponder or consider the message—he simply reacts instantaneously. Considering what little information was available about pheromones, and also considering what we knew of our own experience, it seemed unlikely (at least in the seventies) that humans had such things. But the suspicions haven't gone away.

In 1974, Dr. Lewis Thomas wrote about pheromones in his best-selling book, *The Lives of a Cell*. "What are we going to do if it turns out that we have pheromones?" he wrote. "What on earth would we be doing with such things? With the richness of speech and all of our new devices for communication, why would we want to release odors into the air to convey information about anything?"

Why indeed? Pheromone communication would hardly be necessary among human beings. Compared to other animals, we exhibit a unique mating ritual, quite unlike any other species on the planet. Our complex exercises of love are grounded in intellectual beauty, and soar to spiritual heights of the heart—but smell? Chemical reactions? Never!

Now with dumb animals like field mice, that's different. Field mice, lacking both the power of speech and the sensitivities of spiritual rapport, need some other method to insure the propagation of more field mice. And that's where pheromones come in. You can automatically trigger estrus in an isolated female mouse by spraying a small quantity of male mouse pheromone (found in their urine) into her cage. Such a mechanical, almost mindless reaction to molecular contact is hardly what we mean when we say "love." Ours is far more complex and elevated—or is it?

Obviously, if you are a young man in search of a date for next Saturday night, spraying girls with mouse urine is hardly the recommended way to go about it. But maybe something akin to it is. In December 1986, the discovery of human pheromone at the Monell Center in Philadelphia abruptly blunted our smug, unique claim to complex "love." I can hear Dr. Thomas saying, "What on earth are we doing with such things?"

We may be doing a lot with them in the future. The discovery of a human pheromone has far-reaching implications. Imagine the potential of a perfume containing human sex pheromones. Most perfumes already contain pheromone-based oils derived from either the civet or the musk deer. It's because both of these compounds are closely related to the human hormone testosterone that perfumes exert the mysterious allure they do. But if actual human pheromones were used, the possibilities could be breathtaking—why, it could be an end to all wallflowers or couch potatoes; even lifeless marriages could disappear with a single spray.

Identification and detection of the entire human pheromone vocabulary could provide a whole new world of communication. Specific pheromones are thought to be associated with certain diseases; knowledge of those could greatly assist physicians. The unique identifying smell of each individual, as well as pheromones released by people who lie, could be used by law enforcement (one has mixed feelings about this one). Property boundaries could be reinforced with pheromone "fences," immediately (and in no uncertain terms) informing intruders (man or beast) that their presence is unwanted.

Stranger to me, and certainly more remarkable than the science-fictionlike research under way, is how we could have been influenced so dramatically by smell for so long, and still have been so unaware.

Think of this. There are no words for a person who has lost the ability to smell, like "blind" or "deaf." We don't even have words for specific smells. We have a precise vocabulary for sights like "red," "triangular," or "bright," but not for smells. Even sounds have precise vocabularies: "half note," "shrill," and "thunder." But smells are always referred to by the thing that emits them, not by the smell itself: "pine," "lemon," "diesel fuel," "rose," "coffee"—there are hundreds of them.

But tomorrow things may be different. "The sweet smell of success" might be available in a small atomizer—a smell to bolster confidence and lift spirits before a big exam or difficult job, like thought in a can. Or perhaps it will be in small French cakes called madeleine, and we, like Marcel Proust, might take one whiff and recapture every thought that's been lost to our past.

Vaccinations

NOTHING, ASIDE FROM A FULL-SCALE NUCLEAR WAR, is capable of decimating a population like disease. Death tolls in the wake of disease far exceed the death tolls of any conventionally waged world war.

In this century, a particularly virulent strain of influenza rampaged across the planet and infected an astounding 500 million people. More than 20 million people died from this particular strain of flu. Here in the United States, 548,000 Americans died. At its peak, about one thousand to two thousand people died daily in cities like New York and Philadelphia.

As horrible as such epidemics have been in the past and could be in the future, we happen to be armed with an unusually effective weapon to prevent diseases like this from reoccurring: vaccines. The mass slaughter in 1918 by influenza could have been reduced to only a few cases had people been vaccinated against it.

Vaccinations are the safest, most effective little miracles in the already impressive bag of miracles possessed by modern science. Life, of course, is not without risk. And no vaccine can ever be declared 100 percent safe. Nothing is 100 percent safe. Sometimes, in a miniscule number of cases, people react to vaccinations in adverse ways. But if we step back and look at the big picture, vaccines are, by a very large margin, safer than most drugs. They are certainly safer than risking the diseases they prevent.

Vaccines are more than just safe. The benefits we gain from administering vaccines are exponentially greater than any benefits we could possibly imagine from therapy, and for a patently obvious reason: an ounce of prevention is worth a pound of cure. The whole point of a vaccination is to prevent disease. Obviously, if you can avoid getting a disease in the first place, then it really doesn't make a difference whether you have an effective cure for it or not. You don't need to cure diseases you don't have.

In a way, the stupendous success of vaccinations have made us forget that the diseases they prevent are still very dangerous, more dangerous than any other threat we face, including war. Vaccinations have reduced the threat of disease, but the unfortunate result of reducing disease has been ignorance. People tend to ignore the fact that vaccinations have reduced disease. Take away the vaccines and disease comes back.

The Reagan administration looked at declining rates of infection in a variety of diseases and concluded that it could cut government vaccination programs. So they did. Of course, as soon as they stopped vaccinating American children, the diseases came back and spread.

It has been estimated that between the years 1981 and 1990, fully 168,000 Americans came down with diseases that could have been prevented with vaccines. Most of these sick people were children, and tens of thousands of those infected people died. In 1988, the number of measles cases hovered around 3,000 a year, but by 1989, after the Reagan cuts, the number shot up to more than 18,000 cases a year.

Measles may be, relatively speaking, a fairly benign disease, but it is a very dangerous disease to pregnant women and young children. Measles can cause serious fetal deformity in pregnant women. The sad part is that measles could be completely eliminated in the U.S., but to do that we would need nationwide cooperation coordinated with a massive government program. Local doctors are not going to eliminate measles by themselves.

The first prong in an attack to eliminate vaccine-preventable disease is to eliminate human ignorance. It seems clear—and the epidemiological numbers underline this clarity—that just because infection was low at the beginning of the Reagan administration was no reason to cut funding and stop vaccinating. Someone goofed, and the goof was due to a failure to grasp the nature of vaccination.

I have to admit that this failure to understand how vaccines work seems particularly odd when we consider how long we've lived with vaccines. You might remember the Salk vaccine trials in the 1950s and the mass inoculations of school children against polio. Polio was a common disease before the Salk vaccine, but after the introduction of the vaccine, polio practically disappeared. The contrast between many polio victims and no polio victims revealed to people back in the fifties that the polio vaccine is a miracle.

Perhaps even more dramatic was the earlier development of a vaccine against smallpox by Edward Jenner in the eighteenth century. Salk, after all, introduced a vaccine against polio to a population that already knew about vaccinations. People in the fifties had been vaccinated against typhus with a vaccine that had been created by Charles Nicolle in 1909. But imagine the impact that Jenner had when he introduced the idea of vaccination for the first time.

Jenner noticed that people who had been infected with a relatively mild disease called cowpox apparently did not succumb to the vastly more horrible disease known as smallpox. One sunny day in early May 1796, Jenner met a young milkmaid named Sarah Nelmes. Nelmes, he found, was infected with cowpox. Jenner removed from a lesion on her finger a certain amount of infected, viscous matter.

On May 14, Jenner took this infectious matter and inoculated it into the body of an eight-year-old boy named James Phipps. Predictably, young James developed a slight fever and produced a lesion typical of cowpox. Assured that the boy had contracted the cowpox, Jenner, on July 1, 1796, deliberately inoculated the boy with smallpox. Sure enough, young James failed to develop smallpox—the boy had become immune. (Can you imagine doing that kind of human experimenting now?)

Our word *vaccinate* is derived from the Latin word for cow, *vacca*. Vaccinate may be used today to refer to a variety of preventive inoculations, but to vaccinate really means to specifically inoculate the cowpox in order to prevent the smallpox. Jenner also noticed that people who suffered a mild case of smallpox did not contract the disease a second time. But he was not the first person to notice this. In fact, long before Edward Jenner came along, people had experimented with giving healthy people smallpox in hopes that they would become immune. Unfortunately, the underlying biology was not understood very well and many people died from these experiments. Instead of triggering an immune response that helped the body stockpile antibodies, patients were overwhelmed by the smallpox virus and died. But people living far away from Europe understood this mechanism surprisingly well, and apparently they had understood such things for a long time.

Sometime around the year A.D. 1000, a prime minister of China named Wang Tan had a son who died of smallpox. In order to protect the rest of his family, Prime Minister Tan called a convention of health professionals to find out if anyone knew how to fight the dreaded pox. A religious mendicant from southwest China's O-mei Shan, a mountain not far from the modern capital of Szechuan, knew very well what to do.

This obscure figure (perhaps he was a Taoist priest) presented an effective method of vaccinating healthy people against smallpox. His method was absolutely amazing: he used scabs taken from healed sores that had developed on a special group of patients. This group had received an attenuated form of the smallpox virus and had developed an immunity to the disease. The scabs were further treated to weaken the virulence, probably by being heated slightly, and therefore there was even less of a chance that the inoculated person would contract the real disease.

The scab containing this "vaccine" was wrapped in cotton and placed inside the nostril of a healthy person. Then, through both inhalation and transmission through the mucus membrane, the viral trigger passed. Amazingly, this Chinese account—which predates Edward Jenner by more than seven hundred years—reveals a fully developed system of preventing smallpox. And remember, this is only the first written reference of such a technique. It's anyone's guess how long before the tenth century Chinese medical people had a successful vaccination against smallpox. It could have been a very long time before.

The Chinese discovery was so successful that it spread west. Sometime after the events surrounding Wang Tan and the mysterious figure from Szechuan, some other unknown person in central Asia developed the method of scratching the skin to introduce inoculates. It was this technique that was probably used to inoculate the wife and children of the British ambassador to Constantinople in 1718. Lady Mary Wortley

Montague referred to the process as being "variolated;" variolate being an alternate name for smallpox. Montague was inoculated with a vaccine against smallpox that had been originally developed in China almost a thousand years before. And her inoculation was almost eighty years before Jenner got credit for discovering smallpox vaccines.

In 1977, the World Health Organization announced the very last case of smallpox. As far as I know, no other cases have appeared since then. Smallpox is gone, and the reason it's gone is because humanity cooperated to wipe it out. The threshold percentage of those who could be inoculated was reached, and the spread of smallpox could not be sustained. The smallpox vaccine proved safe and, in this case, 100 percent effective.

It's time that we get busy with other vaccines, too. We can eliminate many diseases with them. We even have newly invented vaccines. A new vaccine against hepatitis B is now a mandatory shot for most babies and should be given to all babies who need it.

Children of all ages should receive a full compliment of all available vaccinations, but they do not. Parents have neglected taking children to get shots, and the government is now neglecting to underwrite costs. We also need further research into much-needed vaccines. We need a vaccine against AIDS. Other viruses are suspected of causing some cancers. It would be nice if we found vaccines against them, too.

Vaccines really work. They are relatively safe; they are dramatically effective; and they're dirt cheap. The United States and other industrialized nations—along with UNICEF and WHO—manage to pass out vaccines for free in poor countries, but here at home American children go without vaccinations. We seem to have developed an immunity to our own success.

CHAPTER FIVE

SCIENCE AND
THE ENVIRONMENT

The Wireless and Its Wonders

SOMETIME BETWEEN 600 AND 400 B.C., the voice of God boomed out of a violent whirlwind and ridiculed a poor wretch named Job: "Canst thou send lightnings, that they may go, and say unto thee, Here we are?" We may only imagine how pathetic Job must have felt in the face of such a challenge. Poor Job could no more send or receive messages by lightning than he could fly.

Mankind remained unable to send messages by lightning for some time after Job's humiliating encounter, but twenty-four centuries later people did begin to send and receive messages by this method. This once seemingly impossible feat was brought about by nothing more than keen observation and rational judgment.

By the early eighteenth century, static electricity could be stored and studied in glass bottles called Leyden jars. In 1820, a Danish physicist, H. C. Ørsted, discovered that a wire carrying an electric current would deflect a pivoted needle on a magnetic compass. In the same year, English scientist Michael Faraday recognized this phenomenon as electromagnetic induction. Suddenly, magnetism and electricity seemed to be different but intimately related forces.

By the middle part of the nineteenth century, a Scot named James Clerk Maxwell made an astonishing proposal. Maxwell suggested that electricity behaves like light, that both travel through space at the same speed, 186,000 miles per second, and that both travel in ever-outward-radiating waves. Armed with a raft of mathematical formulae to support this theory, Maxwell prophesied that invisible electric waves could be reflected off surfaces the same way that visible light is reflected. This exciting possibility proved to be true.

Maxwell's theories were proved by a German high school teacher named Heinrich Rudolph Hertz, whose name today is used to measure radio frequencies, as in *kilohertz* and *megahertz*. Hertz observed that when a coil of wire with a spark gap received enough current to produce a spark, a neighboring coil, which was sitting off to the side and idle and had no current running through it at all, also had a spark. Maxwell's wave theory suddenly assumed enormous practical implications.

We are now talking about the year 1894 and the inventor Guglielmo Marconi. Marconi built upon the work of both Hertz and Sir Oliver Lodge, an Englishman who had sent a "wireless" telegraphy message across a distance of a few hundred yards. Marconi experimented with these discoveries and improved upon them.

One day, accidentally, one of the wires connected to Marconi's primitive contraption fell off the table and touched the ground. Marconi immediately saw a dramatic surge in the signal. He took the hint and grounded the rest of his equipment. Soon he had wires buried deep into the ground and elevated high into the air. This now familiar configuration of a grounded wireless set with an extended antenna permitted Marconi to send and receive messages over ever-greater distances.

Marconi took his device to the Italian government and, in a burst of patriotic pride, offered his services and those of his remarkable wireless set. In an equally remarkable thud of bureaucratic density and dimwittedness, he was told by a faceless government official that wireless communications had no earthly use. Lucky for Marconi and for the rest of us, he had two patriotic allegiances. His mother, an Irishwoman of some means, took him to Britain and introduced him to the technical head of Britain's post office, Sir William Preece.

The British had conducted several experiments in wireless telegraphy (Preece himself had personally dabbled in it), and they embraced Marconi. I might mention here that the word *wireless* was not yet in use in 1896. Marconi's first patent was for "signaling through space without wires." Now that he had both recognition and capital backing, Marconi was welcomed back to Italy, where he set up a land station in Spezia and successfully communicated with a warship that was a full twelve miles offshore.

The very idea of communicating without wires was particularly appealing to ocean craft for the obvious reason that ships cannot string wires back to port. Marconi set up many shore stations and equipped many ships with wireless sets. On March 27, 1899, Marconi successfully communicated across the English channel from Dover to Boulogne. A month later it happened. . . .

The steamship R. F. Matthews, wandering perilously off course in a dense fog, slammed into the Goodwin Sands lightship. A wireless operator aboard the lightship radioed for help, and crews rowed twelve miles out to sea and rescued everyone. Of course, this rescue was a miracle: imperiled sailors had sent lightning through a storm to announce to their comrades ashore, "Here we are!"

These sparks of lightning, effective though they were, underwent even more spectacular improvements. Spark bursts were suitable for carrying Morse code but little else. In 1906, Lee De Forest produced the vacuum tube, permitting communications to travel over a continuous wave. De Forest's tubes also amplified weak signals and made radio universally practical. In fact, De Forest is the real inventor of radio; Marconi pioneered a type of telegraphy.

De Forest once remarked that he had discovered an "Invisible Empire of the Air, intangible, yet solid as granite." One of De Forest's earliest attempts to enter this invisible empire of the air is marked by a humorous event somewhat analogous to the founding of more sacred landscapes like those of Avalon, Tibet, or Eden.

In 1907 in his Manhattan laboratory, De Forest invited some friends to examine a prototype wireless designed to transmit voice. One of his guests was a Swedish concert singer named Madame Eugenia Farrar. Madame Farrar, who knew nothing of radio or what the technology implied, stepped up to the microphone and sang "I Love You Truly." Everyone applauded. She sang an encore, "Just A-Wearyin' for You." Another muffled applause. After the demonstration, even De Forest was unsure if his experiment had worked or not.

But far to the south of Manhattan, in the Brooklyn Navy Yard, a Navy wireless operator was diligently copying Morse code sent from ships at sea. When this sailor heard Farrar's voice come over his headset, he was thunderstruck. Everybody knew that it was impossible to hear voices on the wireless; wireless telegraphy meant Morse code and nothing else. The sailor immediately summoned his lieutenant, who was at first skeptical and then, after he, too, heard the voice, equally amazed. The two of them actually discussed the possibility that the voice they'd heard might be an angel singing. As far as they knew, radio may have opened some mysterious corridor to heaven itself.

As luck would have it, radio turned out to be natural, not supernatural. In 1916, a young and practical man named David Sarnoff, later General Sarnoff, was working for the American Marconi Company and sent a memo to his boss, Edward J. Nalley. (As a teenager Sarnoff had heard the *Titanic's* distress call.) His memo said that radio could be sold "as a household utility in the same sense as the piano or phonograph. The idea is to bring music into the home by wireless. . . . The receiver can be designed in the form of a simple 'radio music box' and arranged for several different wavelengths, which could be changeable with the throwing of a single switch. . . . The same principle can be extended to numerous other fields as, for example, receiving lectures at home; also events of national importance can be simultaneously announced and received. Baseball scores can be transmitted in the air . . ."

At the end of the now-famous memo, Sarnoff added this telling line: "Aside from the profit to be derived from [selling radios], the possibilities for advertising are . . . tremendous." Sarnoff shepherded RCA, the Radio Corporation of America, into the corporate stratosphere. And advertising played no small part in projecting it there. Sarnoff built the National Broadcasting Company, which eventually separated into two networks: the Red and the Blue. Sarnoff also pioneered television— NBC's Blue network ultimately became ABC.

Some people think of radio as a mere prelude to television. It isn't. Radio may not be supernatural, but it radiates a form of magic all its own. Radio can trigger cascades of images in the human mind, which, unlike television images, may overlap one another in mental superimpositions. The colors and textures of radio imagery can exceed the flickering, spoon-fed images served up on TV screens, because the imagination ensures that each listener tailors the suggested image to fit perfectly.

The suggestion of iridescence on a butterfly's wing, for example, can, on the radio, conjure much more than shimmering colors; this particular iridescence might also trigger memories of the subtle powder that coats butterfly wings. We are also free to imagine different butterfly wings at the same time—a myriad number of associations may spring from the memory and attach to the mental sound-pictures interpreted from even the smallest transistorized, wireless set.

There is another, rather odd thing about radio. It is much easier to gain access to this vast Invisible Empire of the Air than it is to enter the televised world. It is possible to take small quantities of sulfur and lead and melt them together in a hot spoon or metal dish. When cool, this mixture crystallizes into Galena crystal, the heart of those crystal radio sets that were so popular in the 1920s and 1930s. The crystal then can be probed with a thin wire, known as a "cat whisker," to find a spot that oscillates on a frequency suitable to receive a nearby radio station.

This simple contraption—the crystal set—when hooked up to a speaker, can actually receive radiated lightnings announcing from afar such messages as "Here we are." Twenty-four centuries ago, God apparently did not think it fit to reveal this possibility to Job.

How Tough Are We?

AMONG THE ENIGMAS of human existence are, on one hand, the relative toughness of human physiology and, on the other hand, the fragility of humankind when pitted against the most ordinary cosmic forces.

When I say "relative toughness," I am thinking of other life-forms and how hardy we humans are compared with, say, rabbits. Rabbits may be beautiful, sensitive animals, but they are not tough. Cats are tough, and the idea that cats have nine lives is not terribly far-fetched, but humans are tougher than cats. Humans, barring infection by some anaerobic bacteria or falls from the tops of tall buildings, are the toughest form of life on the planet. We inhabit all the climates on earth, from the hottest tropics to the coolest Arctic. We've lived in habitats on the bottom of the sea, taking with us, of course, a supply of air to breathe. We even have lived in the vacuum of outer space, again taking along our own life-support systems. We are less vulnerable to disease, generally, than other life-forms.

The gorilla, for example, is not as tough or disease-resistant as his human cousin. A male gorilla is very strong from a muscular stand-point—he can collapse a truck tire at arm's length—but he catches pneumonia easily and cannot survive outside certain limited areas of the globe. Humans are tougher and much more adaptable.

But how tough is tough? It's all relative. We might as well ask how big is big? A basketball among golf balls is big. But compared to a hot-air balloon, a basketball is small, and compared to the moon or the earth, a basketball is miniscule. Human hardiness needs a scale of relative comparisons, too, and there are two sharply contrasting scales that we may apply. In the terrestrial setting—within the biosphere, from the ocean depths to the stratosphere, and compared to other life-forms, as we have noted—a human being is about as hardy as any living thing gets. Our intellect has made us even hardier because it enables us to adapt to hostile environments with suitable technology or with other clever ideas.

We have an astounding range of tolerance for temperatures, pressures, and G-forces outside of most normal experiences. In ocean diving, the human body can stand a pressure of many atmospheres. In the air at sea level, we have one atmosphere of pressure on our bodies at all times, about 14 pounds to the square inch. But every 32 feet down in the ocean, another atmosphere of pressure is added. So at a depth of 32 feet in the water, a diver experiences 28 pounds per square inch instead of the normal 14 pounds. At 64 feet under, adding another 14 pounds of pressure, he would have 42 pounds of pressure per square inch, and so on.

Diver Hannes Keller dove to a depth of 1,100 feet and survived, without a submarine or special suit. The pressure that far down is about 35 atmospheres, or 490 pounds per square inch—490 pounds pressing on every square inch of the body. It does seem miraculous that Keller lived through it. Of course, there are fish that handle these pressures routinely, but nothing in the evolutionary background of humans has prepared us for such a thing, which shows we have a lot of built-in margin that redounds to our benefit.

The same thing is true with temperatures and G-forces. Colonel John Paul Stapp, in his celebrated rocket-sled experiments, underwent very high forces of acceleration (G-forces) and proved that human beings are more durable than the dummies used in crash testing. The dummies tend to come apart—humans tend to stay together.

As far as temperature goes, people have heat strokes, and people can freeze to death, but it's remarkable what extremes of temperature we can handle, considering that we must maintain a core temperature of 98.6°F. If your core temperature goes up by only four degrees, you have a fever. If your core temperature goes down by only four degrees, you are on the way to hypothermia and possible death. We perspire to keep cool, and we invented air conditioning to keep cool in extreme heat. To keep warm, we dress ourselves in woven cloth and the skins of furry animals; we don the down of geese; and, when we need to, we build fires and shelters. We can adapt to unusually severe environments, but our insides have to stay within that narrow range of four or five degrees on either side of 98.6°F.

In this context, we are tough. Historically, we have managed to prevail and to thrive during radical climate changes that wiped out whole species of other animals. Amazingly, we've even managed to thrive in spite of our own history of folly and self-damage. But are we tough or fragile compared to cosmic forces?

Life as we know it can survive, and could only have come about, in tiny enclaves of the universe. We need to be the right distance from a star to get just enough of its warming energy. If we were much closer to the sun, we would fry, and if we were much farther away (like the planet Pluto), we would freeze solid. There are, of course, other places in the universe suitable for life, but they make up a negligible amount of volume in the whole cosmos.

The word *astronomical* has come to mean super enormous, and it applies (almost understatedly) not only to the distances and the size of things cosmic, but also to quantities, temperatures, pressures, and forces known to exist in the universe.

Compare some of these forces with earthly forces: the forces of the planet Earth are, to say the least, impressive. When a volcano the size of Mount St. Helens or Krakatoa explodes, it produces forces that would make a hydrogen bomb blast seem small. Tornadoes, hurricanes, and floods generate forces that, on the scale of human power, or even horsepower, are overwhelmingly immense. But big as they are, there are relative limits to these forces. The greatest pressure in the ocean is, at its greatest depth of seven miles, about eight tons to the square inch. This is puny compared to pressures 4,000 miles down inside the earth, where the nickel-iron core is squeezed from a specific gravity of seven to a much more compacted density of ten. That's the greatest amount of pressure you can find on earth, deep inside it.

The planet Jupiter has more pressure than that on its surface, at the bottom of its atmosphere. In the interior of Jupiter, the core is squeezed so hard that if Jupiter were just a little bit larger, the pressure would create so much heat the whole planet would ignite in atomic fusion. It would become a star—smaller than the sun, but like the sun—an incandescent atomic furnace. When we examine cosmic temperatures, we

find similar astronomical magnitudes. Curiously, the highest temperatures ever to occur on the earth are recent, and they were all caused by
humans. Although its blast may not be as great, the explosion of a
hydrogen bomb is much hotter than any volcanic magma and even hotter than the molten core at the earth's center.

For a list of milestones in temperature, let's start with zero degree
Kelvin, absolute zero, which is no warmth at all—the ultimate cold.
Most of the universe is close to this temperature. Almost three hundred
degrees higher puts us at zero degrees Celsius (32°F). Above this temperature ice melts and becomes water. At 100°C (212°F), water boils
and becomes steam. Metals begin to melt at several hundred degrees
Celsius; glass is molten at 2300°C, at 5000°C, all solids become gas. But
all of the heat that the earth generates, combined, can barely be considered warm compared to the interior of stars. Scientists measure temperatures inside of stars in the hundreds of millions of degrees, and they
mean that literally, on a linear scale where 1,000 degrees is ten times hotter than 100 degrees, and a million degrees is a thousand times hotter
than that.

Stars on their way to becoming black holes have temperatures in
the billions of degrees. They become so compressed that if we were to
slice out a piece of that squeezed material the size of a sugar cube, it
would weigh more than a billion tons. This now-accepted fact is so
amazing that it seems like the work of a wildly extravagant imagination. It isn't.

Ideas that were once the extravagant exercises of science fiction have
been overtaken by the extraordinary realizations of demonstrable science fact. We know today that we live in a terrifyingly violent universe
made up of incredible extremes, and this is our home. To survive we
must remain huddled in our little cove of safety. We must stay exactly
the right distance from a stable star, the sun, and we must be immersed
in a clean and breathable biosphere that shelters us from excessive radiation, pressure, and temperature. Here we can be safe from heat and
cold, but only as long as our core temperature remains 98.6°F and
does not vary by more than a half dozen degrees either way. This

comparatively narrow slice of the cosmos allows human life to flourish and permits strange things like the human intellect to wonder: "Are we tough or are we fragile?"

Immune to Death

IN 1789, BENJAMIN FRANKLIN WROTE to a friend: "Our Constitution is in actual operation; everything appears to promise that it will last; but in this world nothing is certain but death and taxes." Progress and history have shown that what may be certain in one age becomes uncertain in another. Taxes will probably remain a certainty for a very long time to come. There's a surprising twist to Franklin's pronouncement about death and taxes: death might actually be eliminated before taxes are. Recent explorations by scientists working in a new area called life extension have chalked up both theoretical and practical gains that could dramatically retard the aging process and maybe, one day, eliminate death by natural causes. Yes, that's what is claimed: no one would die.

Aging is a complicated process that involves the interaction of several different mechanisms. For example, certain hormones released both during puberty and as a response to stress are known to weaken the body's internal organs. The body's organs age as a result of the deleterious effects of these hormones. But hormones aren't the only reason the body ages, the body ages under the effects of free radicals, too.

"Free radical" is the name chemists have given to an atom, or a group of atoms, with an unpaired electron, the implication being that it is not bound to another chemical compound. Free radicals, however, are prepared (one might say eager even) to bind to other suitably matched atoms once they are found. Chemists describe this ability as being highly reactive. Free radicals are found practically everywhere, including in the food we eat and the air we breathe.

Unfortunately, free radicals find a lot of atoms to which they can bind in the human body. The chemical bond that free radicals make with various atomic structures in the body, particularly with DNA (the "blueprint" used in cellular reproduction) alters our physiology in the well-known process of aging.

Our environment also contains industrial toxins and other hazards that can penetrate cell walls and interfere with the normal health of a cell, causing it to age. Even sunlight plays a part in aging. Sunlight contains penetrating rays that break down the fibrous collagen foundation beneath the skin. Without sufficient collagen to act as a support, the skin wrinkles and eventually sags.

In addition to the effects of hormones, free radicals, and environmental toxins, there seems to be some evidence that the brain may harbor a "clock" for aging, perhaps not unrelated to the biological clock that frequent jet travelers must suffer such pains to reset. According to this theory, when the "aging" clock reaches a certain "time," the body's chemistry shifts into old age and lowers the efficiency of our organs. The lungs no longer breath as efficiently; the immune system finds it more difficult to repel invaders. There is hope that future drugs will reset the aging clock as easily as we can reset the wake-sleep cycle after a long trip in a jet airplane.

Most of this research is very new. It's hard to believe, but only thirty years ago medical science still had no idea what role the thymus gland played in the body. Some people even thought the thymus didn't do anything at all. It is now known that the thymus is the master regulator of the immune system and is crucial for normal development and growth. The search for life-extending drugs has already hit pay dirt in the thymus.

The thymus gland performs its miracles by releasing a selection of neurohormones called thymosins. Thymosins act as chemical triggers that spur into action the three most important types of white blood cells: the T cells, or "killer" cells, which literally attack foreign invaders and cancer cells; the helper cells, which assist in the body's manufacture of antibodies; and the suppressor cells, which stop the immune system from attacking its host.

Thymosins can also trigger three important chemicals produced in the brain: the adreno cortico trophic hormone (or ACTH for short), a stress hormone required for that "fight-or-flight" feeling; beta endorphin (the body's analogue of morphine), which both protects us against severe pain and provides a natural euphoria; and prolactin, a nearly miraculous growth hormone. Thymosins stimulate the production of all three of these.

Interestingly, when ACTH is triggered by adding thymosins, the ACTH instructs the adrenal glands to release the stress hormones for the fight-or-flight response. But then, the stress hormones travel back to the thymus, where they slow the production of ACTH, which in turn shuts down the production of the stress hormones.

In other words, the production of the hormones responsible for aging are part of a complicated brain-thymus loop. Interfering with this loop to produce more of one hormone and less of another promises to extend the maximum number of human years of life—now believed to be about a hundred and twenty—by maybe another dozen years. With a little luck, life might be extended considerably longer. Controlling the critical hormonal balance would also greatly enhance quality of life overall. In the future, pills containing thymosin might be as standard a health accessory as vitamin pills are today.

Yet another promising chemical in the anti-aging arsenal is DHEA, which is produced by the adrenal glands. A study of women with breast cancer revealed that those who developed cancer also had unusually low levels of DHEA, suggesting that more DHEA might reduce the incidence of cancer. DHEA also affects metabolism by shutting down the body's fat-storage facilities, forcing the intake of food, particularly glucose, to be burned up as energy rather than stored as fat.

Metabolism and longevity are intimately connected. Back in the mid-1930s a researcher at Cornell University discovered he could double the life span of laboratory rats by cutting down the amount of food they ate. Just imagine, if DHEA or some derivative of DHEA eventually proves to resist cancer and simultaneously burn fat, it will probably become the greatest retail item in the entire history of capitalism.

If all the goals of life-extension research are realized, fatality could be reduced to accident, and not, as it usually is now, the result of natural biological processes of disease or wear. The scientific approach to immortality might be a very new idea, but the belief that humans might achieve this kind of immortality must be as old as the species itself.

Before biology developed life-extension research, most notions concerning immortality were confined to religion. The religious approach to immortality usually involves one of three separate doctrines. The first doctrine is that of an immortal soul, and this is found as early as the ancient Greeks and Egyptians. The immortal soul theory assumes that human beings are made up of a physical body and a subtle soul. The soul alternately inhabits, dwells in, or is imprisoned by the body. Death simply dissolves the physical shell and releases the soul, which then has no discernible form, and it floats on as a diaphanous, undying entity. The second doctrine is called the "doctrine of reconstitution." This idea supposes that somehow the dead can be brought back. The Christian idea of resurrection falls under the heading of the doctrine of reconstitution. The third most common doctrine of immortality is called the "shadow man" doctrine. This one suggests that a ghostlike entity continues after death. This shadow entity, unlike the soul idea, has a distinct form but one that can only be seen by some people and not by others.

The Chinese religion known as Taoism is somewhat unique in that it makes extraordinary efforts to achieve immortality by perpetuating the physical body. Taoists went to great lengths to extend their natural lives, and these efforts, perhaps, most closely resemble modern scientific efforts of life extension in both rhetoric and experiment.

It isn't that the Chinese Taoists don't believe in a soul or spirit—they enumerate three "upper" and seven "lower" souls in human beings—rather, they believe that both the soul and the body are required to achieve immortality. All they need to do is add a missing medicine to cure death.

As early as 219 B.C., the Emperor Chin Shi Huang Di launched an expedition to find the "fairy islands" (believed to be somewhere in the Eastern sea), where his minions might persuade the immortals who dwelled there to part with their secret recipe for the elixir of immortality. The emperor was certain, absolutely certain, that such islands existed and that they were inhabited by immortal beings who made a drug that cured death.

The emperor wasn't the only person certain about the possibility of immortality. Hundreds of millions of people spanning more than two thousand years of Chinese history were also just as certain. The ultimate irony of this must be that today, in the modern industrialized United States, a growing number of scientists feel almost as certain that they will come up with drugs that will cure death or at least eliminate natural death—they are just as certain as Emperor Chin Shi Huang Di was.

Imagine the impact a genuine elixir of immortality would have on the world. Why, we'd all be forced to rewrite Ben Franklin and go around saying, "In this world nothing is certain but taxes."

Sailing to the Stars

SAILING IS ONE OF MANKIND'S most ancient and useful modes of transportation, and it now promises to be the most efficient way to travel in space. It is easier, cheaper, and ecologically safer to sail to the planets than it is to use chemical rockets. Sailing may be the most efficient way to travel through the solar system and even beyond to explore distant star systems. Sails on space ships will provide propulsion from light. It was a long time before people came up with the idea of solar-powered sailing ships in space, but even the earliest experiments in ocean sailing had fascinating parallels.

By the time of predynastic Egypt, certainly before 3000 B.C., North Africans were already building rafts and dugouts with two long poles attached amidships. The two poles were joined at the top where a cross beam, or yard arm, that could support a sail was affixed. Early sailors experimented with this triangular support for about a thousand years until somewhere around 2000 B.C., when the two poles were replaced by a single stout mast. The Egyptians left the Nile River in such craft and routinely traded with Phoenicia, Crete, and the Baleric Islands off Spain. The Phoenicians themselves had ships that sailed as far away as the British Isles.

Sailing has from the beginning suggested travel to the stars. The Egyptian sun god, Ra, was believed to sail across the day sky in a solar boat. At night, Ra crossed the underworld in another boat. People who early on navigated by stars also believed that they would sail to the stars in boats when they died. Worshippers of Osiris, for example, were carried to their final resting places in boat-shaped coffins. Early Egyptian graves, as well as graves found in Sumer and Ur, contain clay models of barges or are themselves shaped like boats. The dead used these symbolic craft to travel to the heavens.

Over the centuries rigging became more sophisticated, and boats were able to hoist more sail. Improvements in the design of rudders, hulls, and finally auxiliary power, further refined the art of sailing. Most sailing ships need some sort of auxiliary power to travel when there is no wind, so paddles, oars, and the great sweeps on galleons were used as power. Steam and diesel power eventually became so efficient that sails no longer seemed useful, but the principle of the sail was reborn with the invention of the aircraft wing.

Most airplanes use power, but not all of them. Sail planes only need power to get aloft. The sail on a sail plane is the wing surface. Like a ship's sail, the lee side of a wing (the top side) creates a low-pressure zone that draws the craft in that direction: on a plane, this is called lift. Some airplanes, such as jet fighters, have more power than sail: the wings are nearly useless little stubs used to guide the thrust produced by the engine.

Rockets with no wings at all get their lift completely from motors, but once a flying craft is placed in orbit around the earth, there is no need for any motor. Pure light will push a craft through space. The bigger the surface area, the greater the push. So we might think the solar sail as dramatic an evolutionary jump from the airplane wing as the airplane wing was from the wind sail.

Five thousand years ago, and probably a considerable amount of time before that, sailing to the stars was a religious metaphor. But today, sailing to the stars is excitingly real. The rocket is still the only way to deliver a sailing ship into space   we might think of chemical rockets as the auxiliary power of a solar sailing vessel—but once in space, large reflective sails powered by nothing more than starlight falling on them are perfectly adequate to go to the moon, to Mars, even to distant stars beyond our solar system.

Around the turn of the century, Russian space pioneers Fridrikh Tsander and Konstantin Tsiolkovsky first mentioned the possibility of sailing in space. Light from the sun exerts pressure on any illuminated object. If the object is very large in relation to its weight, like a sail, the light falling on it will push it through space—remember, there is no resistance in space, no air, nothing to create resistance or friction. The trick to sailing in space is to build a sail with an efficient surface-area-to-weight ratio. The bigger the sail, the more light, and therefore the more pressure to push the craft.

Ideally, the sail on a space vessel would be many miles on a side and only a few atoms thick. Theoretically, such sails are possible. Sails this thin, obviously, would have to be built in space. Small, electrically powered vanes, like ailerons, could position a sail to receive more or less light—more light, and the craft moves away from the sun; less light, and the craft falls back toward the sun because of gravity. Sailing ships in space can go in any direction practically for free.

A space sail must begin its journey far away from the drag of the earth's atmosphere. Even the one to two-hundred-mile orbits of the American space shuttle or the Soviet Mir space station are too close. A sail would have to be about a thousand miles away from the earth to be free from all atmospheric drag. From that point, it's clear sailing.

Unfortunately, getting the sails off the ground and into orbit, by far the shortest distance they must traverse, has proved daunting. The reasons have nothing to do with science, space, or technical know-how—the reasons are political and financial.

Beginning in 1976, NASA's Jet Propulsion Laboratory was building a square solar sail that measured half a mile on a side. The sail was to carry a scientific package to Halley's comet for its 1986 pass by earth. After two years of tests, scientists were convinced that solar sailing in space is possible using available technology. Despite the potential for scientific success, political budget cuts doused the light on the solar sail, and America missed a golden opportunity.

In 1979, a private nonprofit group called the World Space Foundation decided to take up the slack. The World Space Foundation has been trying to set sail in space for some time. The Halley's comet rendezvous was sacrificed for lack of funds. Another plan to race to the moon in 1992, the quincentenary of Christopher Columbus's voyage, also was scrapped because of no money. But solar sail entrants from Japan, France, and the U.S. are planning another race sometime soon. The only thing that could possibly stop them is—you guessed it—money.

One way the World Space Foundation's Project Solar Sail is trying to raise money is by selling a fascinating book on solar sailing with contributions from Arthur C. Clarke, Isaac Asimov, Ray Bradbury, and many others. *Project Solar Sail*, the book, enlightens readers about the fabulous potential of solar sailing. It also kicks in needed financial support so America can be represented in the upcoming race.

Emerson Labombard, the director of Project Solar Sail, expects that the launch will be on a French-made Ariane IV rocket. Three sailing craft will be locked together and will be released in space after the deployment of the main payload, probably a large communications satellite, which, undoubtedly, is what will pay for the launch. Once far away from earth, the three sails will separate, unfurl, and set a course for the moon. The French and Japanese entries plan to return to earth, but the World Space Foundation's sail plans to go on to Mars. Since the sail requires no fuel, it could get there. And going to Mars is significant for another reason.

Solar sails could deliver heavy cargo to Mars in advance of manned expeditions. Food, water, and return fuel could be parked in orbit around Mars to await the arrival of future explorers. The delivery, once under sail, would cost little but time—about three years to reach Mars. A chemical rocket, taking the shortest trajectory from earth and using enormous amounts of fuel, could arrive at Mars in about four months. *Project Solar Sail* says this will prove the viability of sailing cargo ships in space.

The World Space Foundation's sail measures one hundred eighty-five feet on a side. It is approximately three thousand square meters—comparatively small considering that future cargo sails could measure more than a mile on a side. The force of the light exerted on the planned sail will only equal the weight of two aspirin tablets. But with no friction, the little craft can scoot. During the first few days, the sail will move very slowly, but after several months of constant pressure, the sail will speed up to many thousands of miles an hour. The longer the time, the faster the speed.

Credible scientists have suggested that in the future a solar-powered laser orbiting Mercury could project a beam of light through a huge lens directly at remote sails. They estimate that such a laser could produce more power than sixty-five thousand of the world's largest nuclear generators. A light this bright would propel a sailing craft well beyond our solar system.

Sailing in space will require commitment, jobs, money, and pluck. But even if we fail to provide any of these ingredients, there is still hope. After all, for more than five thousand years mankind has suspected that sailing ships one day would travel to the heavens. What's another budget cut or two? Or even another couple of decades of political myopia? The light from five thousand years of human imagination may eventually propel our species into space regardless of political impediments, budget deficits, or doubts about the value of space travel. Humans will probably explore space not because space is "there," like some unconquered mountain, but because we humans are here.

And God Said: Let Us Make Aliens in Our Image

THE RUSSIANS SEEM TO FEEL they may have been visited by extraterrestrial beings in a spacecraft. At least Tass, the Soviet News Agency, so reported a while back.

It's probably safe to say that the line that separates science fiction from science fact is disappearing before our very eyes. Some ideas that were once silly flights of imagination have become solid scientific realities. In the 1930s, Buck Rogers's ray gun was children's comic-book fare; today, thousands of adults make their living selling, operating, or designing real-life lasers. Space flight between the planets was once scoffed at as an impossible dream, and yet, not long ago, we watched close-up pictures of distant Neptune and her moons broadcast from a very successful *Voyager* spacecraft.

Science fiction still imagines things beyond the reach of science fact; but science fiction's most extraordinary possibility—that some day we will find extraterrestrial intelligence—is moving rapidly toward mainstream acceptability. The universe has turned out to be so much larger than we thought it was even fifty years ago that many sober scientists now believe it would be unlikely if intelligent life didn't exist somewhere else besides earth.

There are more stars known to exist right now than the total number of all the grains of sand on every beach in the entire world. With those kinds of odds, it would seem downright naive for someone to go to a single beach in, say, some out of the way inlet in Baffin Bay, and stoop down to pick up only one tiny grain of sand, and declare that that grain, and that grain alone, was the only place where life could exist.

As early as the third century B.C., an Epicurean philosopher in Greece named Metrodorus said, "To consider the earth the only populated world in infinite space is as absurd as to assert that in an entire field sown with millet, only one grain will grow." Some scientists believe that one in ten thousand stars could have planets situated as the earth is, with suitable conditions to support life. Estimates of the number of stars with possible earthlike planets just in our own galaxy, the Milky Way, range from three to fifteen million.

Perhaps the biggest obstacle to establishing contact with extraterrestrial intelligence is distance, vast distance. We think of our own solar system as pretty vast; after all, it took the *Voyager* spacecraft twelve years just to get to Neptune. But compare the size of our solar system with our galaxy, the Milky Way.

Look at your thumbnail and imagine the sun as a microscopic point in the exact middle. The earth, the third planet out from the sun, would be only the thickness of a single piece of paper away from the center of your thumbnail. Neptune, which is very far away from earth, would be way out there at the edge of your nail.

Now, if the solar system is the size of your thumbnail, then the Milky Way would have to be the size of the entire state of Alaska to be true to scale. That's more than half the size of the continental United States. Our entire solar system, with distant Neptune a full twelve years away, would be a mere thumbnail, a postage stamp, blowing around somewhere inside all of Alaska. And don't forget, the Milky Way is only one of billions of other galaxies.

Pondering relative scale models of the universe can make an individual human feel pretty insignificant. We might feel a lot less insignificant if we were able to contact another form of intelligent life on some other planet, but the task, as you can well imagine, is not going to be easy.

A spacecraft would need millions of years to traverse such distances; a beacon of light, although much faster, would require more power than we are presently able to muster. Scientists believe that to make contact, the easiest, most cost-effective way is to send and receive microwave radio messages. The microwave band lies between one and ten gigahertz on the electromagnetic spectrum, right between long wave radio and infrared. Compared to other frequencies, microwaves suffer the least amount of background interference, which makes them ideal for cheap, clean signals that can travel extremely long distances.

Scientists are scanning the sky in hopes of receiving a broadcast from another planet. Ohio State University has a long-running project, and more people are listening at Harvard University in Cambridge, Massachusetts. The Ohio project, called Big Ear, has been continuously listening for alien messages since the early 1970s. The project deserves acclaim for the sheer diligence of the volunteers who operate it. Money, as you might imagine, is not exactly flowing into their coffers. The Harvard project has a slightly better funding picture, but with only about $100,000 it, too, is limited. NASA has attempted to search for other planets and extraterrestrial intelligence for several years. Unfortunately, NASA's efforts have been thwarted by life-forms on earth.

Congress (a group that mysteriously escapes the "intelligence" label, even when it is deserved) canceled funds for NASA's Search for Extraterrestrial Intelligence (SETI) project, apparently because a Nevada congressman was terrified by the word "extraterrestrial." NASA continues to operate a category of projects under the umbrella name of TOP: Toward Other Planets. TOP wobbles along with the potential to listen, to go, to photograph, to do many things toward understanding other planets. At one point, the earth people in Congress provided $100 million to do this, but life-forms obviously alienated to the idea got it canceled.

With the demise of NASA's SETI project, a privately funded group called the SETI Institute in Mountain View, California, hopes to continue, at least in part, some of this work. They realize that the effort is founded on good science and good engineering and that the time is right. The SETI Institute has already logged time at the giant radio telescope at Arecibo Ionospheric Observatory in Arecibo, Puerto Rico. Measuring 1,000 feet across, it is the largest radio telescope in the world. If the SETI Institute gets enough money from private donors, it will set up listening posts in Australia to scan the southern skies.

The potential for filling gaps in our knowledge by merely listening to space is tremendous. Space is literally full of radio transmissions. Most are part of nature's background noise, but there is a distinct chance that some of that noise could be intentional signals. Considering the enormous number of planets with the potential to support intelligent life, we would be foolish not to monitor radio waves; radio is a simple and relatively cheap method of exploration.

If we ever do discover a signal, we may not have to interpret the transmission to know it was produced by intelligent life. If intelligent life somewhere else happened to be monitoring us (by listening to all the high-frequency radio transmissions from earth as well as the considerable volume of television transmissions), they would notice a vast discrepancy between the energy the earth puts out into space and the surface temperature of the earth. If they interpreted all that energy as natural planetary heat, the temperature of the earth would have to be hundreds of millions of degrees. Since it isn't, the extraterrestrial observers might deduce that intelligent life accounted for the discrepancy. They could guess we had harnessed the necessary frequencies of the electromagnetic spectrum.

Our extraterrestrial voyeurs wouldn't know the name Marconi, but they could tell that broadcasting on earth began only a few decades ago and that it gradually increased. In the last fifty years, broadcast signals have become significant. Outside observers could analyze the frequencies used and the periodicity of these signals and determine that the so-called "brightness temperature" of the earth was not a random event of nature. They might not know what we look like or understand our music or speech, but they could rightly assume that we exist.

Author and futurist Arthur C. Clarke once cast the possibility of interstellar communications as a process of evolution. As technical abilities become more sophisticated, each planet develops the ability to broadcast. Clarke thinks there could be a universal "phone exchange" of sorts that registers these broadcasts as they come "on line." Planets new to the system would also be the least sophisticated, the least developed technically. But once a planet plugged into the network, valuable information could be downloaded according to their capabilities and capacities. Circumventing years of trial and error to immediately seize advanced technical prowess may be wishful thinking, but the profound change sure to come once we realize that we are not alone is very real.

Our lives as individuals are also punctuated with a series of realizations that we are not alone. Psychology confirms that as infants we learn that other people are both separate and distinct from us, but at the same time these other people provide us with necessary things: companionship, models of style, and sources of important ideas. As we develop we tend to define ourselves against the backdrop of other, separate people. If contact with extraterrestrial intelligence becomes a reality, the entire family of humankind may have the unprecedented opportunity to redefine itself in a similar way.

But what if life is radically different on other planets? Some people argue that extraterrestrial life could be so different from life on earth that we might not even recognize an extraterrestrial if it came up and looked us right in the eye. Luckily, there is a precedent for recognizing radically different forms of life right here on earth. The most often-cited example is that of Antonie van Leeuwenhoeck, a Dutch microscopist. Three hundred years ago he became the first human to see bacteria and protozoa. Van Leeuwenhoeck had no difficulty at all recognizing microscopic creatures as living things, even though he had no examples, not even remote examples, with which to compare them. The chances of recognizing life, particularly intelligent life, on other planets are probably just as good.

Now all we have to do is listen.

The Case of the Missing Gray Whales

THE NEWSPAPER HEADLINE READ: Baja Mystery—Gray Whales Missing. The article referred to not just one or two whales but to the entire population of gray whales that migrate from Alaskan feeding grounds down the West Coast to Baja, California, where they breed—a few thousand gray whales. Gray whales are not the largest whales in the sea, but they're not the smallest either. They're anywhere from thirty to fifty feet long, and they tip the scales from twenty to forty tons. Even newborns are fifteen feet long and weigh fifteen hundred pounds.

You'd think it would be pretty hard to miss so many whales that size swimming so close to land, especially with all that whale watching going on, and that includes hordes of federal agencies and private institutions. Many of these authorities confirmed that some coastal observations had failed to spot the migrating grays this year. But the gray whales were out there alright, they were just a little bit late this year, and for some unknown reason many of them took routes farther out to sea than usual. Credible reports from the breeding grounds in Baja claimed that some areas seemed to have a bit fewer whales than in previous years. But they were there, and one lagoon reported as many as six hundred.

This news came as a relief. It wasn't all that long ago that gray whales were nearly extinct. The Atlantic gray whales are extinct; so are the ones that used to roam around Japan, although a small population, I'm told, still exists near Korea.

The Pacific gray whales have been migrating from Alaska to Mexico for at least the last couple of hundred thousand years. But during the last century, in a mere forty-five years or so, almost all of them fell prey to sharp harpoons and were processed into consumer products—mostly oil for lamps, but also stays for women's corsets, fertilizer, and animal feed.

Gray whales were not the first choice of whalers, the much larger bowheads, humpbacks, and especially, the right whales were more profitable. The right whale got its name because, as the most profitable, it was the "right" one—that is, the correct one—to catch. Greed combined with an awesome scientific efficiency in catching whales decimated populations of bowheads and right whales very quickly. When those populations became scarce, whalers set out for the coastal grays.

Whaling off California was lucrative and drew many old salts from the East Coast. By the mid-nineteenth century the Atlantic was fairly well whaled-out. There's good reason why, even today, many coastal towns north of the San Francisco Bay look like towns in Massachusetts or Maine: people from those states built them. The well-known television show *Murder, She Wrote*, which is set in a fictitious place called Cabot Cove, Maine, is actually filmed in Mendicino, California. Mendicino is an old whaling town, and its houses and streets look like they could be in Maine.

By the mid 1840s whalers knew that the gray whales were migrating to Baja probably to give birth and breed. But in 1857, a New Englander named Charles Melville Scammon discovered the jackpot—a bay about halfway down the Baja coast, known in Spanish as Laguna Ojo de Liebre. In English it's called Scammon's Lagoon, because of what he found there.

Scammon eased his ship, the *Boston*, into the quiet waters of the lagoon and saw thousands of gray whales. He had accidentally discovered the main gray whale breeding ground. The reason the grays use this particular lagoon to give birth is because of the unusually high salt content of the water. More salt means things float easier, which helps mother whales deliver easier. Scammon slaughtered hundreds upon hundreds of grays that day, and the next day, and the next.

The slaughter was a holocaust for the whales and an economic bonanza for Scammon. A single gray whale yields anywhere from twenty-five to forty barrels of oil. In 1855, a barrel of whale oil would fetch anywhere from $25 to around $40. That meant Scammon could get a minimum of $675 per whale and up to a maximum of $1,800. And this was in a day when a cowhand might make twenty dollars a month. Multiply the price of one whale by several hundred, and you can

appreciate why Scammon is firmly ensconced as one of the most successful whalers of all time.

Pursuit of the gray whale continued unabated until about 1890. By
that time there were so few whales left that expeditions were no longer
economically feasible. The hunt subsided for almost twenty-five years,
at which point two things happened: steam- and diesel-powered ves-
sels came into play, and the grays had made a valiant comeback by
doing what they do best, making more of themselves. With more gray
wales to be plundered, and more efficient ships with which to chase
them, these now-mechanized Ahabs, Starbucks, and Specksnyders
plunged into the sea like death itself, determined to liberate the gray
leviathans from their earthly existence. And that they did to many.

Luckily, for the whales that is, two world wars intervened, and whaling fleets were needed by the navies. In 1946 the gray whale was recognized as being dangerously depleted and was declared an endangered
species. Today, Scammon's Lagoon is a Mexican national park, and
boats are only allowed to enter with a special license.

The gray whale population has continued to grow, and the best estimates peg their numbers in the low twenty-thousands. In fact, some
whale experts think the saturation level could be reached soon and we
might see a drop in their numbers. This wouldn't be anything to worry
about; it would only be nature seeking its usual balance.

It isn't as if whales were never hunted by man; they've always been
hunted. Coastal Indians and the Eskimos took many gray whales. Some
ancient hunters could have been just as greedy as the whalers of the last
century, but they didn't have the technical means to wreak total devas-
tation. Indians and Eskimos also had remarkable cultural mechanisms
that regulated the hunt like ecological management programs do. The
simplest regulation was that ancient hunters hunted for food, not
money. You can only eat and store so much food. But money? Well, the
more you have, the better.

Imagine setting out upon Arctic waters in a flimsy skin kayak armed
with nothing more than a stone lance to kill a forty-ton, fifty-foot whale.
The Eskimos did that routinely. They were also quite good at it. They

hunted in groups. Each hunter had a line attached to his harpoon (the lines were even fitted with swivels carved from a single piece of wood or bone) and at the end of the line was secured a large bag of air made from sealskin. Once the whale had enough airbags stuck in him, he could neither sound very deeply nor swim very fast. It was only a matter of time until the whale tired and the Eskimos, who had leisurely followed a safe distance behind, moved in for the kill.

Eskimos whaling in this fashion were discovered as late as 1900. The implication of this discovery is that whaling surely dates from the Stone Age. Considering how dangerous it is to hunt whales, it's amazing it happened at all, and yet Stone Age people were clearly masters of this heroic feat. But in all that time they only took what was needed and never threatened nature's gracious largesse. It took the abuse of science to do that.

The real curb on whaling during the last century came from a combination of the depleted number of whales, an ever-increasing demand for oil, and the development of modern petroleum drilling techniques in Titusville, Pennsylvania, by Edwin L. Drake.

It's important to note that the discovery of petroleum was not new either. Petroleum products, like whale products, go back a long time. Drake only invented a new way to get more of it out of the ground faster and in larger quantities than could women and children collecting ground seepage.

The ancient Sumerians, Assyrians, and Babylonians were using ground-seepage oil more than five thousand years ago. The Dead Sea, which produces clumps of seepage oil along its shores, was once called Lake Asphaltites. This is where we get our word *asphalt*. The ancients used asphalt to coat irrigation sluices; to make waterproof bricks, baskets, and mats; to caulk boat hulls; and as an ingredient for paints and in building roads.

The world's whale population was nearly decimated in the last century to fuel the machines of progress. They were eventually saved by the discovery of petroleum. Unfortunately, as we have so painfully discovered, substituting whale oil with petroleum oil did little to slack a seemingly insatiable thirst for power and energy.

A few more spills like that of the *Exxon Valdez* and human beings may start to feel like the whales—threatened. We've already managed to tear a hole in the protective ozone, and skin cancer incidents have increased as a result. It now looks like atomic-weapons plants may have been giving people all kinds of cancers since the end of World War II. Our garbage has to be hidden because there's no proper place to put it. If we are really headed for an ecological showdown with nature, I certainly don't need a bookie to tell me what our odds would be. In this game, as they say, nature bats last.

That's why I was so alarmed to read that headline: Baja Mystery— Gray Whales Missing. The whales have become synonymous with ecological preservation. If they go, how long will it be before humans disappear? How long before some unwritten and unread headline will declare: Earth mystery—humans missing?

Just Say "Nano"

IN THE WORLD OF MANUFACTURING, smaller is definitely better. The smaller the unit of construction, the easier it is for a manufacturer to produce a more sophisticated product. An ancient Egyptian chariot, for example, was manufactured coarsely, using very large things: two large cartwheels, an axle roughly hewn from a tree trunk, a platform with a handrail, and a horse or two to pull it. Ancient Egyptian chariots worked, but by modern standards, the units from which they were made seem gross and unrefined.

Think of the parts used to manufacture even the most ordinary modern automobile. A modern car needs hundreds of little springs and tiny set screws. All modern car engines are manufactured to tolerances measured within microns—one micron is one-millionth of a meter. Measurements this small may have been theorized by ancient Egyptian mathematicians, but one look at Egyptian tools reveals that such measurements were never used by their mechanics or wheelwrights.

Tiny set screws and tiny springs have been manufactured for centuries as parts of fine timepieces, but they are not as small as the insides of computer chips, which now abound in modern cars. Not long ago, the order in which pistons were fired in an automobile engine was determined by a mechanical rotating contraption called a distributor. Not any more. Timing is controlled by a computer chip—so is the climate control, the antilock brakes, the fully independent antidive suspensions, and the speed-sensitive power steering. And let's not forget those new automatic transmissions that can deliver different amounts of power to each of the four wheels depending on driving requirements. It's all done by computer.

The point here is that modern automobiles are worlds apart from ancient Egyptian chariots and are even vastly superior to cars made only ten years ago. This has to do with the size of parts—the small size. The smaller we are able to build things, the greater, it seems is the benefit.

Even the tiny parts found in the finest Swiss watch seem gross when compared to the inside of a modern computer chip. The ability to keep precise time is different, too. Mechanical gears, wheels, and springs will wear out before a solid-state, electronic computer chip will. What we gain from this leap downward, from this dramatic infolding or miniaturization, is a gigantic leap upward in ability. A mechanical watch may tell time and keep track of the date (some even track the phases of the moon), but watches built with computer chips can do that and more.

Computerized watches not only keep time more accurately than mechanical watches, they may keep three or more separate times each, with alarm functions. They can store thousand-year calendars that include leap years. They can store several hundred telephone numbers and even emit sounds to dial those numbers into a telephone receiver. And, of course, they can perform all the standard functions of a sophisticated calculator. Palm-sized computers, only slightly larger than a pocket watch, can process complicated numeric spread sheets, run advanced word processors, and even carry on remote telecommunications. Palm-sized computers are perfect examples of "small is more powerful."

And now we come to a new prediction made by K. Eric Drexler. A new type of technology, called nanotechnology, will accomplish miraculous feats of precision on a level so small that modern computer chips will seem, by comparison, as crude as ancient Egyptian chariots. Nanotechnology promises to catapult humanity to a level of manufacturing prowess that is hard to imagine. Predictions made about nanotechnically produced goods are more startling than predictions we've heard about the electronic revolution.

Nano is the Latin word for dwarf. It means, by extension, something very small. Nano often denotes a billionth part of something. Mathematicians use the word as a prefix, as in nanosecond, to denote a billionth part of a second. Nanotechnology refers to a method of constructing gross things like automobiles or rocket ships or skyscrapers by using specially designed molecules as tools. That's right: molecules used as tools to build big things.

For those of you who might have forgotten your high school chemistry, a molecule is the smallest unit possible that still exhibits a particular characteristic of a substance. A molecule is about as small as a tool could ever get. Anything smaller would be a collection of random atoms. Biologists already use molecules as tools when they recombine DNA to create different types of plants or to design new drugs. But bioengineers use molecular tools that already exist in nature and merely appropriate them for their needs. They do not, they cannot, design specific molecules to do specific jobs—at least not yet.

Bioengineers take molecules called restriction enzymes from bacteria and use them as tools to cut and paste strands of DNA. Drexler believes that by manipulating the genetic code, nanoengineers can produce special enzymes capable of manipulating all matter, atom by atom.

The potential impact this could have on manufacturing is astounding. Drexler tells us that special enzyme machines called assemblers would enable engineers to "add carbon atoms to a small spot, layer on layer. If bonded correctly, the atoms will build up to form a fine, flexible diamond fiber having over fifty times as much strength as the same weight of aluminum. Aerospace companies will line up to buy such fibers by the ton to make advanced composites."

I bet they would. So would automobile companies, bicycle companies, and clothing, camping, and construction companies. A diamond tent would be stronger and lighter than a wooden house. A diamond dome could withstand an avalanche. But the most astonishing feature of a nanotechnically manufactured diamond fiber is the theory behind it: that a diamond fiber could be "grown" by manipulating matter one atom at a time. Nanotechnology gets down there where it really counts.

Manipulating matter on the atomic level requires that the enzymes assemble the atoms according to specific instructions, somewhat in the way DNA is instructed by a "code." The code is a mathematical plan similar to the codes used by computer programmers who plan software. The molecule-sized tools, the assemblers, can be guided by another molecule that contains instructions for assembly like a computer. This is what Drexler calls a nanocomputer.

A computer is nothing more than a very large number of on/off switches. The first nanocomputers don't even have to have electronic switches to be faster than a modern supercomputer. Nanocomputers, using switches made from rods only a few atoms long (rods that would physically slide one way for "on" and another way for "off"), would be blindingly faster than any computer made to date. Eventually, nanocomputers could also use electrons, like their big cousins, and achieve speeds as yet undreamed—providing better chariots, houses, buildings, bridges, everything.

A nanocomputer would store plans to instruct assembler molecules as to what to make and how big it should be. In Drexler's book *Engines of Creation* we find a breathtaking description of how this might work in the case of manufacturing a rocket motor inside a large vat. Imagine a broth of molecular-sized nanotools—assemblers—sloshing around in a milky consistency. Drexler says: "At the center of the base plate, deep in the swirling, assembler-laden fluid, sits a 'seed.' It contains a nanocomputer with stored engine plans, and its surface sports patches to which assemblers stick. When an assembler sticks to it, they plug themselves together and the seed computer transfers instructions to the assembler computer. This new programming tells it where it is in relation to the seed, and directs it to extend manipulator arms to snag more assemblers . . . a sort of assembler crystal grows from the chaos of the liquid."

Pumps attached to the vat draw off used-up fluids and dump more raw materials in as they are needed. Eventually, the shape of the engine becomes clear, and the little molecules go to work converting carbon into diamond pipes, ducts, and pumps. When aluminum oxides are needed, the little molecules could make them in the stronger form of sapphire. The finished rocket motor emerges from the vat in about a day. No human need attend the growth, and the work is as flawless as one might expect from nature. There is no seam anywhere in the entire motor.

The tolerances inside the motor could be made to within a wavelength of light. We are told that this motor will have "iridescence like that of fire opal. . . . Tap it and it rings like a bell of surprisingly high pitch for its size. Mounted on a spacecraft of similar construction, it flies from a runway to space and back again with ease. It stands long, hard use because its strong materials have let designers include large safety margins."

Nanotechnology will permit designers to achieve equally thrilling advances in the human body. We might look forward to the reconstruction of organs, even the reconstruction of nerves, by using nanotechnically designed machines, billions upon billions of which would fit into a shirt pocket. A nano-sized machine is small enough to kill a virus. The machine itself would probably be a virus, but one designed in a lab. Today's drugs are too large to attack viral infections, but tomorrow's drugs could be small enough to cure viral diseases like AIDS, herpes, pneumonia, and more.

So the grandest plans of the future seem to depend on the most miniscule machines imaginable. There is something strangely fitting about this. Big and small are obviously opposite qualities and are not the same. And yet, in an ironic way—a way worthy of some great wisdom—our mastery over both big and small things appears to lie in the same direction.

CHAPTER SIX

HUMAN NATURE

Tipping

THE CUSTOM OF TIPPING prevails in spite of a strong feeling (and a feeling one suspects is universal) that it should decently disappear for the sake of everyone. Why in the world do we tip?

Lest you suspect that my attack on this practice is because I'm a skinflint who wants to deny his fellow creatures their just due and save himself petty sums of money, let me rush to explain that I have no objection to proper compensation for services rendered. It's all right with me to let those who provide satisfactory service be paid 15 percent or 20 percent more than a bill reflects, and let the customer pay it. But don't you ever feel we could abandon the hypocritical posturing of extra cash offered as though it were deserved, when so often it is not? And wouldn't it be nice not to have to undergo the embarrassment of leaving too little or too much just because we don't have the right change?

Tipping is, technically, voluntary. We are free to abandon it whenever we wish, and sometimes under extreme provocation we do. But there is such enormous pressure to avoid looking cheap, to curry favor, and to dodge the danger of an embarrassing faux pas, that we often add a prescribed percentage to an already exorbitant charge. It makes many people feel as if they are being taken.

I'm not proposing that restaurants merely widen the practice of printing "service included" on their menus so that a 15 percent gratuity is automatically added to the bill. That's merely a forced tip. Forced tipping seems suspicious. I never know if that 15 percent goes to the person who serves me or not. Do you? I suppose it does, but I'm never sure.

The question is, why not do away with tipping in all forms and simply compensate service people adequately and fairly to begin with? They'd have the same income as the tips provide (apparently that's what the job's worth anyway), and people obliged to tip would be spared a lot of annoyance and embarrassment. Sensible suggestion. But it's not likely to come about anytime soon.

Humans are strange animals, and over the years I've observed a number of customs that fall into a category I call: "Things we do that nobody wants to do or have done but nevertheless we can't seem to stop doing no matter how much we complain or what action we take against them." This is one of the neater category titles I've managed to mint lately.

Another example of a social custom that everybody hates but that no one seems able to get rid of is dinner music. How often have you been at dinner in a hotel, just settled into a fascinating conversation with your dining partner, when a large band, assembled for the purpose, strikes up an amplified level of sound sufficient to threaten the more delicate stemware on the table? All human communication beyond sign language becomes impossible. During the first lull in the music everyone at the table grins and shakes their heads, and someone inevitably wishes there was a place to put a quarter for a few minutes of silence. But the dinner music custom is so strong that people who plan private dinners, and who admit that it would be nice to be able to talk during them, will book dinner music anyway for fear that not having live music might make their dinner seem less important. For some reason, people believe that it is more important to have an important dinner than a delicious dinner. Dinners are no longer eaten for nutrition or taste or even arranged as opportunities for conversation. They are for importance.

Anyway, until very recently, I have firmly believed tipping was one of those activities that falls into the neatly titled category of which I spoke a moment ago, whose title (in case you forgot) is "Things we do that nobody wants to do or have done but nevertheless we can't seem to stop doing no matter how much we complain or what action we take against them."

Why do we tip? In societies with clearly marked social strata where there is a servant class, tipping is a symbol of dominance. But Americans are not segmented into inferior and superior classes (or they're not supposed to be), and most Americans don't feel inferior simply because they serve. Why aren't they offended when offered a tip? In Japan ten years ago, when I last visited, I was told that many people felt accepting a tip implied a loss of face. A gratuity in any form was charity, and it was offensive to imply that someone needed charity. I learned of a rule in Tahiti that frankly and universally forbids the practice.

Americans see it differently. Almost all Americans feel they are underpaid, so a tip is merely oblique compensation that can make them slightly less underpaid. In other words, nobody feels the extra isn't deserved. And since the person giving it is not regarded as superior, the question of dominance never arises.

So much for the recipient, and now to the tipper. There's still embarrassment, confusion, annoyance, and resentment on the part of those called upon to tip. Not everyone I'm sure, but for those of us easily bullied by custom, and set off-stride by arrogant expectations, tipping can be an anguish. I finally worked out my own formula and can usually apply it without awkwardness.

First of all, the 10 percent tip in this country is now out. Tips are expected to be between 15 percent and 20 percent. If the service is so bad you feel less than 15 percent is deserved, then you should make your comment by not tipping at all. To leave more than 20 percent is ostentatious or vulgar or both. The recipient may appreciate it, but dinner partners may think overtipping odd, or worse.

Two factors govern the percentage I give as gratuity: one is what degree of gratitude or warmth I feel about the service or the individual providing it, and the other is how convenient and rounded-off the change-making process is. If an even-dollar amount comes out to 16 percent, I let it alone. Even if the service was not worth a 19 or 20 percent tip but the even-dollar amount brings it to that, the convenience of not waiting for change (or facing the waiter again) determines the tip.

You are not expected to tip gas-station attendants, airline flight attendants, hotel managers, or assistant managers (even those who may see you to your room), establishment owners who may personally serve you, ushers, busboys, or bank clerks. But we do tip doormen, waiters, hat- and coat-check people, cab drivers, barbers and hairdressers, chauffeurs and croupiers. Is there some reason for this? As for wine stewards, when I run into them in fancy eateries I consider them tipped along with captains, headwaiters, maitre-d's and other restaurant personnel under the tip for "service," which can be the full 20 percent, and let them make the division. This may sound chintzy, but to tip each one of these people a full 20 percent of the bill would require more money in tips than I paid for the food.

Alexander Cockburn has written that tipping is a paradox: "formal yet informal; public yet private; commercial yet intimate; voluntary yet in reality so close to compulsory that most people across the years have little difficulty in remembering the times they felt compelled to leave no tip at all. If tipping becomes an entirely mechanical act, beneath government supervision, it loses its vitality and provokes that dull resentment one experiences at the sight of the words 'a fifteen percent service charge is included in the price of the meal.'"

There must be some room to maneuver so that individual expression is possible in the gesture. Sometimes companies take advantage of the situation by reducing employees' salaries to adjust for tips the company knows they are getting. This has gone so far that some car-hops, waiters, and others actually pay the management for the privilege of working at establishments known to generate generous gratuities. It would take a hard-hearted person to withhold all tipping in such a circumstance.

Still, there are people who would like to do away with the custom. As far as I know no organized groups existed before 1905, when the Anti-Tipping Society of America was formed. It attracted more than 100,000 members, most of them traveling salesmen. There was some effort to pass anti-tipping laws, but all these were declared unconstitutional in the same year the Volstead Act outlawed liquor and created the rumrunners, who didn't mind at all accepting big tips for providing bootleg liquor to a desperately sober America.

Much of tipping, like those tips to rumrunners, seems like bribery. Even today it is not so much a gesture of gratitude as a fee for not being neglected. Originally, one theory goes, the letters T-I-P stood for "to insure promptness." Maybe. But if given before the service, it is a bribe, and not a tip as we think a tip should be.

It sure looks like the custom will be around a very long time, however egalitarian the society. It may in fact grow as the work force shifts from resource exploitation and manufacturing to service industries. Soon we'll be serving each other all over the place. Will we be tipping each other? And be annoyed with the practice? I don't know.

Incidentally, if you feel like slipping me a gratuity for the rather splendid service I've rendered through this enlightening dissertation (which you could not have gotten anywhere else), then you should know that I would feel a loss of face if I accepted anything at all in the way of a cash gift—even a full 20 percent of whatever you felt this essay was worth. I absolutely won't be offended if you send nothing at all.

Of course, you also should know that I sat up all night preparing this thing on your behalf and got carpal tunnel syndrome typing it all out, and I sweat blood looking up all these silly facts for your amusement, but—no, on second thought, just forget it. Don't send anything.

Practical Jokes

THE DIFFERENCE BETWEEN a practical joke and an ordinary one is whether you tell it or play it. You tell an ordinary joke—you play a practical joke. Also, a practical joke has a "victim," who serves as the butt of what may or may not be a funny prank. In a civilized society, a cruel practical joke is not the civilized thing to do—certainly not to the "victim." Crude wedding pranks, like kidnapping the bride, have all but passed from the scene.

Early (perhaps prehistoric) practical jokes (human laughter obviously predates civilization) may have been as simple and blunt as one caveman surreptitiously lobbing a rock on another caveman's head and guffawing when his skull thwacked loudly. Given the right circumstances, this had the potential of being uproariously funny to all but the victim.

A seventeenth-century Spanish nobleman is reported to have built an upside-down room in his castle, which he furnished lavishly with beautiful carpeting glued tight to the ceiling along with chairs and tables. The doors were cut down from the ceiling, and, in the middle of the floor, a welded, rigid chain rose to an inverted chandelier, every crystal spike of which stuck up in the air. When a guest passed out from drinking too much, the nobleman would carry his inebriated victim to this room and deposit him in the middle of the "ceiling."

The host then watched through a peephole as his subjects woke up. They invariably freaked, clawing at the wall to get to the doors, which were up, out of reach. We are asked to believe that this nobleman actually died laughing at the antics of one of his victims.

I have a friend who is very big on practical jokes and very skilled at perpetrating them. But he is also clever and sensible and lives by the code that a practical joke should be as funny to the jokee as to the joker. He demonstrated this on several occasions. He also has been the butt of some notable pranks produced for his benefit by his friends and his victims (who overlap).

Jim Moran, who worked as a PR man, mounted some lavish practical jokes in connection with publicizing products or productions. I was in one. He invited me to ride in a vintage touring car with the top down in a parade in Washington, D.C. This ticker-tape procession was connected the movie *The Mouse that Roared*. Remember it? It came out back in the 1960s. The film told the story of a tiny fictional principality called the Duchy of Grand Fenwick and starred the late Peter Sellers. To publicize the opening of the picture, Jim staged a Washington extravaganza that must have cost almost as much as the picture.

He bought cases of wine, which he relabeled, bottle by bottle, with a fictional vineyard and emblazoned with this fictional country's crest. He mailed invitations on engraved stationary from Europe. The envelopes were stamped with a bogus postage stamp of the Duchy of Grand Fenwick. The postal systems of France and the U.S. canceled the stamps and delivered them all. He scheduled an enormous cocktail party, where he appeared as a diplomat from the Duchy in a uniform that would have made any doorman envious.

Leading up to it all was this twenty-block-long parade with borrowed school bands. One of the bands was costumed with the Grand Fenwick Crest, and the touring car had a cast bronze license emblem reading G. F. (for Grand Fenwick). I sat beside Jim in his resplendent uniform, and, at one point, waving to a rather sparse crowd, he turned to me and said, "All I have to do now is get assassinated and start World War I over again."

At first, people didn't take the invitations to the cocktail party very seriously, but a couple of days before, Pearl Mesta, then the prima hostess of all Washington, got wind of it and realized that she had not been invited. Jim hastily got an invitation to her and then everybody who was anybody in Washington wanted to come. They all did.

Most of them were not in on the joke and figured Grand Fenwick was one of those places like San Marino or Andorra. The party and the premiere were huge successes. There were no victims of this joke except maybe the postal systems of France and the U.S. (if they can be victimized). At the fancy reception, more than one Washingtonian sidled up to me to ask if I knew what it was all about. I pleaded ignorance but said I thought the ambassador was going to say something before it was over. Moran explained, in character, that he was proud that an American film company had come to his country to film a feature-length movie which was to premiere, et cetera. I think some guests went away still believing there was a Duchy of Grand Fenwick. The reception was a great party and everyone enjoyed it, but for those in the know it was absolutely side-splitting. And Jim, ever the publicist, got great press for carrying off one of Washington's more memorable acts of cunning. Even the wine was good.

I have been both the victim and the perpetrator of practical jokes. Let me share one of each. In the mid-1950s, I went to Florida with a writer from NBC's *Home Show* to do a segment on hotels. The segment producer was my friend (who is so good at practical joking I'm going to hide his true identity and call him Jack Miller.) The writer who accompanied me to our Miami Beach hotel said, "Be on the lookout for Miller. He strikes fast." I knew he was right, and as the car stopped, I looked up the stairs expecting to see Miller burst through doors. A bellhop opened the car door and started to help me out. I was still watching the hotel doors when suddenly the bellhop twisted my arm until I went down on the pavement. It was Miller in a bellhop's uniform.

Sometimes a well-meaning practical joke can get out of hand. I lost control of one once, and it scared me before it was over. A friend of ours had a ranch in Wyoming. We'd been going there in the summers to explore the wilderness and punch cattle and enjoy the wide open spaces. One summer, two other sets of friends were invited and one arrived a few days late. He brought his family—his wife and two little daughters. We had arranged a charter flight in a small plane from Laramie to an airstrip on a neighbor's ranch, about three miles from my friend's main ranch buildings. The road to the airstrip was good enough for four-wheel drive vehicles, but we decided to traverse it with a team of horses and a buckboard wagon.

As we planned this transportation, we drifted into the idea of a practical joke on Clint, our late-arriving friend. He and his family would remember it for a long time. So would I.

I recruited some of the ranch hands to stage a fake robbery on the trail. Making sure all guns were unloaded, we headed up to the airstrip, the ranch owner and I on horseback, the foreman driving the team pulling the wagon. We met the plane, and Clint and his family piled on the wagon with their luggage. Halfway back to the ranch, we were duly robbed. After taking our money and valuables, two "robbers" ordered the owner and me to get off our horses and turn them loose. This was not in the script, and it was a mile and a half back to the barn. I shot a warning look at one of these desperadoes and found myself looking right down the barrel of the Colt revolver he had drawn and set on the pommel of his saddle. I got off my horse. Now I was afoot. I was furious. The robbers clattered off toward the hills, and the wagon, which had no room for me or the owner, trotted off for home.

Fifteen minutes later, a rider at full gallop came at us from the ranch with the news that as soon as Clint and his family got there and announced the robbery, the other ranch hands, who knew nothing of the prank, had grabbed guns off the walls, loaded them, and scattered in search of the "robbers." We had to get back to the wranglers who had posed as robbers and tell them not to come in, that they might get shot. It crossed my mind that this development might be a practical joke on us—but it wasn't—and we had a sticky situation rounding up this impromptu posse and getting their guns back on the wall. Nobody got hurt, but as I said, I was scared. I breathed a sigh of relief when all the artillery was rounded up and the wranglers were back and everybody's money and jewels and wallets were returned.

Clint and his family would look at these guys, now cleaned up and honest-looking, and say, "Boy, it's hard to trust you, even now—hard to believe you didn't rob us." They finally conceded that there was a little disappointment in having it turn out a practical joke. For a time there, they thought they'd had an experience they could tell their grandchildren, since being robbed Old West–style is a pretty rare event, even back in the 1950s. They said it would have been worth the money.

My practical jokes are of a milder nature nowadays and also less frequent. The last one I remember involved securing the cooperation of an entire symphony orchestra to make not a sound at first downbeat of a rehearsal session. The conductor later told me it felt like getting hit hard in the neck to give that powerful sforzando downbeat and have no one make a sound.

I don't have the ambition anymore to mount a real production-type joke. I always seem to have other things to do. But I can still enjoy a good practical joke, even if it's on me. And I always try to live by "Moran's rule": a practical joke should be as much fun for the jokee as for the joker.

What to Say

THERE ARE SITUATIONS THAT CALL for an appropriate spoken response, and how we all envy the person whose skill with language allows them to return the pithy, the witty, the cutting, the memorable bon mot quickly, as if without thinking. Such folks seem to deserve adjectives like civilized, urbane, and clever. Through misadventure or bad luck, we sometimes come up with exactly the wrong thing to say. I've had some of those. Some of them I remember painfully.

Once, years ago in Chicago, I borrowed the car of a colleague. I needed it for an hour and he insisted that I take it, gave me the keys, and told me it was a new, black Studebaker Land Cruiser parked directly in front of the Merchandise Mart—the building our studios were in. I descended in the elevator and came out of the Mart on this winter evening and there, directly in front, was a new, black Studebaker Land Cruiser.

I inserted the key but couldn't turn it. I tried the other key. Same thing. Finally, knowing locks can freeze, I got down on one knee and blew in the keyhole to melt any ice there and then tried a key again. While I was doing this, I sensed a presence behind me. Looking up, I saw a man and woman standing close, watching me. My embarrassment was heightened by my kneeling position.

I thought I should explain, so I said, "This isn't my car." The man said, "I know." I realized that I had the wrong new, black Studebaker Land Cruiser, and, kneeling away from the scene, I spotted an identical car a few spaces away. As I unlocked the door of this car, I looked back, and saw the couple still standing . . . watching me. They figured I'd finally found one to break into.

I've always had trouble with saying the right thing in automotive situations. Once when a car of mine was being repaired under warranty, the dealer was kind enough to lend me an identical model. He said it belonged to another customer, who was out of town. I was stopped that evening by police patrolling a residential area and was asked whose car it was. I said, "I don't have the faintest idea." That took a little while to unravel, including a trip to the station house and a call to the dealer. I usually answer questions with less awkwardness.

There are people who seem to dig themselves in deeper, even with remarks calculated to correct a gaffe. Remember the character of Dr. Watson played by Nigel Bruce in the Sherlock Holmes movies? Basil Rathbone played Holmes. The good doctor could refer with innocence to someone being broad in the hips. Then, when offense was taken, he'd say, by way of an inept apology, "Sorry, didn't realize you were sensitive about it." Bruce played a wonderful and refined buffoon.

My son had a friend in college who was very shy but who knew there were times when he should say something. At least he felt he was obliged to put in a comment. He felt this way whenever a lull occurred in a conversation, or a silence of more than three beats. He always inserted the same remark, which was, "Well, I'll tell you one thing! I just don't know." It seemed to fit all occasions. First of all, it was probably true. Second, it conveyed the idea that he was impressed with the importance of whatever element of conversation had been left hanging, and it managed to make him a part of the general discussion.

Sometimes a proper response is simple silence. George Washington said, "The best way to treat calumny is with silence." I always took this to mean, "Don't dignify a ridiculous accusation with an answer." (That may mean the same thing, but Washington said it better.)

The punch line of one of the most famous of all radio jokes was silence. Jack Benny established a character who found parting with money extremely painful under any circumstances. When he was held up at gunpoint by a robber, the robber screams, "Your money or your life!" After a long pause, the sentence was repeated and Benny said, "I'm thinking! I'm thinking!"

Silence can even convey gallantry. Alexander the Great was once handed a note saying his physician was in on a plot to kill him. The note arrived just as the physician handed Alexander a cup with a medicinal draft for a cold the king had. Alexander read the note, passed it to the physician without saying anything, and drank the draft. He must have really trusted the fellow. The gesture seems remarkably silent and gallant at once.

Alexander also heard the elegant expressions of others. He went to a public square in Athens once to meet and pay homage to the philosopher Diogenes. Diogenes happened to be sunbathing that late spring day. Alexander dismissed his retinue of bodyguards, walked to the center of the square, and woke Diogenes by nudging him with his foot. "I am Alexander, the great king," he said. "What can I do for you?" Diogenes answered, "Stand out of the sun." At a time in his career when Alexander could have bestowed whole countries on whomever he chose, the only thing he could do for this philosopher (who no longer owned even a begging bowl) was to move and not block the sunlight. That was a retort that revealed a wealth greater than kings, the only real wealth, a complete disinterest in material possessions.

On an old radio program, the late Tallulah Bankhead said, in her whisky voice, to the late George Sanders, "I've always believed it was important to grow old gracefully." Sanders replied, "Did you?"

Winston Churchill also was a master of the putdown. He hated Clement Attlee, onetime British prime minister. Churchill, giving an account of a certain social function, wrote, "An empty limousine pulled up, and out stepped Clement Attlee."

The British can wither a person they don't like with great subtlety. A single word can convey that what a person has just said is actually utter rot. The word, pronounced with exaggerated precision, is: "Exactly." By drawing out the "a" and adding a twist of extreme boredom to one's voice, the person is left with the firm impression that anything else they say will be as worthless.

British culture is a veritable treasury of withering remarks. Another example: A London author received a manuscript from a writer whose works he detested. He wrote back, "I am in receipt of your latest manuscript. Rest assured I shall lose no time in reading it." One wonders which meaning the author took.

Another masterful putdown has to do with England's King Edward

VII and is supposed to be a true story (I prefer to believe it is). Early in Edward's reign, he fancied himself a singer and went to England's foremost vocal coach for an opinion of his talent. This teacher was noted not only for his musical and teaching ability but for his frankness. All of England wondered what this man would say to the king. Edward sang for him, and apparently he was pretty bad, at best he was mediocre. The vocal coach listened patiently, and then the king asked for an opinion. The coach said, "Your Majesty would have the most thrilling voice I have yet encountered if the upper register had the power and clarity so desperately lacking in the lower."

Dealing with verbal abuse is another matter. The old Chinese maxim that "He who strikes the first blow has lost the fight" is certainly true, but there are ways to parry and counter vituperation with words that can be effective and make you feel triumphant. One technique is not to give your assailant the satisfaction of knowing his words have riled you. I have a line I use when another motorist, imagining that I have cut him off or otherwise taken advantage of him, pulls alongside and hurls abusive language my way. I listen patiently and then say something like, "You shouldn't be so upset because it wasn't entirely your fault. Is there any way I can help you?" The air goes out of their tires, figuratively, as you pull away. I don't recommend this technique in states like California, where drive-by shooters abound, nor should it be used against pickup trucks equipped with gun racks.

A personal favorite putdown, perhaps the greatest I ever heard, was delivered by the late Robert M. Hutchins. Hutchins (at age twenty-eight) was dean of Yale Law School and later president of Chicago University. He presided over a forum on foreign policy in Los Angeles at which several of us delivered papers. Mine was titled "Television and Foreign Policy." There was an audience of more than a thousand, and after all of the contributors had spoken, Hutchins summarized our offerings in about six minutes and threw open the floor for questions. As often happens at this kind of thing, about the fourth question was not a question at all, but a speech, and in this case, a weird one.

The man launched a diatribe that was hard to follow. He criticized Hutchins for listing only nine points in his summary and went on to tell of a tenth point, which was so off the wall the audience got restless. Twice, Hutchins signaled for quiet to let the man finish. The man finally ended with a question, rather truculently saying, "And I want to know, Dr. Hutchins, why you didn't mention that tenth point?" Hutchins said, "I forgot it." It brought the house down.

It's a Gamble

A FEW YEARS AGO I WAS IN MACAO, the Portuguese colony that's physically attached to China in much the same way that Hong Kong is, although by a narrower neck. A hundred years ago Macao was a wide-open place, redolent of license and of most vices known to humans. Time and outside pressure have simmered the place down considerably. China lets it alone (it makes big bucks off of Macao), and Portugal never exploited it in the classical sense of colonial exploitation (I'm thinking of King George III and the original thirteen colonies before the American Revolution).

We had gone there with Chinese friends from Hong Kong who could give us a better inside glimpse of Macao than if we had gone as tourists. On the hydrofoil on the way over I saw an American from New Mexico who, heading for the casino, naturally thought everyone else was, too. He recognized me from television and said that he never realized I was a gambler. I'm not, really, not in any high-rolling sense of the word, but I failed to convince him that I wasn't headed for a big-stakes night at the gaming tables.

The Macao casinos made most Las Vegas places look brittle and formal. They were wildly opulent in an old-world way; they had everything from slot machines to roulette tables and everything was wrapped in genuine Baroque rococo (the rococo of Vegas is all fake, you know). Stalking these contraptions of greed were legions of gamblers working feverishly to unload their money. This is the real link between the Macao casinos and those in Las Vegas: gamblers, the people who manufacture a hope of winning and, more importantly, act out their need for losing.

None in our party was what you'd call a gambler. We had earmarked small sums of money for amusement, and when it was gone, we were ready to depart—although a couple of times small wins pulled us deeper into greed and made us want to stay for "the big one." We flirted with this tangible lure of gambling.

I got to thinking about gambling on the jet boat back to Hong Kong. I guess it's still true that there are basically three kinds of gamblers: the professional, the recreational, and the compulsive. The professional has enough skill and discipline to work systems and to come out somewhere on the plus side. There are those "memorizers" who (if they are discovered) are barred from casinos because they can remember cards well enough to win against the house in blackjack. Actually, this is perfectly legitimate, but memorizers are feared by gambling establishments, especially when there are no limits to the size of the bet. Limits are common now, but before limits were imposed, it was possible to break banks by consistently doubling the stakes. At some point you would win, recoup your losses, and go beyond the bank's resources. I've been told that doubling was first outlawed at Monte Carlo.

The professional gambler doesn't hope. He knows. He knows what the house take is; he knows what the odds are; and he knows that the house comes out ahead, and the gambler will lose. It's as simple as that. In roulette, played to eternity, you will win 35 and lose 37. Those are the numbers, and professionals usually avoid roulette. Of course, some people have rigged the game or have cheated otherwise, and some have even devised successful systems to defeat it, but those systems are outlawed, too.

Roulette is not a game for the professional or the amateur. The great casinos have everything stacked in their favor. Evidence of this favor is found in the enormous wealth of these casinos. The obscene capital that constructed these palaces of pure venality is precisely the money that nonprofessional gamblers thought they might win back—at roulette or at any other game with a built-in house take.

The second type of gambler wants to amuse himself with the occasional jackpot or the chance of hitting it big. This recreational bettor knows that in the long haul his money will be forfeited. This kind of gambler considers his risk (and his loss) as an entertainment. The gamble is considered a straightforward expense, and, as a result, he walks away from the tables with his realism intact, maybe confirmed.

The third type is the compulsive gambler whose pathological

optimism causes a deep belief that the next throw of the dice, the next turn of the wheel, the next card dealt, will shower him (and there are a lot of hers out there, too) with unimaginable wealth. The compulsive gambler will bet bread money, company money, the home mortgage, even a grandmother or two for that next big strike (as in "strike it rich"). Unfortunately, compulsion is pathological by definition. People who believe that gambles are sure things take too big a chance with life.

It is widely believed that the compulsive gambler is driven by a hope of winning big. But psychologists suggest that reverse may be true. The motivation—subconscious and hidden from the gambler himself—is a self-destructive wish to lose. This seems true when you look at what compulsive gamblers do with big winnings. Whenever compulsive gamblers really do hit it big, they can't wait to plunk down all their winnings and bet again. There is no desire to consolidate gains by holding on to winnings. "Shoot the works," "Go for broke," "Let it ride." You sure don't have to be a psychologist to understand the inner meaning of such pathetic metaphors. The meaning seems to be: "Destroy the winnings, because they are damaging my need to lose."

This syndrome is so common and so destructive that an organization, structured very much along the lines of Alcoholics Anonymous, exists for gamblers. It is called Gamblers Anonymous. Pathological gambling is a pernicious habit that seriously interferes with the gamblers' lives and with the livelihood of their families. Gamblers Anonymous has helped many people afflicted with what is recognized now as a disease.

But consider this: if you're fortunate enough not to have this disease, if you're not a professional gambler, and even if you don't care to amuse yourself by waging small amounts of money from time to time, you might imagine that you are not a gambler. But you are probably wrong. We all gamble, we all take chances, and we all assume risk.

Just being alive forces all of us to gamble. We take chances in everything we do—in our jobs, in romance, in travel, anything. We can't avoid it. If you seek to escape risk by not doing anything, by not going outdoors, say, or by staying in bed, you are still gambling big, with your health. For one thing, you'd get osteoporosis, bedsores, and wither from boredom if you lived your whole life in bed.

So we have to gamble. How do you judge what is a good gamble and what is a foolish one? One rule of thumb might be found in the way a lottery works. Most states, whether they regard lotteries as legal or illegal, assume that a lottery must comprise three things: consideration, chance, and prize. Without any one of these elements, the game is not defined as a lottery.

Consideration is what the player invests to play the game. It's what you have to buy, or put up in cash, or place in jeopardy in the hope of winning. Chance is the probability that you will win something. If there is no chance of your winning, then it's a scam, it's thievery; it's certainly not a lottery. The third element is the prize. There has to be something to win. The prize must be real and the winner must be able to take possession of it.

Sometimes contests can be held legally in states where lotteries are illegal by eliminating one of these elements. If all the components of a lottery are present, but you don't have to put up any money or buy anything or subscribe to a magazine, or whatever, then it isn't a lottery because there is no "consideration." This is the "nothing to buy" or "no purchase necessary to win" contest, and we find them in areas where local laws prohibit lotteries. They always seem a bit suspicious, though. Suppose you get one of these propositions in the mail, and it lists a number of magazines you can subscribe to and also promises a chance to win millions. Somewhere in the material it will make clear that you can enter (and have just as good a chance of winning) without subscribing to any of the magazines. If the contest is run honestly, it really doesn't make any difference whether a contestant subscribes or not. But even so, the implication in the mind of the applicants is often that they will have a better chance of winning if they sign up for one of the magazines. These games always strike me as slightly coercive.

No one ever got anything in the mail to win a life on earth, we're all born into life. Nonetheless, life's gambles also have three elements. But for clarity's sake let's rename consideration, chance, and prize to *investment, odds,* and *stakes.* Suppose you decide to drive to a neighboring town to visit a client that you believe is interested in closing a real-estate deal. You invest a lot in such a trip: time, energy, gasoline, and the wear and tear on your car. This investment is your "consideration."

The odds (the chance) are that you might waste your time, gas, and your car. You even, to a certain extent, risk your life on the highway. The stakes (the prize) would be the potential reward of successfully closing the deal. You weigh all these things and if you decide it's worth it, you go. But you are gambling.

Now consider this example. Suppose someone asks you to drive a car 130 miles an hour. You might think the request unreasonable and probably ridiculous. Why in the world would you ever drive a car so fast? Well, you can't really say "yes" or "no" until you know "what for?" If you're going to risk a front tire blowout or an accident at that speed for no other reason than to go 130 mph in a fast car, then you'd probably say no. (I realize that some daredevils actually do like to go that fast and their payoff is the sheer thrill of it. That kind of thrill might seem worth it to some people, but not to me.)

Now suppose we change the stakes. The investment remains the same: a substantial risk to your life. The odds remain the same: the chance of a bad accident. But now imagine that someone you love, a child or a mate, is in desperate need of your help. Suddenly, the stakes are very high. You would weigh things like road conditions, weather, abilities of the car, and assuming such high speed was possible, you might very well slam that accelerator through the floorboards to save the life of your wife or husband or son or daughter. Depending on the car, you might even go faster than 130 mph. So then the question, "Would you drive a car at 130 miles an hour?" would have an entirely different meaning. You might try it.

Anything we do is a gamble and combines these three elements. Fortunately, much of daily living is relatively low risk with reasonable stakes and minimal consideration. But because our day-to-day gambles are low key, we don't see them as gambles. We cross the street and the risk of being hit by a truck is low, but it is there. We can even reduce some of the risks we take: we can be more cautious crossing streets, we can quit smoking, we can improve our diet, we can, in short, stack the cards in our favor. There are no guarantees in life, and we can improve the odds, but gamble we must. In fact, if we resist gambling, we risk becoming very uninteresting people.

Tomorrow and the next day and ten years from now—or the next second—all have uncertain outcomes. We leap into our future with the same liability that a gambler leaps into his game. In fact, if life had no chance about it, if we were not required continually to risk things we value, if there were no stake of potential winnings, then it wouldn't be much of a life at all.

I remember returning from Macao that summer's day (I actually won a little money)—crossing Hong Kong harbor aboard the high-flying hydrofoil, engines screaming, salt spray in my face—and thinking, "Good God, at any moment this boat could blow up and sink." But the minimal investment seemed worth the ride, and the chances of an explosion seemed pretty minimal, too. Best of all, the prize of a safe arrival, the company of good friends and a wonderful wife seemed to me like a great wealth.

Phobia

NORMAL FEARS ARE NOT PHOBIAS. If a person is literally fearless—has no fear of any sort ever—then that person is not normal. I suspect that completely fearless people might not last very long in a world where fear is so obviously useful to stave off disaster.

It is not acrophobia if you're afraid when you find yourself on a window ledge fifty stories up. If you desperately wish you were inside and you suffer anxiety, you are entirely normal. The fear becomes acrophobia when you are terrified on the third step up on a stepladder. And it's not claustrophobia to feel panicky if you get locked in a coffin, but a person who cannot be in an ordinary small room without feeling panicked anxiety probably does have claustrophobia.

There are so many specific phobias that the American Psychiatric Association enumerates a very long list of them. They define such phobias as nystophobia, fear of the dark; ochlophobia, fear of crowds; xenophobia, fear of strangers; zoophobia, fear of animals; and a great many more impossible-sounding, multisyllabic Hellenic compounds.

The whole subject of phobias got me to thinking about the interplay between the rational thinking processes and emotional needs. This interplay is clearly present even in ostensibly normal people who seem otherwise free of neuroses or phobias. I have what I think is a touch of acrophobia: heights bother me a little more than they should.

Some years ago my brother worked as a radio engineer at a small broadcast station in Ohio. The transmitter tower was one hundred feet high, and he occasionally had to climb to the top to change a light bulb, the little red light required by law for aviation safety. This is something he did with no fuss. One day he invited me to go to the top for the view. From the ground it didn't seem too much of a challenge. The climbing spikes stuck out at right angles along the edge, and they seemed anchored firmly enough. I started up, and found that at about forty feet I did not feel comfortable. Before I got to fifty feet, halfway up, I was so unhappy and fearful that my wrists began to shake, and I was actually afraid I might lose my grip. I had to climb back down.

Once on the ground, I couldn't believe I had been afraid up there, and I tried it again—with the same result. I finally had to admit that I could never climb to the top of that tower. Maybe I could have made it to the top if the tower had a stairwell, even a semi-enclosed one, but I sure couldn't do it out in the open like that. The fear seemed irrational, but it was real.

But here is something even more irrational (and I don't think I'm unique in this): being in an airplane at any altitude does not frighten me at all. In fact, I don't feel any sense of height. The little houses and barns and factories down below seem like dolls' houses, remote and quite objectified. Of course I know better, but I don't feel as though I'm really five thousand or ten thousand feet up in the air. As a result, being in a plane or glider or balloon has never factored into my mild case of acrophobia, if indeed that's what I have. I've never discussed this with a psychologist.

Since heights do not bother me in aircraft, there are things I could do at great heights without anxiety that I absolutely could not do at lesser altitudes. Stay with me, because I'm about to prove that I'm bonkers. I really believe that if there were some reason to do this as part of a project—let's say a broadcast project—that if I were required to climb out of the open cockpit of a biplane at an altitude of, say, ten thousand feet, and climb down a rope ladder to the cockpit of another biplane that matched the speed, I could do it. I'd want to wear a parachute in case the ladder broke or I lost my grip or something, but I could do this. But if you offered me $50 million to wash the outside of an office-building window seven floors up, even using a window-washer's belt, I'd never collect a penny. I'd feel pretty bad about not getting $50 million, but I know I'd become a basket case before I ever climbed out over that sill. (It makes me fearful just to look down from an open window at that height.)

I think I finally figured out what makes the difference, why one circumstance produces so much fear in me and the other does not. It came to me during a balloon flight in Arizona a couple of years ago. I am a licensed balloon pilot, and for a publicity project in a balloon owned by one of the Pointe Resort hotels in Phoenix, I took some people on a balloon ride which terminated on a farm northwest of Scottsdale.

In a balloon I have no trouble sitting on the edge of the gondola, leaning out and hanging on to the rigging—again, regardless of the altitude. There is no sense of height in this for me. But I made a discovery as that flight neared its end. I was hanging out over the edge of the basket as we were clearing around three hundred feet over some tall trees and shouting down to our ground crew. There was a mild breeze, and we were drifting toward some barns that I wanted to avoid.

A balloon carries a long mooring line, a tether that can be deployed downward so that the ground crew can control the movement of the balloon during the last few feet down. The tether is usually two hundred feet long. On this occasion I decided to throw it down and be reeled in before drifting into the barns I saw looming ahead. As soon as I saw the tether go spinning down and a ground crew member reach up to grab it, I realized then (emotionally, as well as rationally) that I was two hundred feet up in the air and leaning out of a balloon basket—and I freaked. I got back in the middle of the basket, almost afraid to look over the side. And it finally came to me that the rope made the difference, it was a tangible connection to the ground.

I suddenly had grasped, on some emotional level, what my true altitude was, and it immediately made me scared. So when you're leaning out of an upper-story window, and you see all those converging lines streaking downward toward the sidewalk, you immediately feel how high up you are, and if you have a touch of acrophobia—or even if you're normal but leaning out a bit too far—you feel panic, too.

Ordinary fear is, I suppose, like pain, something you don't want to avoid totally. If you were incapable of feeling pain, you might not notice your hand on a hot stove until you smelled burning flesh. With no pain you'd probably damage yourself in short order. Fear is pretty useful, too. Fear removes us from situations that are harmful or risky.

Curiously, almost no one is afraid of going into the water as an infant.

We broadcast a segment on NBC television many years ago called "Water Babies," in which little tiny babies were flung into a swimming pool that had water warmed up to almost body temperature. The infants left their eyes open and did not breathe while under water—they also exhibited no fear. In fact, it seemed a little eerie. But since they'd just spent the first nine months of their existence immersed in amniotic fluid, they were probably more used to being under water than being in the air.

The psychologist who gave this demonstration said that after two or three years, children are usually subjected to fearful admonitions about going near the water from parents who want to be sure they don't wander off into an untended swimming pool or pond. Kids hear grownups say, "Oh, no! Don't go anywhere near the water! Water is BAD!" And so they associate water with images of doom. This association can stick with us for the rest of our lives.

Fear of flying is something else again. Some experts claim that the fear of flying is almost always a referred fear —— that is, the real fear (too fearful to be allowed into the conscious mind) camouflages itself and comes out as a fear of flying in planes. I broadcast a segment on a school that helps people overcome the fear of flying. The school has been pretty successful, but the regime is hard work for the students, and the process can take a long time to unfold. Again, it has nothing to do with the soundness of these people's minds. Aside from their fear of flying, these people appear totally rational. They may understand that their fear is nonsensical. They may realize that flying coast-to-coast is about six times safer than driving, but they don't want to get in an airplane. Some of them could drive coast-to-coast and never bother to fasten a seat belt and not feel uneasy, but fly in a plane? Never. Irrational behavior from a rational mind.

So, if you have some fears that seem somewhat lopsided, fear not! Of course I can only speak for myself, and right now I'm suffering inordinate fear that I've already written too much and will have to use another page. Or maybe I'll ramble, or not pick the right word for you to read, or . . . well, hey, I'm just not going to worry about it.

SOCIETY

The American Free Press

IT'S SOMETIMES HARD FOR US AMERICANS to appreciate what life is like in other countries. Sandwiched between two enormous bodies of water, we are isolated by the Atlantic and Pacific oceans. We have only two foreign neighbors with which to compare our lives. We enjoy so many unusual freedoms compared to most other countries that (it's often been observed) we tend to take our freedoms for granted. This seems somewhat amazing, because I think we should appreciate our freedoms as fresh. As far as freedoms go, we are living in a very new and revolutionary experiment that is scarcely two hundred years old.

Every ten years or so when the census bureau goes out and counts everybody's head, there is always an article in the paper about suspicion and resistance to having a government official come over to the house and ask a lot of personal questions. There's more than just fear of officialdom regarding the census. The fear of the census is an ancient one, and it strikes deep.

The Roman Empire established the office of the censor back in 443 B.C. The censor not only went around and counted everybody's head, he was also responsible for policing everybody's morals. Fear of the censor was a perfectly justifiable fear. Getting rid of the censor concept is one of the brilliant achievements of the American experiment.

In ancient Rome, immorality and treason were closely linked. The censor was established to maintain the virtue of the Roman state. In those days, before the industrial revolution and the Age of Enlightenment, religion and politics were so closely intertwined that they were virtually the same thing. Being a victim of censorship in ancient Rome was a very serious matter, it meant being stripped of your rights as a citizen. There was no trial, really. Usually a lone official sat in judgment over the alleged crimes of immorality and treason. He was assisted in his judgment by the person who was doing the accusing—the informer, or delator. Interestingly, the delator was paid for informing on people.

Reporting your neighbor's dalliances to the local praetor and ruining your neighbor's life in the process was an easy way to pick up a little extra cash in ancient Rome.

Flagrant and immoral behavior like adultery wasn't all that could strip you of your rights and ruin your life forever. Speech was censored in ancient Rome. Criticism of the government, or even of historical figures, was censored. So were innocent statements that weren't necessarily critical—a mere allusion to criticism could be considered treason.

Censorship, as an official practice, predates the Romans and has existed in other cultures as well. But it was the Romans who, almost five hundred years before Christ, gave us the word *censor* and established the office that ultimately migrated throughout Western culture. The spirit of this moral-political census was rooted in the whim and greed of rulers rather than in impartial justice. What began as Roman censorship continued for a very long time.

After Rome fell to the marauding hordes of Vandals and the various Goths, censorship was pretty much an ad hoc affair. Vandals and Visigoths preferred to minimize legal proceedings. Rather than establishing an official bureau of the census, they found that a simple, swift sword blow censored people a lot faster.

Europe lumbered on through its dark ages and suffered the tyranny of church censorship. Monasteries kept classical learning alive, it's true, but the temporal power of the Church censored and judged with a fist as heavy as that of the old Roman Empire.

Even after the colonization of the New World and freedom from Rome and its heirs we didn't escape the censor. American colonists censored "witches" by killing them after speedy trials. The Salem witch hunts were motivated by an blend of bent morality and warped politics. I've never been sure what a witch was supposed to be. Colonists were not allowed to write about witchcraft and witches rarely wrote about themselves. I haven't read anything by a person I was convinced was a bona fide witch, and considering the general tenor of the seventeenth century, witches didn't discuss openly what they did. Colonial America only permitted certain opinions and censored all the other opinions.

The narrowness of opinion in those days is difficult to imagine today. When the government burned the books of the peaceful Quakers, the people who turned them in were themselves fined half of the ten-pound fine levied on people who possessed such literature. Seems incredible.

The American colonies in the seventeenth century were about as anxiety ridden and as repressive as ancient Rome. You could, after all, be taken to a public square and hanged by the police if you were thought to be in league with the powers of darkness. You could be severely punished for joking about witchcraft. You didn't have to actually say or do anything criminal yourself to get in trouble—other people's unfounded accusations were often quite enough to cause you harm.

Expressing any opinion other than the party line was so fervently feared in colonial America that Sir William Berkeley, the governor of Virginia in 1671, was moved to thank God that he did not have printing in his colony. Sir William said: " . . . learning has brought disobedience and heresy . . . into the world and printing has divulged them and libels against government." Before the American Revolution, the government in Virginia *was* Sir William Berkeley. He had little room for opinions other than his own.

Sixty-three years after Berkeley's remarkable statement about the liberal press, New York had big trouble with printing. William Cosby, the governor of New York in 1734, became livid after reading a series of articles about him and his government in the *New York Weekly-Journal*. He called the articles, "Scandalous, virulent, false and seditious reflections." The governor of New York has always been a powerful individual, but back in 1734 he was unrestrained by civil rights laws or the First Amendment or any of the guarantees we enjoy today. His power was simply immense back then. The publisher of the *New York Weekly-Journal* was an insignificant German immigrant named John Peter Zenger. The *Zenger* case is one of the more elegant events in American history. During his trial, Zenger demonstrated that what he had printed was simply true. The jury, already showing the seeds of a revolutionary spirit, decided that since what Zenger said was true, he was not guilty of libel. Libel, by definition, is something that is untrue and designed to damage the reputation of a person. Amazing! Nothing like it had ever happened in history. Zenger went free and in doing so, laid the cornerstone of American free press.

This decision, in the remote colonies of the Americas, was a great departure from traditional English law. Americans were tiring of many aspects of English law, which, after all, had a tradition of censorship dating all the way back to the Roman census of 443 B.C. What seems particularly American to me about this famous trial is how the jury in the *Zenger* case put truth above everything else. They ignored the differences between a powerful man and a powerless man. They limited their inquiry to what was true and what was not.

Cosby, the governor of New York, had presented to the public only one side of the case. There was another side, and that side not only had a right to be heard, it was important for the American mind to know it. To know both sides of an issue and to decide freely and independently between them is a fundamental strength of American democracy, and it fosters freedom.

Can you imagine a public forum in the modern United States in which the opinions of governments and of people we don't like were not allowed on television or radio or in the papers? Free access to many sides of an issue allows us to decide intelligently. Other countries prohibit information outright or manipulate information in ways that maneuver their populations into narrow channels of thinking. America was founded on the expansion of liberty and on unfettered thought. It has worked for two hundred years, and if we don't succumb to the very real dangers of spin doctors, intentional distortions, blatant censorship, or if we don't simply throw it all away, it will work for another two hundred years.

We might remember just how long ago the old Roman office of the censor really was. It was only a few hundred later, after that office was founded, that another figure who was considered by officialdom to be a dangerous revolutionary, said: "And ye shall know the truth, and the truth shall make you free." If I remember correctly, the government lied about that guy, too.

Dress "Codes"

In very ancient times humans wore no clothes, not even neckties. The custom of clothing the body appeared well before civilization and must have come with the development of intellect. The first reason for putting on clothes, I presume, must have been very practical: clothes offer protection. Garments protect against the cold, against brambles and stones, and against tree bark when you have to scramble up a tree to get away from a bear.

Even when we had more body hair than we have now, we were not well protected from environment, in northern latitudes particularly. Somebody must have noticed that you didn't die as fast from freezing if you were bundled up in the skin of a furry animal (it probably felt pretty good, too) and that racing through a raspberry patch at full speed with a saber-toothed tiger on your tail was a lot more comfortable if you were wrapped in tough buckskins or leather hides. Even with heavily calloused feet, walking must have been easier if some leather or straw intervened between your soles and all the flint shards that littered the ground.

After the practice of wearing clothes was fairly well established, humans developed a sense of privacy that came to be called "modesty." Increased self-consciousness combined with sexual jealousy (and an irritation with other people's sexuality) to elevate modesty to the powerful force of propriety we have today. (I don't know why, but everyone seems to think their own sexuality is beautiful, even necessary, and that other people's, or some other people's, is revolting.) These developments gave clothing a role beyond the protection it afforded.

Then a third element came into play: clothes began to mean something. Clothing became symbolic of rank, status, degrees and types of authority, and group identification. The blue collar, vestments of the priestly class, smocks of artists, white jackets of professional scientists and medical doctors, police and military uniforms, purple-and-ermine robes of royalty, the straitjacket, designer jeans, and other humble chic, including threadbare snobbery—all of these styles emerged to make specific statements: statements of self-importance, of rebellion, of power or delegated authority, and more.

Attire exudes a powerful charisma that can change not only our own attitudes with our own clothes but our behavior in the presence of other people's clothing. We may be willing, in the presence of a physician we've never met before, to take off all our clothes and submit to probing indignities that would certainly be intolerable if not for the doctor's reassuring white jacket. We may feel uneasy or vaguely guilty in the presence of a police uniform, even if the officer has approached us merely to pass the time of day.

So clothing does three things: it shields the body from environmental harshness, it covers and hides the animal nature of our physical makeup, and it gives sanction and potency to whatever authority we claim to wield. Clothing is a kind of advertising.

No wonder there are so few nudist colonies. People lose too much status, power, and panache if they trot around completely bare in public. I heard that President Lyndon Johnson, when there were men he wished to bargain with or influence, would invite power brokers to the White House swimming pool to swim without suits. Then Johnson would show up late—clothed. These erstwhile shakers and movers were immediately plunged into a deep and distinct psychological disadvantage.

Remember when some fashion experts predicted that female toplessness would become popular? Designer Rudi Gernreich even brought out a line of topless dresses. It never caught on, and no wonder. Men may say they love to see women parade around topless, but the same men may also feel uncomfortable if the woman happens to be their wife or their mother or sister or their daughter. And women, obviously, are not so stupid as to intentionally parade around at a psychological disadvantage (remember Lyndon Johnson). I can't imagine that toplessness would become mainstream fashion anytime soon. If it ever did, women undoubtedly would demand an equal amount of skin from men.

And that's hardly likely either. There is a term: "clothed and in his right mind." Intelligent people rarely relinquish their sanity for a fad.

What you wear is important, and clothing clads you in social advantage or disadvantage. Job seeking, meeting one's in-laws for the first time, religious gatherings—all seem to go smoother for the better attired. That said, I am often maddened by the requirement of certain restaurants that men must wear neckties. Is a necktie really that important for a man?

Why is a man regarded to be likely to pay his bill or to be a good worker if he is wearing a necktie? Some of the greatest deadbeats and goof-offs in history have worn neckties. Great embezzlers and confidence men have beautiful necktie collections, and yet the custom persists. I used to argue with headwaiters about wearing a tie in restaurants. It was a futile, and perhaps sophomoric, exercise. I finally gave up. Now I merely put on a tie or go elsewhere.

You can get away with breaking these rules but only if you are firmly and universally established as successful and important. Albert Einstein could go around without a haircut, with chalk dust on a frumpy jacket that ill-concealed a baggy sweater, and with no necktie. He was Albert Einstein, a known brain. But he did not dress like that back in 1904, when he was applying for a job as a patent clerk in Bern, Switzerland. He had a necktie and a haircut; if he hadn't he would not have been able even to apply.

But we still haven't answered the question of why the four-in-hand necktie became—and remains—such a powerful symbol in male attire. It is required so often that it must stand for something very important. Sometimes items of clothing are used to hide something. Sometimes they accommodate vanity, as in the case of padded shoulders. But the necktie? What in the world does it do, anyway? Add color? Fashion may be frothy, but it usually has some practical roots.

The transition from knee breeches to long pants in the upper classes in England and America came about, they say, when Queen Victoria's Prince Albert, who hated the shape of his legs, decided not to wear knee breeches any more. He wore only long pants. The Prince Consort of England has always been a trendsetter, so predictably British tailors commenced making long trousers for gentlemen. Working men had worn long pants for quite awhile (a foreign fashion, long ago inherited from the ancient Scythians, who invented them), so it was a bold step for royalty and nobility to adopt a plebeian practice from the so-called lower classes. It was a complete "make-over."

Outside of golfers' plus fours, adult males abandoned all forms of knee pants in favor of trousers. The name *trousers*, by the way, appears to have come from Scotland. Scots wore kilts, of course, but when the weather was extremely cold, they would wrap wool tartans tightly around each leg. This wool leg-sleeve was called a *trewes* or *trowse*. Two of them were called *trowses*, and the word became *trousers* (with a second "r"). And despite being joined at the waist as a single garment, they retained a plural name. Eventually, and luckily, the Scots adopted the more traditional Scythian version with its immensely more useful full-pants design, which included the gusseted crotch.

But I digress from examining the necktie. The tie evolved from the "stock," a wide scarflike band of cloth wound around the neck outside a high collar and fixed with a pin. Later the stock became thinner and was tied in a knot instead of being pinned. The method of tying allowed a slipknot to tighten the whole thing to make certain the wearer's neck would be firmly constricted and that there would be no hope of comfort while out in public. I do not mark this event among the greater insights of the human mind; indeed, the tie itself constricts the blood supply to the brain in sufficient quantities to preclude insight on any meaningful level.

I would estimate that it takes the average American boy about three years to master tying a necktie so that it appears neat. He spends the rest of his life either perfecting the knot and the evenness of the two ends, or he gives up entirely, turning to pretied, clip-on bow ties or gold chains or bolo ties or, most recently (gad!), decorative pins.

The modern four-in-hand necktie is a particularly barbaric device in the summertime. When a man is dressed in a suit with a shirt and tie and thermometers are at their longest extension, consider the number of layers of cloth around a man's neck. The jacket collar itself has two layers of wool between which is a buckram lining. This whole assemblage is brought up to neck height and doubled over. The suit coat alone puts six layers around his neck. Under this is a shirt with a double layer of cotton fabric, lined (and often starched). That's three layers with the collar standing up—when it's folded over, then it's six layers. Inside the fold of the shirt collar is the necktie, which has a lining inside doubled silk (or whatever the tie is made of)—that's five layers of necktie. The total brings us to seventeen layers of cloth wrapped or cinched tightly around a man's neck. It could be 102°F in the shade, but we may be sure that the man's I.Q. will usually fall well below this number.

How can a culture that calls itself civilized inflict this cruel and unusual punishment on a human being just because he was born male? Neckties have assumed a life of their own, at least in certain circles, and I don't imagine the habit will slough itself off of my neck anytime soon.

Considering the unnatural bindings and curious prostheses that women are urged to wear (usually for no other reason than to inflate the male ego, or more likely, something actually below his necktie), I guess I should feel lucky to get off with only seventeen layers of cloth around my neck. I often wince at women's wear.

I wear a variety of garb for TV when I'm in the field, mostly without neckties. but I wouldn't do my studio work in shirt sleeves or without a tie. Somehow I would not be taken as seriously if I didn't. I have worn a variety of outfits designed for protection: fireproof auto-racing suits, flight suits, pressure suits, arctic gear, diving suits—including the hardhat full diving suit, the kind that predates scuba gear. And I've worn scuba gear, wet suits, and dry suits. I have never worn a full suit of armor or a bulletproof vest, and I'd rather not find myself in a situation that calls for either.

The heaviest clothing I ever had to struggle into was a Greek spongediver's suit I wore at Tarpon Springs, Florida. It was the only dive I ever made in a full diving suit. These things are frighteningly claustrophobic, and I had to talk to myself while they were bolting the helmet onto the neckring. I actually had to convince myself that it was clothing and not a contoured coffin. Once I was under the surface, it didn't bother me, but out of water I felt uneasy until I got out of the suit.

The most necessary clothing I have ever worn was full arctic gear that I donned in Siberia in the winter of 1969. I was filming a TV special on the woolly mammoth hunters of 15,000 years ago. The temperature was sixty-six degrees below zero. From inside out I had on thermal underwear, a quilted undershirt, a wool shirt, a heavy-knit sweater, a down vest, a parka made of thick down trimmed in wolverine fur, lined chinos, wool trousers, and down arctic pants, plus a couple of pairs of socks and felt-and-fleece boots. I knew that even dressed like that, without an artificially heated enclosure nearby, I still would freeze solid in a matter of hours. I didn't dare exert myself much, because at that temperature rapid deep breathing could have frosted my lungs, and any sweat I produced could have frozen and killed the top layer of my skin.

Incidentally, I had no necktie on during that shoot. But I did have on a heavy scarf. It's very hard to escape that dratted noose.

Left-Handedness

I REMEMBER IT ALL VERY WELL. It was back in the 1940s. We were living in Chicago then, and our eldest child, a son also named Hugh, reached out in his first coordinated eye-and-hand movement. Shock followed fear as we both realized that our son had been born—*gauche*.

Up to that moment I had had little experience with the left-handed. It was always discomforting to watch them bumping their elbows against right-handed tablemates in restaurants, and I knew that when they wrote with a fountain pen, they smeared the words as the heel of their hand followed the nib—something like a street cleaner nudging along a curb. I tell you, seeing our child like that, waving his little rattle at us with his left hand . . . hey, that's tough.

I remember having been frightened as a child by stories of the chronically left-handed. They say that in state homes for the left-handed, the screams last all night from the agony of using right-handed scissors as they cut out paper chains of dolls. Apparently, this product is the sole export from homes for the severely sinister.

It was painful to think of such things; my son looked like such a nice child. But even if he avoided one of those homes, there would always be the stigma to live with: "Hey, lefty!" "Hey you, the southpaw!" My God, I can still hear it. Our only hope was to be better informed. So I read up on the subject.

I discovered that the very word *left* has troubling roots. The Middle English *lift* and Old English *left* means "weak or worthless." The Anglo Saxon *lyft* means "weak or broken" and is related to *lopt* or *lopped* and is probably related to the German *licht* and *leicht*, conveying the sense of "fragile." You can be assured that those definitions may not be on the tip of everyone's memory, but they laid a strong foundation for our modern word *left*, and much of that sense is still with us.

Even the *Oxford Dictionary* deals the phrase "left-handed" a derogatory hand. Defective; awkward; clumsy; doubtful—they're all there. In medical terminology, left-handed can mean spurious, and of course there was that awful word *sinister*. Can you imagine how embarrassing it is introducing your son as sinister?

Sinister is a derivative of *sinus*, which means *pocket* in Latin. This originally referred to the pocket of a Roman toga, which was always on the left-hand side. Before sinister came into common Latin parlance, the ancient Romans used another word, *laevus*, which means not only the left hand but also shield. That's not such a derogatory meaning, more descriptive really; it referred to the traditional soldier's armor—specifically to the shield, which was held in the left hand (presumably to guard the heart). The sword was grasped by the right hand.

Sinister seems to have acquired its maligned association from Greek methods of fortune-telling that were imported to Rome. The oracle, or augur, faced north during these seances. Aligning oneself on the compass this way places the rising sun on one's right side. That would be the east side and, therefore, the fortunate side. Because east is the direction of morning light, it traditionally has been considered an auspicious direction. The east brings light. Conversely, the sun is extinguished every evening in the west, associating that direction with death.

In Britain, the term *cack*-handed is even more inauspicious, cack being a colloquial term for excrement. But separating the duties of each hand goes beyond Britain and is also found in the Middle East and most all of Asia. Eating is usually reserved for the right hand, while the other hand, the left, is left to perform hygienic duties that are, for the most part, unmentionable. The ritual impurity associated with the left hand in those cultures is so strong that it exceeds any scientific explanation for simple hygiene. In fact, my son was once shopping in a market in India and was innocently fondling some oranges with his left hand to find the juicy ones. The Brahman running the stall took such umbrage at this act of defilement that the poor boy received a painful roundhouse punch to the ear—left hand of the Brahman, right ear of my kid. Considering that you peel an orange before you eat it, there is hardly any risk of contamination, but such is the plight of sinistrals in our unfair world. Of course, I had known long ago that my son would suffer.

A ritual discrimination between right and left hands is not something exclusive to Muslims, Hindus, and Buddhists. Christianity is rife with exalting the right hand to the detriment of the left. Christ sits on the right hand of God, after all. The bread and wine of communion are carried from the right of the altar and dispensed from left to right to recipients. In more folksy Christian lore, the inauspicious event of spilling salt (which you may remember Judas doing in da Vinci's painting *The Last Supper*) can be rectified by taking a pinch of salt with the right hand and throwing it over the left shoulder, thereby propitiating the devil in his direction.

There are no lack of examples of the devil's association with the left hand. In medieval iconography the devil blesses people with that hand and devotees are often shown making sinistral offerings. (I'm sure all this talk about satanic cults these days is only a persecution of left-handed people.) These traditions die hard. They also go back much farther than the Middle Ages.

In the Bible the Israelites even fought a war against an army of left-handed warriors, the Benjamites. There are some curiously contradictory things about this encounter. First of all, the name Benjamin comes from Ben-Yamin, which means "Son of the Right Hand." But the Bible describes the army of Benjamites (in Judges 20:16, if you're interested) this way: "Among all this people there were seven hundred select men who were left-handed; every one could sling a stone at a hair's breadth and not miss."

I always considered the Benjamites' excellent marksmanship to be a redeeming feature of the legions of the gauche. And just to show that even this tribe of left-handed people weren't all bad, the Bible records that one of the Benjamites, Ehud, was drafted by God to perform a righteous assassination. At God's behest, Ehud killed Eglon, the cruel leader of the Moabs. Although not exactly the wittiest retort a left-handed person might sling back to a denigrator on the street, this does have an interesting background. ("Who you callin' southpaw? At God's behest, Ehud killed Eglon, the cruel leader of the Moabs! You S.O.B.!" You see? It just doesn't work.)

The sinistral Ehud was used for this assassination because he could elude the search for weapons that preceded an audience with King Eglon. Having strapped his dagger to his right thigh, he was able to pass the compulsory search for weapons undetected. The guards only searched the left thigh, of course, because that's where a dextral swordsman would conceal a weapon. So even God found a use for the left-handed. There may be more to this biblical story than meets the eye. I certainly hope so, because a redemption would hold great promise for my son and others with this affliction. In fact, the left-handed may very well represent a special vision and be worthy of preservation.

Although Benjamin Franklin was right-handed, he wrote a remarkable piece in defense of the left hand called "A Petition to Those Who Have the Superintendency of Education." It was an appeal recommending the acceptance of gauche children in school. Forcing a left-handed child to switch to the right is now known as a possible cause of stuttering, or worse. But in Franklin's day this was not so well known. He writes from the point of view of a left hand: "I address myself to all the friends of youth, and conjure them to direct their compassionate regard to my unhappy fate, in order to remove the prejudices of which I am the victim." He signed his petition "Your obedient servant, THE LEFT HAND."

Several charismatic figures throughout history were known to be (or thought to be) left-handed. The ancient Egyptian reliefs at Abu Simbel show Rameses clubbing enemies with his left hand. At Karnak, Thothmes III holds an offering in his left hand. Pharaohs may have been despotic, but we can hardly deny them charisma.

C.P.E. Bach and Cole Porter were left-handed. F. Lee Bailey is left-handed, so are both Paul McCartney and Ringo Starr. Charlie Chaplin even played the violin that way, not an easy thing to do. He had to string his violin backward to make it work. Babe Ruth was another famous, and skilled, left-handed person, and in fact, it was baseball that gave us the term "southpaw." In an old Chicago ballpark a left-handed pitcher faced west to pitch, thereby aligning his left hand with the south. Only later was the term applied to boxers. And now, of course, "southpaw" is applied to any left-handed person.

But the all time great charismatic sinistral was Leonardo da Vinci. Here was a left-handed–vegetarian–bodybuilder–inventor–artist, whose use of his left hand exceeded all bounds of the ordinary human imagination. Da Vinci not only wrote with his left hand, he penned his notebooks in mirror fashion, writing from right to left.

He may have done this to conceal discoveries that, although scientifically demonstrable, were nonetheless radical departures from accepted Christian superstitions. The left hand seems to have a particular skill in such innovative and unorthodox deviations. Many sinistrals fall easily into mirror writing or simply get it back to front.

Lewis Carroll, author of *Through the Looking Glass*, was as skilled at mirror writing as was da Vinci, and he spontaneously performed it to the amusement of his friends. Carroll, who also stuttered, incidentally, gives us a rare peek into the world of the other hand in his classic book about Alice. The left-handed must often feel they are in a world as uncommon and unorthodox as the inside of a mirror. And that may be their greatest contribution and saving grace. I have to admire anyone who can break out of the staid molds of the familiar and leap into the imagination. The left-handed vision offers this leap as a constant inspiration for us dextrals.

But you know what the hard part is? How does one adroitly give those lefties, who constitute up to 8 percent of our population, a positive left-handed compliment? Believe me, it's tough.

Brutes and Their Rights?

WHEN YOU CONSIDER THE VOLUME of public outcry generated by animal rights activists, you might be persuaded to believe this is a new phenomenon—it isn't. It's true that concern for animal suffering has been well documented for the last several thousand years (there is evidence of concern for animal suffering in the Bible), but the roots of the modern animal rights movements only go back a few hundred years. The surprising thing about the origin of modern animal rights movements is that they were created more as a result of dispassionate science than by compassionate religion. Ironically, public concern for animal welfare was triggered by scientific discoveries. Only later was it perpetuated by religious groups.

You certainly don't have to be an animal lover to be shocked at how animals were once treated in Europe. Even today's confirmed meat-eating, fur-wearing crowd can be appalled. Sport hunting was not a particular problem then, because it was limited to the very rich, and hunting was still considered a source of food. The problem was animal baiting. Animal baiting was common during the Middle Ages, and after, that most people hardly gave it a second thought. Cockfights, for example, were once so ordinary that much of the vocabulary it produced still exists in English: phrases like "pit against," "a clean pair of heels," "cut out for," the verb *to scoot* and, of course, the word *cockpit* all come from cockfighting, a sport that fortunately has few boosters today.

In 1526, a large theater was built in London at a place called Paris Garden. The only events scheduled at Paris Garden were public torturings of animals. One spectator who saw a performance in the late sixteenth century wrote how bulls would kill bulldogs that had been tied to their tails and how new dogs were immediately thrown into the ring to replace those that died. He went on to say, "To this entertainment there often follows that of whipping a blinded bear, which is performed by five or six men standing circularly with whips, which they exercise upon [the bear] without . . . mercy, as he cannot escape his chain. He defends himself with all his force and skill, throwing down all that come within his reach . . . and tearing the whips from their hands, and breaking them."

One British advertisement in the eighteenth century announced, "At His Majesty's Bear Garden at Hockley-in-the-hole, on Monday, 14th September, 1730, a mad bull is to be dressed up with fireworks all over him, and turned loose. . . . Also a bull to be let loose at the same time, and a cat to be tied to the bull's tail." This advertisement ends with the telling words, "Note—The doors will be opened at four, as the sports begin at five exactly, because the diversion will last long, and the days grow short."

People back then considered animal torture about the same way we think of ball games or thoroughbred racing. And animal torture events were not limited to the uneducated lower classes; most British kings and queens as well as peers and aristocrats of all levels were frequent visitors at Paris Garden. I was especially surprised to discover that King James I was sufficiently fond of animal torture that he included this activity as part of his official receptions. The very name "King James version" of the Bible always left me with the impression that the man must have been more compassionate than that—but most Europeans who participated in animal baiting considered themselves religious people.

Christian philosophers, especially St. Paul, St. Augustine, and St. Thomas Aquinas, maintained that animals didn't have souls. If anyone still felt squeamish about the way animals were treated, they could always read what God told Noah, "The fear of you and the dread of you shall be upon every beast of the earth, and upon every fowl of the air . . . and upon all the fishes of the sea; into your hands are they delivered. Every moving thing that liveth shall be meat for you."

Despite rhetorical claims of compassion, religion remained one of the greatest justifications for cruelty, at least for brutes. What happened to change that (most modern religious people are very much concerned with compassion for all life) was a series of scientific discoveries that unfolded at about the same time. Certain discoveries in biology and specifically in zoology had a tremendous effect on the way Europeans regarded animals.

First, in 1628, William Harvey discovered blood circulation. His book, *On the Movement of the Heart and Blood in Animals*, reinforced an earlier suspicion that animal and human anatomy were extremely close. More confirmations quickly followed. Sir Thomas Browne considered the newly developed microscope to be one of the most effective weapons against superstition. Browne, using his microscope, discovered that snails have eyes and that even pigeons possess a gall.

In the words of historian Dagobert de Levie, "While the Middle Ages consciously turned away from the human body and from beasts which they regarded as mean and sinful, the interest in beasts now increased. An impressive number of famous philosophers suddenly had concern for beasts and felt induced to reflect thoroughly on the animal problem. Thus the beast established its position also in the realm of spirit."

De Levie points out that science shattered organized religion's monopoly of God by revealing miracles of its own—scientific miracles. He says, "When God was understood to be the substance of the world, and the body and soul were regarded as its modifications, [animals], as a part of [the] godly substance, appeared . . . as worthy of respect . . . as any other living being."

This realization threw the ball back into the court of religion. The issue was picked up by a group of breakaway heretics called Free Churches. The Free Churches were not only free from the state religion politically, they were free to craft their own ideas about morality. Their new vision owed a large debt to the scientific discoveries of their age. The result of this mix was several very powerful movements for social change. Most of the modern animal-rights movements, certainly the thrust behind them, trace their roots back to the Free Churches of eighteenth-century Europe. (Not coincidentally, it was the Free Church Protestants who were largely responsible for the abolition of slavery.) Despite the progress made since, the questions have not gone away entirely. Are people who eat animal meat or wear animal fur or skins somehow evil? What about animal testing in laboratories—is that evil?

Perhaps the wisest course to fairly judge issues like these is for each person to personally reflect on them. What everyone should bear in mind is that people who use animal products have a vision, too, a legitimate vision.

Mankind has been wearing and eating dead animals for, maybe, hundreds of thousands of years. For almost as long, certainly for the last fifty thousand years or so, animal slaughter was considered a kind of ritual sacrifice. In the broader sense, for prehistoric people ritual killing confirmed a symbiotic unity of life with death. Consider these points:

Out of Newton's laws comes the conclusion that matter cannot be created or destroyed; it just changes and gets moved around. This reflects the central idea of sacrifice. The universe can only perpetuate itself by eating itself.

In the great Indian epic poem "The Mahabarata," the god Shiva says, "There is no one in the world who does not kill. He who walks kills innumerable insects with his feet. Even when sleeping, lives can be destroyed. All creatures kill one another . . . it is not possible for anyone to live without killing."

In a passage from another famous Indian poem "The Taittiriya Upanishad," we find a saint psychologically united with the universe. In a swoon, he says, "I am food, I am food, I am food! I am the eater of food, I am the eater of food . . . I am the uniter!" Maybe that's what God was telling Noah all along.

Admittedly, there are abuses in scientific labs, fur farms, and slaughter houses, but conditions are dramatically better for animals than they once were, and abuse, after all, is a relative term. Most of the people involved in the animal trade are sane and reasonable people. The difference is that they focus more on the welfare of animal populations than individual animals.

They also realize that animals who live in the wild don't just die of old age; they starve, get sick, have accidents, or more commonly, are torn apart and eaten by another animal occupying the next higher link in the food chain. These people tend to be realists and understand that life is more complex than it is pretty.

Animal industries have also benefited from the same objective scientific discoveries that spawned the animal rights movements. Biologists specializing in wildlife management can justifiably claim to have actually saved many animals by using scientific methods. Sometimes though, as any farmer will tell you, managing animal populations requires a selective and conscious pruning of the population.

We are guaranteed to see animal-product people and animal-rights people clash more often and with more severity in the future. There is an increasing possibility that public opinion will be swayed and the market for animal products will simply die its own death. Leonardo da Vinci once said he believed that someday killing a sentient animal to eat it would be regarded as immoral as killing a human being to eat.

If the market in animal products ever does grind to a halt, let's hope it happens in the same peaceful spirit we should lavish on animals. Stopping animal trade cannot be accomplished best by breaking the law. The destruction of private property, assault, and terrorist bombings committed by extremists are not in anyone's interest because violence is a poor foundation upon which to build a compassionate edifice.

At least we now know that animal furs are not necessary for warmth. And animal protein is not necessary for human health. The road is open for a better deal for the world's animals.

Dope Hope for the Oil Imbroglio?

IN 1990, VOTERS IN THE STATE OF ALASKA made marijuana illegal again for the first time in fifteen years. If Alaska turns out to be like the other forty-nine states, the law will do little to curb use or production. Despite the legal prohibitions against marijuana, many Americans continue to buck the trend. Some pro-marijuana organizations, in fact, tell us that marijuana, also known as hemp, could, as a raw material, save the U.S. economy. Not by smoking it—that's a minor issue. Would you believe that marijuana could replace most oil and energy needs? That marijuana could revolutionize the textile industry and stop foreign imports? Those are the claims. Some people think marijuana, or hemp, may be the epitome of Yankee ingenuity.

Jack Herer, for example, is the national director and founder of an organization called H.E.M.P. (Help End Marijuana Prohibition) located in Van Nuys, California. Herer is the author of a remarkable little book called *The Emperor Wears No Clothes*, wherein (not surprisingly) he urges the repeal of marijuana prohibition. He is not alone. Throughout the war on drugs, several organizations have consistently urged the legalization of marijuana—*High Times* magazine, for example, and the National Organization to Reform Marijuana Laws, or NORML for short, and an organization called BACH (Business Alliance for Commerce in Hemp). There are others.

But the reasons the pro-marijuana lobby wants marijuana legal has little to do with getting high and a great deal to do with fighting big oil interests. The pro-marijuana groups claim that hemp is such a versatile raw material that its products compete not only with petroleum, but with coal, natural gas, nuclear energy, pharmaceutical, timber, and textile companies.

It is estimated that methane and methanol production alone, from hemp grown as biomass, could replace 90 percent of the world's energy needs. If this is right, it is not good news for oil interests (and could account for the continuation of marijuana prohibition). The claim is that the threat hemp posed to natural resource companies back in the 1930s accounts for its original ban.

At one time marijuana seemed to have a promising future as a cornerstone of industry. When Rudolph Diesel produced his famous engine in 1896, he assumed that the diesel engine would be powered "by a variety of fuels, especially vegetable and seed oils." Diesel, like most engineers then, believed vegetable fuels were superior to petroleum. Hemp is the most efficient vegetable.

In the thirties, the Ford Motor Company also saw a future in biomass fuels and operated a successful biomass-conversion plant that included hemp at its Iron Mountain facility in Michigan. Ford engineers extracted methanol, charcoal fuel, tar, pitch, ethyl acetate, and creosote—all fundamental ingredients for modern industry and all now supplied by oil-related industries. The difference is that the vegetable source is renewable, cheap, and clean, and the petroleum or coal sources are limited, expensive, and dirty. The market advantage enjoyed by petroleum is that it is still easier to exploit and use than biomass sources, which will need startup and conversion capital to compete.

By volume, 30 percent of hemp seed contains oil suitable for high-grade diesel fuel and for aircraft-engine fuel and precision-machine oil. Henry Ford's experiments with methanol promised cheap, readily renewable fuel, and if you think methanol means compromise, you should know that many modern race cars run today on methanol.

About the time Ford was making biomass methanol, a mechanical device to strip the outer fibers of the hemp plant appeared on the market. This machine could turn hemp into paper and fabric quickly and cheaply. Hemp paper is superior to wood paper. The first two drafts of the U.S. Constitution were written on hemp paper. (The final draft is on animal skin.) Hemp paper contains no dioxins or other toxic residue, and a single acre of hemp can produce the same amount of paper as four acres of trees. Trees take twenty years to harvest and hemp takes a single season. In warm climates hemp can be harvested two or even three times a year. It also grows in bad soil and restores the nutrients.

Hemp fiber-stripping machines were bad news to the Hearst Paper Manufacturing Division and to a host of other natural resource firms. Coincidentally, in 1937 the DuPont chemical company was granted a patent on a sulfuric-acid process to make paper from wood pulp. At the time, DuPont predicted its sulfuric-acid process would account for 80 percent of its business for the next fifty years. Hemp, once a mainstay of American agriculture, became a threat to a handful of corporate giants. To stifle the commercial threat hemp posed to timber interests, William Randolph Hearst began referring to hemp in his newspapers by its Spanish name, marijuana. This did two things: it associated the plant with Mexicans and played on racist fears, and it misled the public into thinking that marijuana and hemp were different plants.

Nobody was afraid of hemp. It had been cultivated, processed into usable goods, consumed as medicine, and burned in oil lamps for hundreds of years. But after a campaign to discredit hemp in the Hearst newspapers, Americans became afraid of something called "marijuana." By 1937, the Marijuana Tax Act was passed, marking the beginning of the end of the hemp industry.

In 1938, *Popular Mechanics* ran an article about marijuana called "New Billion-Dollar Crop." It was the first time the words "billion-dollar" were used to describe a U.S. agricultural product. *Popular Mechanics* stated, "A machine has been invented which solves a problem more than 6,000 years old. . . . The machine . . . is designed to remove the fiber-bearing cortex from the rest of the stalk, making hemp fiber available for use without a prohibitive amount of human labor. Hemp is the standard fiber of the world. It has great tensile strength and durability. It is used to produce more than 5,000 textile products ranging from rope to fine laces, and the woody 'hurds' remaining after the fiber has been removed contain more than seventy-seven percent cellulose, and can be used to produce more than 25,000 products ranging from dynamite to Cellophane."

Since the *Popular Mechanics* article appeared over half a century ago, many more applications have come to light. But back in 1935, more than 58,000 tons of marijuana seed were used just to make paint and varnish, all nontoxic, by the way. When marijuana was banned, these safe paints and varnishes were replaced by paints made with toxic petrochemicals. In the 1930s, no one dreamed about poisoned rivers, deadly landfills, and children dying from chemicals in house paint.

People did know something about hemp back then because the plant and its products were so common. All ships' lines were made from hemp, and so was much of the sail canvas. In fact, the word *canvas* is the Dutch pronunciation of the Greek word for hemp, *kannabis*. All ropes, hawsers, and lines aboard ship, all rigging, nets, flags and pennants were also made from marijuana stalks (so were all charts, logs, and bibles). Today, many of these items are made, in whole or part, with synthetic petrochemicals and wood. Most oil lamps burned hemp-seed oil until whale oil edged it out of first place in the mid-nineteenth century. And then, when most of the whales were dead, lamplights were fueled by petroleum, coal, and recently, radioactive energy.

This may be hard to believe (in the middle of a war on drugs), but the first law concerning marijuana in the colonies, at Jamestown in 1619, ordered farmers to grow Indian hemp. Massachusetts passed a compulsory hemp-growing law in 1631. Connecticut followed in 1632. In the mid-eighteenth century, the Chesapeake colonies ordered their farmers, by law, to grow marijuana. Names like Hempstead or Hemphill dot the American landscape and reflect areas of intense marijuana cultivation.

During World War II domestic hemp production became crucial when the Japanese cut off Asian supplies to the United States. American farmers, even their sons, who grew marijuana were exempt from military duty during World War II. A 1942 U.S. Department of Agriculture film called *Hemp for Victor* extolled the agricultural might of marijuana and called for hundreds of thousands of acres to be planted. Despite a rather vigorous drug crackdown, 4-H clubs were asked by the government to grow marijuana for seed supply. Ironically, war plunged the government into a sober reality about marijuana: it is very valuable.

In today's antidrug climate, people don't want to hear about the commercial potential of marijuana. The reason is that the flowering top of a female hemp plant contains a drug. But from 1842 through the 1890s a powerful, concentrated extract of marijuana was the second-most prescribed drug in the United States. In all that time, medical literature did not list any of the ill effects claimed by today's drug warriors.

Today, there are anywhere from twenty-five to thirty million Americans who smoke marijuana regularly. As an industry, marijuana clears well more than four billion dollars a year. Obviously, as an illegal business, none of that money goes to taxes. But the modern marijuana trade only sells one product, a drug. Hemp could be worth considerably more than four billion dollars a year if it were legally supplying the fifty-thousand safe products that proponents claim it can.

If hemp could supply the energy needs of the United States, its value would be inestimable. America has an opportunity to say farewell, once and for all, to oil spills and the expensive brinkmanship in the desert sands of the Middle East.

CHAPTER EIGHT

HISTORY

Myth

MYTH CERTAINLY SEEMS TO BE the antithesis of science. Science is knowledge of something and myth is simply a story; that seems pretty well accepted. But as science expands its frontiers, it's interesting to notice that many myths of the past have more than just a kernel of truth to them. Myth doesn't mean untrue, but rather appears to be a device for making the unknown intelligible. Take the outlandish stories of werewolves and vampires, for example. Superstition? Perhaps, but possibly (in the beginning) the stories were based on observation, the way science is.

Myths of werewolves and vampires stretch back into great antiquity. Pliny, Herodotus, and Virgil all reported them. Stories of werewolves and vampires also are widespread geographically; they are found in Asia, Africa, and South America, not just in Transylvania and Hollywood.

The English word *werewolf* is a combination of the Anglo-Saxon *wer*, which means man, and *wolf*. The idea of people turning into animals is not so unusual in folklore. It originally may stem from prehistoric man's identification with particular animals, most especially animal qualities, an ancient tenet known as totemism.

We here in the Americas are familiar with Native Americans calling themselves Sitting Bull or Running Deer. These names identified a person with a particular image found in the animal world. Totemic belief was a useful way to prepare a child psychologically for adult life. We may smugly think Native American names a little quaint, but are we all that different? Sylvester Stallone made a movie about a powerful cop named Cobra. The name instantly telegraphs to the audience the fear of a large, poisonous, fanged, hooded viper. Sports teams—such as the Bears, the Rams, the Dolphins—link the teams with qualities associated with these animals. It's inescapable. I don't think any of us is completely without some totemic imagination. But there is a difference between assuming a name (and emulating a quality) and actually transforming into an animal. At one time, actually transforming into an animal was believed to be not only real but punishable by law. And indeed it was punished.

During the sixteenth century, a French judge named Bouget sentenced more than six hundred witches and werewolves to death. Bouget records in his *Discours de Sorciers*, a work he penned in 1590, that he once had tried a case involving a farmer's wife who had changed into a wolf and attacked a neighbor. During the fight with this wolf, the neighbor was able to lop off one of the wolf's paws. And voilá, as the wolf turned back into a woman, she indeed was missing a hand! What more proof could the court hope for, I ask you? It's incredible to us that such a thing was believed at all, but we must remember that most people of sixteenth-century France believed justice was being impartially meted out and that their lives were protected because of it. They believed this in exactly the same way we look at the deliberation of the Supreme Court in Washington. And as history repeats itself, it's probably only a matter of time before people will laugh at decisions made in our courts, just as we laugh at those of the sixteenth century.

There were several ways a person could transform into an animal. You could put on the skin of an animal and turn into that animal, or you could apply an ointment or mutter certain incantations. In fact, it was also possible for some people to change someone else into an animal, presumably against their will.

Greek legend says Lyeaon was turned into a wolf by Jupiter as punishment for eating human flesh. Saint Patrick turned Veretricius, then Prince of Wales, into a wolf, and in Christianity generally, angels (or those with angelic power) could do things like this. Saint Thomas Aquinas once commented that "all angels good and bad by some natural virtue have the ability to transmute our bodies."

Sometimes these transformations were not complete. Sometimes only parts of the body were affected and the other parts left human. Another sixteenth-century authority on witches, a priest named Bodin, categorized these partial transformations (nearly all of them) as involving only the teeth or the hands. Teeth and hands are significant in these stories.

It's one thing to have St. Thomas Aquinas describe details of a mental or spiritual vision (what angels do or don't do), and it's quite another thing to claim to have actual eyewitness accounts of sightings in the down-to-earth, concrete world. A big difference.

Marcellus of Sida was a physician who lived around the year 117. He mentions werewolves being in the habit of visiting the tombs of Athens at night. He notes they had yellow complexions, dry tongues, and hollow eyes, a frightening spectacle to describe, but Marcellus seems to be describing something he really saw. He wasn't trying to condemn anybody, as later exorcist priests tried to do.

Another description comes down to us from a scholar of Leipzig University named (quite coincidentally) John Frederic Wolfeshusius. When a werewolf was brought before a sixteenth-century Duke of Prussia, Wolfeshusius described him as "an evil favored man, not much unlike a beast, and he had many scars on his face . . . although he was vigilantly watched, this werewolf never cast what little he possessed of human shape." This may be a frightening description, but it makes me feel more pity than fright.

In fact pity may be the appropriate response. Contemporary medical science knows of a rare blood disease called porphyria. Porphyria may possibly be the kernel of truth buried in such a richly embroidered and widely dispersed myth as the werewolf. Porphyria is caused by a recessive gene that makes it impossible to convert porphobiliogen to porphyrin in the bone marrow, disrupting the heme biosynthetic pathway. Heme is an iron complex that pigments the blood with its characteristic red color. There are several different types of porphyria, and they have varying degrees of severity, but the most extreme type bears a number of symptoms that, when considered as a group, are fascinating in their implications.

Exposure to light, especially sunlight, produces pain and a reddish or yellowish discoloring of the skin in a porphyria patient. The skin ulcerates, attacking cartilage and disfiguring the patient's nose, lips, eyelids, ears, and fingers. With the lips changed like this, the teeth appear to protrude more than they actually do, and the patient takes on a kind of permanent grin. The teeth are further affected by deposits of porphyrins, turning them red. Since a good deal of the porphyrins are passed out in urine, even that becomes reddish in color. These patients also grow excessive amounts of hair, and this hirsutism makes them appear more animal-like. If you can imagine a person who suffers all of these symptoms at the same time, you will have a hairy, deformed individual with a mutilated face displaying protruding red teeth, bearing hands with curled nails on twisted fingers. Also, this person would feel ill at ease in the daylight and comfortable outside only at night.

It has even been suggested that victims of porphyria might have had a desire to drink blood in order to replenish the blood element of heme that they were so desperately lacking. Indeed, one modern treatment for porphyria is an injection of heme. A big question is whether sufferers in the Middle Ages were actually drinking blood and whether heme could pass through the stomach without being destroyed. But the need for an important ingredient found in blood might explain the peculiar thirst attributed to vampires.

Sadly, in addition to the physical disfigurement, these patients may also suffer serious mental disorders, ranging from mild hysteria to profound psychosis and delirium. Madness would make these people seem even more bizarre, and in the mind of a superstitious society, perhaps confirm preconceived notions of evil. A study in 1961 of 2,500 psychiatric patients admitted consecutively to a hospital showed 35 of them to be victims of porphyria. They had originally been diagnosed with schizophrenia, depression, alcoholism, and even acute brain syndromes. Four hundred years ago they would likely have been believed to be possessed by the devil.

As a genetic disorder, porphyria would most likely appear in localized outbreaks. This would have been especially during the Middle Ages, when people traveled less and when there was a tendency toward inbreeding. Possibly, imaginative stories were spun around this frightening physical phenomenon in order to make sense of it. Without an explanation, porphyria seems confusing, and the behavior would represent chaos—a state the human mind rejects. People need order, and they need to explain things.

But there is a fascinating epilogue to our story. Ancient people created myth to make sense out of confusion. The word *myth* itself means story in Greek, and we certainly use stories, even today, to explain the unknown. Sometimes only a story, not science, will do.

Now consider this: today nuclear energy is the most advanced application of science. Nuclear energy has obvious problems (as news events have all too painfully shown). But even if nuclear energy were somehow (improbably) perfect and free of accident, there would still be a problem. disposal of radioactive waste. Nuclear waste is a deadly poison, with a staying power of thousands of years. The smallest amount of nuclear waste has the power to poison hundreds of thousands of human beings. Storing such a horrible poison is difficult enough now. But what about the people who will follow us? In the event of another dark age, successive generations might become unaware of the horrors of nuclear waste. People forget. How will future generations know to steer clear of a dump? Well, the Nuclear Energy Commission, NEC, has seriously considered the creation of a myth. A myth to cross through vast stretches of time, a myth to serve a useful scientific purpose: to warn people of a terribly dangerous place. Maybe, thousands of years later, science might reappear, and someone else might find a kernel of truth buried in those future myths.

That Was the Week That Was

FOR A PEOPLE WHO PRIZE FREEDOM from superstition, it's remarkable how often we invoke the names of ancient Roman and Norse gods. The gods who lent their names to our days of the week may no longer have organized followings as they once did, but they continue to endure as we follow them religiously through the calendar. In addition to the sun's day and the moon's day, our days are ruled by Tyr, Woden, Thor, Frigg, and Saturn. Once these god were potent symbols used to understand a troubled world. Today the days of the week may signify nothing more than a convenient way to plan for the future or trace events in the past. But by merely uttering the names of these long-forgotten gods, we perpetuate a religious incantation that once exerted a powerful grip on the human mind. And the grip remains; it's just more subtle than before.

Contributions from several different cultures were necessary before the week assumed its present familiar shape. The ancient Jews, Egyptians, Chaldeans, Romans, and finally, northern European Germanic tribes, all had a hand in fashioning the seven-day cycle by which we live. The week is a complex synthesis of strange gods and widely differing mathematical systems. Untangling the meanings woven into our week is, to say the least, an adventure. The ancient Jewish cycle of seven days that we see in the Old Testament and the seven planets of Chaldean astrology dovetailed neatly and together they firmly established the seven day plan we have today. Eventually Christianity, Islam, and Hinduism spread this calendrical pattern to just about every place on earth.

Since Judaism recognizes only one god, the ancient Jews used numbers to distinguish the days of their week. The practice of naming the days after different gods came from Chaldean astrology. In their case, the sun, moon, and planets (which they believed were gods), took turns at ruling different days. There was considerable traffic between ancient Israel and Chaldea (Abraham was born in Chaldea), so it's not surprising to find instances where the cultures either seamlessly mix or, coincidentally, arrive at the same idea, like the number seven. Seven seemed to dominate the ancient world. Several references to seven-day time periods dot the Old Testament: seven days of mourning or wearing particular clothing, seven-day ritual purifications. The Chaldeans imagined the universe to be a seven-layered affair ruled by an amalgamation of seven deities. To give you an idea of just how profoundly this magic association with the number seven affected humanity, consider this: even though very few of us today could give an accurate description of Chaldean cosmology, we continue to describe a pleasurable experience as going to "seventh heaven."

The most important idea about the seventh stage is that everything starts over again. The seventh day of the Jewish week, the *shabbath*, is derived from a verb that means to stop effort, the implication being that effort begins anew after the seventh day. Following the days of the week we progress from a beginning, through a sustained development, to a pivotal point where things once again return to a beginning. Ideally, the ancients very well may have experienced each week that way, as a progression where the world is created, dissolved, and recreated again .

The twenty-four hour day, divided into sixty minutes of sixty seconds each, is a legacy of Chaldean sexagesimal mathematics. The sexagesimal system of reckoning assumes a base of sixty, rather than the more familiar base of ten that we use today in our decimal system. One Chaldean astronomer, a man named Naburimannu, using the sexagesimal system, determined that a year was exactly three hundred and sixty-five days, six hours, fifteen minutes, and forty-one seconds long. Not bad when you consider that three thousand years and a whole scientific revolution later, Naburimannu was found to have over-estimated the length of a year by only twenty-six minutes and fifty-five seconds. Sophisticated mathematics like this, which included accurate predictions of eclipses, exerted a compelling influence for acceptance of the seven-day week, even though the number seven played more of a symbolic, not scientific, role.

By the time the week was adopted by the Romans, the astrological emphasis had practically eclipsed the sophisticated mathematics. There was a sun day, a moon day, a day for Mars (our Tuesday), a day for Mercury (our Wednesday). Thursday (later Thor's day) was originally ruled by Jupiter. The day of the goddess of love, Venus, fell on Friday, and lastly, Saturday was ruled by Saturn.

As the Roman legions spread the seven-day week across Europe, the Celtic and Romance languages simply adopted the Latin names, giving them phonetic equivalents. But the Germanic tribes actually substituted their own for the Roman deities; in other words, they translated the system as opposed to merely borrowing it. This translation from Roman gods to the old Norse gods is how English arrived as its curious names for the days of the week.

Sunday and Monday you already know about, but beginning with the name Tuesday we enter the strange world of Norse mythology. For the Romans, Tuesday was ruled by Mars, the god of war. The Germanic tribes saw a correlation between the Roman Mars and their god Tyr, and they translated him accordingly. In Old English, Tyr became Tiw, which is how we get Tuesday, or Tiw's day. Tyr was not simply a god of war, he was the spirit of treaties, good faith, and the guardian of oaths. Tyr is often depicted with only one hand because, according to an old story, he once placed his hand in the jaws of a wolf-monster named Fenrir as an act of good faith, while other gods played with Fenrir. But the other gods only pretended to play, in fact they were trying to capture Fenrir. When Fenrir realized the deception, he bit off Tyr's hand. I don't know about you, but somehow I manage to think about other things when Tuesday rolls around. That is until I looked all this up.

Even before I looked all this up, I had heard that Wednesday took its name from the Norse god Odin. Odin, or Wodan in his older form, was a tall, slim man with a long, flowing white beard. Odin rode an eight-legged horse called Sleipnir; he carried a spear and was accompanied by a raven and a wolf. Even though Odin traded one of his eyes for wisdom (he wore a wide brimmed hat to cover that deformity), he possessed the vision of poets. Odin managed this because he stole the poet's mead, a fermented honey concoction that effectively eroded normal sobriety and propelled the imbiber into the visionary world of art. Odin is also a god of war, and heroic warriors slain in the heat of battle followed him and his horse Sleipnir to the warrior heaven of Balhalla, or Valhalla. Presumably they all quaffed copious amounts of mead en route to ease the pain of their mortal wounds and to conjure the visions of inspired poets. They do this (if they ever do this) on Wednesdays.

Thursday is reserved for yet another warrior, Thor. The name Thor simply means thunder. He was envisioned by his Teutonic followers as a middle-aged man with a red beard who possessed terrific strength. Thor was locked in an eternal struggle with Jormungand, the serpent of evil who, constrictor-like, holds the world captive in his coils. The low rumble of distant thunder traced the path of Thor's mighty hammer, Mjollnir, across the stormy north sky. As a sky deity, Thor was a good substitute for the sky-god Jupiter, who ruled the Roman Thursday.

Friday is the only day of the week ruled by a female, Venus. Venus is the goddess of sexuality, fertility, and beauty. These qualities, so necessary to preserve the species, are immensely powerful, and as such have both benign and wrathful manifestations. As she moved north, Venus was gradually replaced by the Norse goddess Frigg. Frigg was also known as Friia, from which the name Friday is derived. Frigg was the wife of Odin, and, like the powers she represented, had two very different and ambiguous personalities. Frigg is sometimes portrayed as a loving mother doting on her offspring, and at other times as an unbridled, sexually licentious tart.

There was no such ambiguity when it came to Saturn's day. Saturn, the Roman god of sowing seed, was the epitome of licentiousness. Saturn managed to retain his name and identity when the week went north, perhaps because his cult was so much fun. (Saturday is still this kind of a day, except in those religious groups that observe it as the Sabbath). Saturn's festival, the Saturnalia, was clearly the Romans' favorite. The Saturnalia was held in late December, and its celebration was distinguished by turning practically everything in society upside-down. Normal customs, conventions, and even laws were suspended. All work stopped, slaves ordered their masters about, and moral restrictions that normally held sway through out the year were ignored. This had the effect of unleashing waves of intoxicated revelers, who unabashedly played out their deepest libidinal fantasies. The seemingly chaotic aspect of the Saturnalia was actually designed to produce a powerful psychological change in the participants. As the old year died and gave way to the new, the Saturnalia plunged society into chaos, out of which a new and pristine year could emerge. Not coincidentally, the Saturnalia itself lasted seven days.

Perhaps the greatest value in discovering the symbolic meaning of celestial phenomena is the hope of gaining a deeper knowledge of oneself. We find this thought echoed in the beginning lines of a poem by Wallace Stevens called "The Sun This March," which reads, "The exceeding brightness of this early sun/Makes me conceive how dark I have become, And re-illuminates things that used to turn/To gold in broadest blue, and be a part of a turning spirit in an earlier self." We know that traces of that earlier spirit remained embedded in our days of the week. What we don't know is what tomorrow will bring.

Dogs, Gods, and Health

IMAGINE A CAVE OR A SMALL WOODEN SHELTER back in the Pleistocene ice age. As the fires dim after dinner, the people inside chuck their leftovers outside onto a heap. Wild dogs emerge from the shadows of the surrounding forest to continue the feast. That scene was probably repeated so many times that eventually people noticed a practical use in having dogs hang about their perimeters. Dogs are born scavengers, and they're excellent early warning systems.

Dogs have walked by the side of human beings for more than ten thousand years. They are the oldest domesticated animal. Dogs have not only become our friends, they have become an important part of human society. They help us work; they have been part of humanity's religious life; and they are even recognized today as a health benefit.

The first person who threw a bone to a receptive dog, way back in the ice age, unwittingly set in motion a profound relationship. Part of the reason that first dog might have been receptive to human contact at all has to do with the nature of dog society. In the wild, dogs hunt in packs led by a single, dominant leader. That's where we come in. The Pleistocene man, or woman, who enticed the first wild dog into their dwelling unknowingly assumed the role of canine leader. Our relationship with dogs relies heavily on playing that role. Dogs depend on a pack leader for both their food and defense. Ice-age dogs must have thought they had a good deal. God knows we throw out enough useful and edible garbage, and human beings are notoriously better at giving orders than taking them—a happy coincidence for the dog.

Those ice-age people must have thought they had a good deal, too. Dogs proved to be of more use than merely alarms and trash scavengers. Pleistocene hunters used (in fact, cultivated) the instinctual tracking skills of dogs, and by practicing more efficient hunting, they stored up more food. Wild dogs are pretty good hunters anyway, but with the enhanced direction of human pack leaders, they became part of a unique and extraordinarily capable team. Today the modern pointers, springers, and grousers who go off to the hunt with human pack leaders reenact that unique prehistoric drama.

We continued to provide enhanced leadership for dogs, and we even taught old dogs new tricks. Today dogs find land mines during war, and guide soldiers through the night. In more peaceful uses, they guide blind people in broad daylight through their eternal night. Dogs herd livestock by responding to an impressive repertoire of commands executed by nothing more than whistles or subtle gestures of the hand given by faraway masters. Dogs even have served as draft animals. They pulled the travois litters of Native Americans, and the wheeled carts of Dutch and Turkish merchants. They still pull sleds in the Alaskan Iditerod, a race more than a thousand miles long over vast, trackless wastes of snow and run in sixty-degrees-below-zero weather.

But the most amazing use to which dogs have been put is as companion and friend. Dogs are committed to their masters for richer or for poorer, in sickness and health—and there is a persistent belief that dogs remain with their masters even after death. Because of the unusual friendship between dogs and mankind, and dogs' affinity for things abandoned by man, the dog passed from the simple status of companion and rose to a mythic magnitude. The ancient Egyptians believed that jackals (another member of the genus *canis*) prowled burial grounds for reasons other than mere scavenging. Jackals, like their dog cousins, are natural guides. In the early days of Egyptian history, Anubis, a jackal-headed deity, was the guide and lord of the dead—he led departed souls to be judged at the court of Osiris. It was the custom in those days for Egyptians to bring offerings to the dead in the predawn hours of the morning. It must have been a moving and hair-raising scene to witness, because the lament for the dead involved imitating the jackal's distinctive cry. This shrill dirge invoked Anubis and encouraged his acceptance of the gifts.

The solemnity surrounding this intense respect for the dead was transferred to the common dog. Dogs, particularly the saluki, were venerated in Egyptian households. If not exactly a deity, the saluki enjoyed an elevated social status and was known as the "royal dog." The death of a saluki compelled family members to shave their heads and bodies and then mourn its passing as if it were one of their own. These dogs were mummified, placed in expensive coffins, and returned to Anubis.

We may laugh at the elaborate dog burials in modern Los Angeles, but we shouldn't fail to appreciate the extreme antiquity of this practice. In fact, the Egyptians themselves had an entire city devoted to the cult of the dog. It was known as Cynopolis, which, loosely translated, means "dog city," and this site was loaded with dog mummies. Most Egyptian communities reserved sections of their burial grounds for dog mummies, thousands of which have been unearthed.

If Los Angeles is any measure of archetypal models for the man/dog relationship, then I wouldn't be surprised if the Egyptians had dog hairdressers and dog psychiatrists, too. Certainly five-star-style hotels catering to pampered pomeranians and mollycoddled collies are to be found in other American cities beside L.A., so it may be only a matter of time before some Egyptologist digs up a dog beauty salon or psychiatric couch.

Despite the primping and benign demeanor of dogs, we can never forget their ferocious capabilities. Dogs are equipped, even the little ones, with an impressive array of hostile dentition. And it was this aspect of the dog, its potential hostility, that was emphasized when the baton of Western civilization passed from the Egyptians to the Greeks. According to Greek mythology, when people died they passed to the underworld over the River Styx, the river of death. It was the custom in ancient Greece (as, indeed, it still is in parts of the world) to offer coins and cakes to the deceased. The coin was to pay the ferryman, and the cakes were to pacify Cerberus, the watchdog of Hades. The Greeks depicted Cerberus with anywhere from three to fifty heads. He had a dragon's tail and a strident howl like ringing bronze. This fiendish hound of hell secured the gate of the underworld, permitting no one to escape and providing an ordeal of terrifying proportions to those who were to enter.

Not many people today remember these old myths. But there's no doubt that encountering a modern Alsatian guard dog with his dander up will stimulate the same fear felt by the ancients. Indeed, training guard dogs has become a big business for that very reason. And whether dogs are used to protect an air force base, a bank, or a home, the image of a hound from hell is pretty much the image intended for any would-be thief. With the spread of Christianity throughout the Middle East, the image of the frightful guard dog and guide was softened slightly. A fascinating example of this was a dog-headed figure known as Saint Christopher. St. Christopher became the well-known patron saint of travelers, but in many early representations he was indeed dog-headed. A fifth-century statue of a dog-headed St. Christopher is recorded in a monastery on Mt. Sinai. By the sixth century, St. Christopher's tremendous popularity had spread throughout most of Europe, Russia, and the Middle East. Wall paintings of dog-headed St. Christophers (done around the sixteenth century) are still to be seen on the Mount Athos monastery frescoes in Greece.

It's no coincidence that St. Christopher would have a dog's head. When the Greek god Hermes was combined with the Egyptian god Anubis, a new deity was created, Hermanubis. He was dog-headed, wore a military uniform, and carried a palm leaf. Hermes carried souls across the river of death and also carried Christ as a child. St. Christopher crosses rivers, and his name means "bearer of Christ." The wall paintings show him dressed in military uniform and carrying a palm frond.

Despite his tremendous popularity, it has been very difficult to prove an actual historical St. Christopher. Unfortunately, due to this difficulty, the Catholic church dropped him from their calendar back in 1969. I always regretted that. When I was a kid, St. Christopher medallions used to be as common in automobiles as gear shifts. A lot of people who had them dangling from their rearview mirrors or stuck to the dashboard or pinned to the inside of luggage weren't even Christian. I'll bet very few of those people realized St. Christopher was a distant cousin of the jackal-headed Anubis. But forgetting is one of the consequences of change.

Anubis himself went through enough changes. By the later dynastic period in Egypt, his jackal head was replaced by the head of a dog, and Anubis became the physician and pharmacist of the gods, because dogs were thought to have unusual therapeutic qualities. The belief that dogs have health benefits for humans was not limited to Egypt by any means. It's a belief that has persisted right down to the present day. There are French stories of dogs curing skin ulcers by licking them. In the Indian Punjab, milk is poured onto wounds to induce dogs to lick them as a cure. The Italians believed there was a medicinal property to a dog's tongue. And in a 1921 issue of the British medical journal *Lancet* was a story about the Durham family from Scotland that had been cured of scabies, owing to the affectionate licking of their pet dog.

Do Americans today believe the dog is therapeutic? We sure do. Recently it has been shown that a dogs' companionship will cure depression, anxiety, and stress, even in severe cases. Keeping a pet dog is extremely therapeutic, and it can develop a bond of extraordinary devotion—something, I guess, like that slightly misanthropic bumper sticker—you know the one—that reads: "The more I get to know people, the more I love my dog."

Ghosts from Christmas Past

THERE IS SOMETHING COMPELLING and universal about Christmas as a festival whether you are a Christian or not. Christmas has a timeless attraction that underlies the superficial nonsense of plastic Santas, fake trees, and the commercialism that degrades our appreciation of what is really a sincere and edifying custom. The message of peace and the deeper religious meaning, all too often drowned out by the clang of cash registers and the frenzy at checkout counters, are sophisticated and enlightening messages, to be sure. But there is something else permeating this winter festivity, something more ancient than Christianity. The Christmas festival has pagan roots.

Christmas is a curious celebration. It is a happy holiday, a message of peace and good will, gifts, seeing old friends, days off from work, good food. It's the Norman Rockwell vision of bubbling equanimity. The thing that makes Christmas so curious, though, is its other side, its wrathful and ancient side. Besides little annoyances like eating too much and pitting your abdominal girth against the tensile strength of the seams of your clothes, and children tiring of new toys eleven minutes after unwrapping them, Christmas can be marred by a serious, almost ritual violence. The most obvious is the danger on highways when high blood-alcohol levels are mixed with gasoline. The other odd and violent thing about Christmastime is that it coincides with the highest rate of suicide of any period in the year. The violence seems anomalous compared to all the good cheer. It makes you wonder.

Merely walking through jungles of plastic and tinsel or bearing the burden of mandatory cheer (when we might not feel cheery) isn't enough to explain this curious, dark side of Christmas. Buried deep but shining brightly within Christmas is the behavior of the sun, rising later and setting earlier than any other time in the year. Hugging a lower horizon than usual, the sun grows wan and pale before the new year, when it will again lengthen the days. The sun dies and is reborn at this darkest time of winter. In ancient times there was unease about whether the sun would come back at all and provide those longer days and spring season. Simultaneously, the winter solstice has also been a time of ease. When harvests were in and larders full, livestock were slaughtered to adapt to the lack of grazing grass. There was a lot of meat to eat. People reaped the fruit of their yearlong labor and celebrated the return of the sun in wild revelry. We have, at least, retained the wild revelry.

Many gods who preceded the Christian interpretation of the winter festival were associated with drunken and salacious behavior. People imitated the acts of gods to draw their rejuvenating powers down to earth; the powers above became incarnate below. Saturn, the Roman agricultural god, was worshiped at this time of year in the Saturnalia, a raucous and bawdy display of unbridled consumption and indulgence. Saturn's festival was symbolized by Janus, the two-headed god of transition often found over Roman doorways.

These ideas die hard, and even during medieval times we find Geoffery Chaucer describing a fifteenth-century Christmas like this:

> *Janus sits by the fire with double beard,*
> *And drinketh of his bugle horn the wine:*
> *Before him stands the brawn of tusked swine,*
> *And "Nowel" cryeth every lusty man.*

Nowel means new birth and implies lusty behavior and regeneration. This celebration was such a permanent fixture among our ancestors that the Christian church found the solstice eminently suited to be adopted as the Nowel of Christ. The first official recognition of Christ's birth took place in Rome three hundred years after the actual event in Bethlehem. The Roman Saturnalia was reinterpreted with the softer message of a Prince of Peace.

By the year 601 we find Pope Gregory trying to make use of the winter festival as a vehicle for the Christian message. He tells Augustine of Canterbury to festoon the churches with evergreens and holly in the manner of the pagan temples and admonishes him: "Nor let them now sacrifice animals to the Devil, but to the praise of God, kill animals for their own eating, and render thanks to the Giver of all their abundance. . . . For from obdurate minds it is impossible to cut off everything at once." Pope Gregory wisely saw that it would be impossible to "cut off everything at once." By co-opting the solstice Saturnalia he eventually tamed many of its outrages. Even though the Saturnalia was in its own way a celebration of good cheer, there were outrages more disturbing than just insensible drunkenness. Saturn, in myth, ate his children as sacrificial victims.

Like little gods, children given in sacrifice mimicked the death of the sun. The Christian message succeeded in reversing the symbolism of human sacrifice. The tradition of giving dolls on Christmas may likely be a nonviolent memory of these sacrifices. As religious historian William Sanson says, "This connection with children as themselves gifts, becoming over the years the recipients of gifts, seems of likely significance."

Not all religious leaders were as perceptive as Pope Gregory in transforming objectionable practices. Some leaders have tried to "cut off everything at once." And if there was ever a Grinch who tried to steal Christmas, it must have been Oliver Cromwell. Cromwell unleashed his Puritan armies to eliminate Christmas. Puritan firepower closed churches and forced shops to stay open. It was against Puritan law to perform traditional pageants, and if discovered (because Christmas continued to be observed in secret), massive bloodletting ensued. In 1647 an observer at an Oxford Christmas celebration noted, ". . . there was a world of skull-breaking; and at Ipswich the festival was celebrated by some loss of life." The clash between the faithful and Cromwell's Puritans saw the Mayor of Canterbury beaten, during an anti-Christmas riot, as "senseless as a pocket of hops."

The Puritan "Grinch" wrought havoc on this ancient festival for eighteen years, and many Christmas traditions atrophied as a result, never to be resurrected. The vitality of Christmas did not atrophy, though, and official observances returned with Charles II. Christmas was changed and sapped of some of its former glory, perhaps, but at least it emerged triumphant as an irrepressible necessity.

After Cromwell, Christmas in England hobbled through the next two centuries like Tiny Tim. But during the 1800s the spirit of Christmas was rekindled in a huge rediscovery of its significance. And Tiny Tim had a lot to do with it. For it was then that Charles Dickens's *A Christmas Carol* gave the world a picture of the inner workings of the Christmas spirit. Compassion, generosity, and the feeling of well-being may have been maimed by Puritan swords, but those qualities were restored with the might of the pen. Dickens's tale is read, performed, and enjoyed today with a solemnity much like that of the ancient Christmas pageants before Puritan repression. And its characters Tiny Tim and Ebeneezer Scrooge have been elevated to archetypes rivaling those of the most venerated myths.

Perhaps even more mythic than *A Christmas Carol* is a short poem of only fifty-eight lines written by an American, Dr. Clement Clarke Moore, in 1822. "A Visit from St. Nicholas" (sometimes called "The Night Before Christmas") immediately gripped the imagination of this country and has propelled an image of the most powerful and generous gift giver of all, Santa Claus.

There really was a St. Nicholas but he is not quite our Santa Claus. In the fourth century, in a small port city in southern Turkey, there lived a bishop noted for his generosity. This original St. Nicholas, so the story goes, once gave three bags of gold to a poor man who had been forced to sell his three daughters to a brothel. This story was very popular in Lombardy, where certain Lombards operated loan houses. The Church of St. Nicholas, on Lombard street in modern London, still displays three gold balls at the top of its spire. Pawn shops the world over display those same three balls as a symbol of the Lombardian profession of lending.

St. Nicholas is also credited with bringing to life three slain boys who had been dismembered and pickled in vinegar. He is clearly connected with children and gifts, but Moore's St. Nicholas, and the Santa Claus he has become, is much more than this fourth-century Turkish bishop. Santa Claus is a memory, a resurgence, of the solstice god of northern Europe who presided over the ancient winter festival.

Moore saw Santa as an elf. Elves were the tree spirits of the Druids—spirits who sanctified evergreen, holly, and especially the mistletoe, making them sacred plants. For Druids, mistletoe was the most sacred of plants, and even today we still set mistletoe off by itself. Modern households might be trimmed with abundant evergreen boughs and holly, but there is usually only one sprig of mistletoe. The round wreath, a symbol of the sun, is pegged to the door. The wreath is the same device that adorns the head of many a Father Christmas like a Druid halo. Santa may seem strange because he uses chimneys instead of doors, but he is not alone in this. The ancient hearth gods did that, and the tree spirit that lived in the Yule log did it, too.

You might say that one of the miracles of Christianity is how well it uses, absorbs, and transforms these ancient practices. Santa may have a pagan heritage far older than Christianity, but who can say he is not an essential part—through his spirit of love and giving—of the true Christmas experience?

What is not sacred is the recurrence of those violent effects. There is no doubt that the world is better off with a message of peace and compassion that eliminates human sacrifice. But the barbarity of Saturnalian (or Druid) sacrifice seems repeated today through the dangers we face from drunk drivers or suicidal depression. Both are torments from the spirits of "Christmas" past—and both can be turned around and stopped.

If you partake of the ancient sacred libations of wassail or punch, eggnog or mulled wines, let someone else drive your sleigh during the holidays. And if you find Christmas dark, plastic, or commercial, don't despair. The days will lengthen, and your good cheer will return. The ghosts of Christmas's most ancient past need not haunt us any more.

A Pocket Full of Coins

IF YOU ARE MALE, YOU MAY REMEMBER the intense pleasure of having a pocket full of coins. Seems like anyone who wears pants has had that pleasure—fingering and turning a stash of substantial metal. Hearing coins clink and jingle inside a cozy sock of pocket cotton; there is a real sense of wealth in that. Even today, with coins not worth as much as they used to be, they seem more like money than paper does.

I remember having, as a boy, a pocket full of silver dollars once—probably only four or five, but it was a treasure. Large flat cakes of weighty silver. History was written all over them. They bore dates like 1865 and scratch marks that told stories of many hands trading for things now long forgotten or useless.

The word itself, *dollar*, seemed weighty. Originally dollar came from *taler*, which means dale in German, referring to the dale of Saint Joachim in Bohemia, where large silver deposits were mined during the sixteenth century. The first of these coins (struck back in 1519) were called Joachimstaler, which mercifully was shortened to *taler* and then to *dollar.* Shortly after the taler made its appearance, a special issue of the coin was struck in Mexico. This coin was known as the Emperor Charles the Fifth, and on its reverse side had a picture of the pillars of Hercules wound with a ribbon and printed with the words "plus ultra," which means something like "even farther" or "beyond the beyond." This design, one theory has it, gave birth to the dollar sign, the familiar S with two bars through it. Another account says that the capital letters US, superimposed, came to form the dollar sign, omitting the bottom curve of the U.

Over the last five hundred years, the dollar has become almighty in the United States, Hong Kong, Canada, Australia, Liberia, and Ethiopia. As legions of faces passed across its obverse side, the dollar framed the great and the mighty in an engraver's gallery of recorded history. The last face a dollar framed here in America was that of Susan B. Anthony.

A giant in American history, Anthony paved the way for the Nineteenth Amendment to the U.S. Constitution, which allowed women to vote. She spearheaded the American Revolution for Women. She organized demonstrations, was civilly disobedient, and not only went to jail but even refused to pay her fines. Anthony won a place in our hearts, but her dollar lost its place in our pockets. It was never accepted by the public. It was small for a dollar, and was too easily mistaken for a fifty-cent piece. Eisenhower got one of those big flat cakes of real silver, but poor Susan B. got stuck somewhere in the size range of Kennedy's half-dollar, and that proved fatal for it. The reason for the small size was compelling enough: big flat cakes of silver are expensive. It takes the mint 8.3 cents to make an Eisenhower dollar, but an Anthony dollar only costs 3.3 cents. Multiplied by millions, that's a pretty big savings.

Ironically, the Eisenhower dollar never really caught on either. It was too big (I guess you really have to be a twelve-year-old to appreciate the feeling of a pocket full of silver dollars). Unfortunately for the mint, the public hoarded both Anthony and Eisenhower dollars and put their faith in George Washington, whose face is printed, curiously enough, on a material that is expensive to make and worth almost nothing— paper. Paper bills are worth something only because we all agree they're worth something. Physically, they are simply disposable. The average paper note lasts eighteen months. You can see why the mint keeps dreaming up ideas for silver dollars—coin lasts about fifteen years before it wears out and has to be replaced.

Paper is easy to give away; it's not a hunk of silver. A hundred-dollar bill may seem more exciting than a single silver dollar when you think of what it can buy, but you have to think what it will buy—you don't feel it, like a coin. Paper money used to pay silver "to the bearer on demand." Now all we have to do is think it into existence. Imagine, somewhere in the government someone merely has to mutter the appropriate mantra over some paper, and people will kill for that paper. An extraordinary phenomenon.

In the broader sense, the modern idea of wealth has become so abstract that a bank account now isn't money at all. At least the paper stuff is printed with mystic designs and arcane Latin incantations, making paper bills a lot easier to believe in. But bank accounts aren't even paper, they're memories in a computer—binary electronic impulses nestled in tiny chips of silicon or magnetic media, a completely artificial structure of thought, mixed with lightning.

In some nostalgic way, I suppose, I mourn the loss of the chunky clinks of dollars (not to mention ducats and doubloons) ringing on counting-room floors. Those ponderous sounds have faded and have been unsatisfactorily replaced with the click of plastic computer keys.

When you stop to think that coins have been with us since the days of the ancient Greek city of Lydia (about seven hundred years before Christ), you have to admit, that's a lot of ringing. It dawned on some bright soul back then that it would be more exact to trade goods against a standardized coin than to swap unwieldy piles of unorganized freight. It was a brilliant idea. If two people had goods of unequal value, they couldn't swap them evenly, but they could use coin to make up the difference.

People had, of course, traded goods against a standard measure (usually against the weight of gold or silver) long before they actually began striking coins. In biblical times, personal ornaments changed hands as a currency by weight: when Abraham's eldest servant presents to Rebekah a "golden earring of half a shekel weight, and two bracelets for her hands of ten shekels weight of gold," he is actually bestowing a kind of cash gift. Before the Lydians showed everyone how useful coinage was, the shekel was merely a Babylonian weight. Only later did it become a coin.

Equating goods to an abstract standard had been used for millennia, not only with gold ornaments but with cattle, salt, opium pills, knives—even twelve-foot limestone disks have been used abstractly as money, really as money and not just as something for barter. But with the advent of coin, abstraction achieved a remarkable polish, and true commerce was born.

The coin endures to make up differences in complicated tax schemes at the retail counter and to surrender to coin-operated robots that lie in ambush at highway rest stops or lurk in office hallways. But not even the vending robots are considering electronic credit as currency of the future. I have that, incidentally, on good faith from an actual robot who has taken over a retail counter near my office.

Many grocery stores and gas stations already sport a computer terminal designed for an automated teller card or a regular credit card. You pay the cashier by putting your plastic bank card in the machine and punching up your secret identification number. Lightning flashes between terminals, and suddenly your bank computer is poorer by eight dollars and fifty-three cents, or whatever the amount, and the cashier is richer. When the machine tells the cashier that, yes, indeed, you are worth the eight fifty-three, you leave with the goods and never once have to soil your hands with filthy lucre. No coins to fondle, no ringing of metal, no flat cakes of burnished silver, no paper, no need even to crumble and count—just a light or two and a small pip-squeak from the computer's speaker.

Up to now, those little plastic cards have had a relatively modest impact on us. But believe me, they have ambitions to invade a lot more areas of our lives. You can't put much information on a simple magnetic strip like those that exist now, but these cards are scheduled to receive sophisticated electronic brains.

We will see, very soon, an entire central processing unit (the computer's CPU) in between the plastic laminates of a credit card. That means the card itself will be an honest-to-god computer. Once all the banks, machines, phones, services, and stores convert, a lot fewer coins are going to be needed, maybe none at all. Pockets will become roomier, and hands will be left free to play with lint and the occasional stray thread.

A "smart card" won't be just a fancy credit card, it has the potential to be a whole lot more. It could hold not only your bank balance, but your entire credit history. Every bad check, every late credit card payment, complete IRS tax history—everything. Even (perhaps especially) all the mistaken reports about you, too.

To prevent anyone else from diving into your savings and taking a trip to Las Vegas, there can be some real showstoppers to ensure absolute identification: voice print, your fingerprints (of course), and even a digitized image of your face. These would surely thwart would-be counterfeiters, (except, perhaps, those mysterious battalions of computer hackers who can slip into the most sacred and protected memory banks). The bureaucratic ethos (being intrinsically committed to generating records), reels in religious swoon at the very thought of such a card. Combine that swoon with the very real momentum of a technological imperative, and we have an incredible identification system—all from the idea of money.

Your police record, your record at work, even your school records will all fit, eventually, onto these "smart cards." So will your political affiliations, travel movements, phone records, medical history—it will all fit. Technically these cards could be used for everything. Realistically we may want to think about that very carefully, about our right to privacy.

Somehow, the inscription "plus ultra" on the 1519 Charles the Fifth taler has become downright prophetic. Computer technology has suddenly opened the door for the idea of mutual credit to go "beyond the beyond." The newest American dollars have already gone beyond the beyond. The new $50 gold piece, the Eagle, is a full one-ounce slab of indestructible mineral wealth. Of course it's worth way beyond the $50 stamped on it. It will cost you more like $440 if you pay with silver (or with paper or electrons). But in an age when substance is in danger of being gobbled up by the pure mathematics of an unfeeling machine, it's still possible—obscenely expensive perhaps, but possible—to dig your finger into a hoard of gold coins clanking in a warm cotton pocket. Yes, I think I'd like that.

The Durability of Stones

THERE'S A STORY, POSSIBLY TRUE, about a gem merchant selling a diamond. His customer thought the diamond mediocre, certainly nothing spectacular and obviously very small. The customer was therefore surprised when the merchant quoted a price five times what the gem seemed worth. "My good man," said the customer, "this diamond isn't worth a fifth of your price." The merchant quickly replied, "Oh, I'm afraid you don't understand. This is an antique diamond." The merchant was right, of course, all diamonds are antiques—a couple of hundred million years old is definitely antique, to say the least.

I've heard this story a lot. Someone once told me he had a friend who went through customs here in the U.S., and the customs agent discovered two diamonds. The man claimed they were antiques and therefore exempt from duty. But the customs agent pointed out the undisputed antiquity of all gemstones—and then charged him the duty. The duty of course was on the setting.

I asked a U.S. Customs agent about this and was told there isn't any duty on loose gems. "Yeah, it's pretty funny, actually. We have people trying to smuggle jewels to avoid duty all the time. But there is no duty on them—all they have to do is declare them."

I think there's a reason people try to smuggle jewels. People think jewels are more valuable than mere money, so valuable it's hard to believe customs wouldn't want a huge cut. The real value, though, is measured in charisma. For thousands of years humanity thought of stones as being alive. If not consciously aware of this, we have subconsciously inherited the attitude. In a poem written in 1574, a Frenchman named Jean de la Taille de Bondaroy attributes all manner of life to gemstones. Gems can get sick, they can get old, and they can die. De Bondaroy goes so far as to say, "They even take offense if an injury be done to them, and become rough and pale."

A little later, in 1609, the court physician of Rudolph II of Germany,

Anselmus De Boot, wrote that the life witnessed in stones is due to supernatural inhabitation, both divine and infernal. De Boot warned of the danger of idolizing stones but seemed convinced that stones exert great powers. He writes, "That gems or stones, when applied to the body, exert an action upon it, is so well proven by the experience of many persons, that anyone who doubts this must be called over-bold." These medieval and early Renaissance writers were themselves inheritors of these beliefs. Attributing talismanic or magic properties to stones appears to be very old, as discoveries of gems in prehistoric graves seem to attest. By the time of the ancient Egyptians, the use of stones in medicine and as portents and protectors was well established.

Stones were thought to be like people to such an extent that they possessed individual virtues or vices, exhibited characteristic abilities to protect or harm, and were even associated with specific seasons and times of the day. This recognition is probably why people started wearing stone jewelry in the first place. Stones were originally charms and only later became decorations.

In the twenty-eighth chapter of "Exodus," in the Bible, there is an elaborate description of how to make the "breastplate of judgment." This was an actual garment worn by the high priests of the Israelites, and it was studded with twelve precious stones. In the first century A.D., Jewish historian Flavius Josephus describes this breastplate as if it were an oracle. The reflected light from these twelve stones was capable of "announcing" future events, such as victory or defeat in battle. The "breastplate of judgment" apparently acted as a direct communiqué from the Almighty. Unfortunately, Josephus tells us, this rather handy source of intelligence had been lost a full two hundred years prior to his writing (Josephus died in A.D. 95). God disconnected this direct line to earth due to his displeasure with mankind's excessive disobedience. This account tends to confirm the theory that all ages of history are thought of, in their time, as corrupt, and that later, in hindsight, the times are remembered as virtuous. Hopefully that will happen to us and our times.

Three hundred years after Josephus, Saint Epiphanius, the Bishop of Constantia, writes again of a stone possessing oracular powers that adorned the neck of the Jewish high priest—a single stone this time. It was probably a diamond, since St. Epiphanius calls it *adama*, Latin for diamond. The priest made three public appearances a year wearing the stone—each appearance at the beginning of certain festival days. If the population had been sinful, the stone took on a dark and clouded color, an unfortunate portent of death by disease. Or worse, it could turn bloodred, which signaled a more violent death by sword. But if the light from the stone looked like that of fine and freshly driven snow, then it was understood that the people had been virtuous, and the congregation immediately plunged headlong into the festivities.

There is an obvious connection here between divination with the stones on the breastplate of the Jewish high priest and gazing into crystal balls or mirrors. Fixing one's vision on a single point of light tends to visually dissolve the object seen and emphasizes instead the activities of the mind. This almost-hypnotic condition is related to dreaming. And as we know from psychology, dreams are direct taps into the subconscious. Dreams allow an unclouded examination of how we honestly feel. It was, theoretically at least, due to this process that crystal or mirror gazing was so immensely popular in the past and enjoyed such a widespread geographical distribution.

Hollywood generally has misunderstood this process and routinely depicts it as images appearing inside the crystal. But the technique has been used with polished metal, drops of mercury, even pools of ink—a point of concentration is all that is needed. A fourteenth-century Persian, Ibn Kaldoun, has left us an interesting, and rather specific, portrayal of this peculiar phenomenon. He says:

Some believe that the image perceived in this way takes form on the surface of the mirror, but they are mistaken. The diviner looks at this surface fixedly until it disappears, and a curtain, like a mist, is interposed between him and the mirror. Upon this curtain are designed the forms he wishes to see, and this permits him to give indications, either affirmative or negative, concerning the matter on which he is questioned. He then describes his perceptions as he has received them. The diviners, while in this state, do not see what is really to be seen (in the mirror). It is another kind of perception, which is born in them and which is realized not by sight but by the soul.

There is a faint echo of this in engagement or wedding rings that have stones. These stones not only symbolically represent the love between two people, but they also have the power to reflect deeper feelings that can't be spoken or merely represented with sign or symbol. Ralph Waldo Emerson's poem, "The Amulet," suggests this:

> *Give me an amulet*
> *That keeps intelligence with you*
> *Red when you love, and rosier red,*
> *And when you love not, pale and blue.*

Perhaps Emerson had the ruby in mind—or more specifically, corundum, the mineral that when red, is called ruby, and when blue, is called sapphire. However, even alchemists could not change a ruby into a sapphire. Corundum is second in hardness only to the diamond and is one of the most prized gemstones, sometimes even placed above the diamond in value.

In a book called *Lapidaire*, written during the fourteenth-century reign of the French king Phillipe de Valois, the ruby is described as, "the lord of stones; it is the gem of gems." At various times in Indian history the ruby was known as the Ratnaraj, or "the king of stones." Both in Europe and in Asia the ruby assumed the one preeminent quality of the king: it could protect its wearer from harm. Of the four grades of rubies described in Indian literature, the the most highly valued Brahmin ruby was thought to protect its owner from physical harm. In Europe, Sir John Mandeville, author and traveler during the 1300s, said very much the same thing. He said the ruby guarantees peace and protects the owner from material disaster. In Burma, the home of the very best rubies in the world, the ruby was thought to make its owner invincible.

Attributing protective, almost martial qualities to the ruby was probably due to its red color. The ruby embodied the properties of both blood and fire. Held in the hand or strung around the neck, it gave the beholder a kind of sympathetic power over blood and fire. It's one of those strange coincidences of life that the first successful laser used a ruby to create a powerful laser beam. The laser has military applications as a martial fire and medically has uses ranging from the photocoagulation of blood to surgery on the eye.

There is a lesson to be learned in the study of the history of stones. Stones themselves are not the real source of power, the mind is. Stones may be catalysts of communication, permitting a better understanding of ourselves and others, but the activity is psychological. Slowly, tragically, we have lost a good deal of this understanding. But the antiquity of the collective mind may be as old as that of stones. One day we may remember this lost understanding. As the brilliant medieval thinker Meister Eckhart reminds us: "The stone is God, but it does not know it, and it is the not knowing that makes it a stone."

The Post, Its Past and Future

HUMAN BEINGS ACHIEVE A DEPTH and subtlety of communication that is unparalleled by any other species. How many other animals have postal systems? None. We grumble about late deliveries and high rates. We grumble about lost letters and stolen packages. We throw away pounds of unwanted junk mail and anguish over the size of the forest that died to supply it. But few of us appreciate the antiquity and the beauty of the post. Even fewer appreciate that the mail system is undergoing a profound change and that it will soon be transformed into a radically new and severe form. Let's start with the past of the post.

The earliest forms of mail service, about 2000 B.C., were organizations of relay runners who transmitted government communiqués in ancient Egypt. Governments require communications to tie together far-flung localities into a single, cohesive empire. A thousand years after the Egyptian runners, officials of the Chou (pronounced "joe") dynasty in ancient China invented stations for their runners. The Chinese relay stations were the first true "post" houses. Confucius alludes to an efficient post when he tells us that "the influence of the righteous travels faster than a royal edict by post-station service."

The Roman mail system, the *cursus publicus*, could forward military messages one hundred and seventy miles in less than a day and a night. Europe had to wait until the nineteenth century for a postal system as efficient as the old Roman *cursus publicus*.

Postal relay systems were used everywhere. The Persian emperor Cyrus operated one in the sixth century B.C. The Mayans had a messenger system that lasted more than a thousand years. And the Incas surely maintained runners and post houses along the extensive roadways they built in the Andes mountains. These message systems conveyed military or government communications almost exclusively. But just before the Renaissance in Europe, when the mercantile class became powerful, business communications became important, and business had the means to operate good postal systems of their own.

During the 1400s and 1500s, large, efficient mail services were operated by private families like the Paar family in Austria. In northern Italy a family named Taxis developed a gigantic postal network that, at its height, employed twenty thousand mail carriers and spanned the entire length and breadth of Europe. Remnants of the Taxis postal system lasted in Germany through 1867.

In 1639, the Massachusetts Bay Colony General Court decreed that all mail coming in from and bound out for England was to be left at Richard Fairbank's tavern in Boston. It's hard to imagine that "Richard Fairbank's tavern, Boston" was once the only address for what was to become the entire United States of America, but it was. Eventually, post roads were established between major communities in the American colonies, and half a century after Richard Fairbank's tavern address became a post office, an official postal service was created that linked together all of the colonies.

In 1753, the king of England appointed Benjamin Franklin and William Hunter joint postmasters general for the North American colonies. Franklin held this office for twenty-one years, until 1774, when he was ousted by crown authorities as a dangerous liberal and revolutionary. Luckily, Franklin's side won the Revolutionary War, and he was reappointed postmaster general of a new postal system in 1775, this time by the Second Continental Congress. In 1789, Samuel Osgood became the first postmaster general of the United States of America.

Sending letters in those days was awkward, expensive, and not very fast. For example, postage was based on the number of sheets of paper being sent and not on weight. In 1835, the rate was a whopping twenty-five cents a page: fifty cents for two pages, seventy-five cents for three, and so forth. This exorbitant rate was in an age when an ordinary person might earn less than a dollar a day. The mail was reserved for important communications, mostly by businesses. Another odd thing about the mail back then was that the recipient, not the sender, paid the postage—and the recipient paid only if the letter was actually taken away from the post office. People quickly learned how to avoid paying postage. Since nobody was required to pick up a letter, recipients would merely look at the letter and notice prearranged codes on the envelopes. The sender would put a secret mark on the outside cover—a dot or a dash or a squiggle, even misspelled words were used as codes. One mark might mean "yes," and another "no." Yet another mark might mean "this letter is important, pay for it and read it." The post office got stuck with tons of mail it had been forced to transport and for which it received not one cent in compensation.

Then in 1837, in England, a man whose name is known to every philatelist in the world, Rowland Hill, published *Post Office Reform: Its Importance and Practicability*. Hill scrutinized the economics of the mail system and discovered that distance really didn't matter as much to a post office as the volume of mail it transported. Postal employees wasted valuable time gauging distances between cities and applying a complicated rate schedule and then justifying these decisions with useless paperwork. Flat rates were simpler and more cost effective.

Hill's statistical analysis revealed that the actual cost of transporting a letter from London to Edinburgh was not the one shilling and one pence then being charged, but a mere one-thirty-sixth of a pence. He based postal rates not on the number of pages being sent but on a flat rate linked to weight. As postal rates went down, volume went up and so did the profits to the government. Hill also stumbled upon an elegant solution to all the deadbeats who refused to pay for their mail on delivery: he suggested that post offices sell prepaid stationary in varying amounts of postage. That way every body would pay up front. Almost as an afterthought, Hill suggested that post offices might also accommodate people who wished to use their own stationary by supplying them with "a bit of paper just large enough to bear the stamp and covered at the back with a glutinous wash, which the bringer might, by applying a little moisture, attach to the back of the letter." Hill had invented the postage stamp as we know it.

Prepaid covers and optional stamps (penny blacks) were launched in 1840. This dramatic reform of postal services in Britain did not go unnoticed in the United States. In 1842, the first American postal adhesive was issued by a private company. Later the government got into the act, and the postal system began a rapid explosion that continues today.

The Pony Express gave way to the stagecoach. The stagecoach gave way to the railroad. Then steamships and air mail followed the rails. Each new method of transport added new dimensions to the post. Faster service made the world seem smaller. Mail order was born. Increased communication allowed business and government and family to prosper and to deepen their understanding of distant events. Then came along a strange type of telephone that sent and received facsimiles of mail—fax machines.

The impact of fax machines on the post is profound. In the past, we could hardly think of sending or receiving letters during times of great social unrest, like war, but as long as telephone lines are intact, fax machines can disgorge miles of printed or handwritten messages. Fax machines worked overtime during the 1989 Tiananmen Square crisis in China, and they continue to send messages in the midst of wars and civil strife all over the world.

But the days of the fax machine are numbered. Computers are about to consume us all. The modem, a word which abbreviates *modulate* and *demodulate*, is about to project us in into the realm of outrageous imagination. The near future promises that gigantic computing power will be available to the most humble consumer. Instant real-time audio and video missives of stunning clarity will be personally produced by neighbors and relatives and faraway friends. Previously formal business meetings will take place in the palm of a dozen hands, and the hands might be at home or at the beach.

A Christmas card, a valentine, or a simple note of thanks might, in the not-too-distant future, resemble the most complex animations of a modern Hollywood production house. Business communications surely will be that elaborate. An expanded satellite system promises to link together every spot on earth—the Gobi, the Sahara, the Pacific, and Main Street. All this is a far cry from the humble postal reforms of Rowland Hill. We are forced to wonder if this new threshold in communications might lose something in translation.

We certainly lose a certain ambiance with this new technology. We do not speak with a fax machine or a modem the way we once did with a fleet-footed messenger. And instant communications destroy the notion of a considered response. We now blurt answers the way knees jerk when struck with rubber mallets. But worse is that so much of the new technology is simply cold, empty, and lifeless. Voice mail bears none of the texture of the fine, handcrafted papers that bore penny black stamps and were franked in crude ink. Special embellishments of old-time mail, like the exuberant flourishes of the pen at the bottom of people's signatures—those special things that molded communication to the uniqueness of the sender's character—seem violated in the extreme with today's frosty, gear-ridden machinery.

The human traditions of writing and the postal service seem demeaned every time we hear that terrifying, ubiquitous, disembodied drone of the voice-mail person. Just once I'd like to hear that cold voice say something different, something like, "If you are calling for a salesperson, please press 'one' on your Touch-Tone phone. If you are calling for a technical person please press 'two.' But if you miss the faint watermarks of fine crisp papers and the beautiful writing of dear friends engaged in intimate exchange, then stay on the line and an actual human being who shares your views will commiserate with you in person."

We, the Iroquois . . .

ONCE, ON A TRIP TO THE SOVIET UNION, President Ronald Reagan told students at Moscow State University that preserving Native American culture might have been a mistake. His exact words were: "Maybe we made a mistake. Maybe we should not have humored them in that, wanting to stay in that kind of primitive life style. Maybe we should have said, 'No, come join us. Be citizens along with the rest of us.' "

Many Americans agree with President Reagan's interpretation. Our histories, movies, and literature remember Native Americans as primitive warlike savages tormenting white Europeans who were busy forging the miracle of the American government. Some historical research looks at it differently. Much of what we regard as unique to American government came not from Europeans but more likely from the Native Americans—specifically the Iroquois.

Perhaps as early as A.D. 1000, and certainly no later than the mid-fifteenth century, five warring Indian nations were unified under an extraordinary constitution called the Great Law of Peace. In the early part of the 1700s, these five nations—Seneca, Onondaga, Mohawk, Oneida, and Cayuga, collectively known as the Iroquois—were joined by a sixth, the Tuscarora. After that they were known as the Six Nations. The principles in the ancient Great Law of Peace are familiar to any modern American.

In his book *Forgotten Founders*, historian Bruce Johansen writes, "The Great Law of Peace rested on assumptions foreign to the monarchies of Europe: it regarded leaders as servants of the people, rather than their masters, and made provisions for the leaders' impeachment for errant behavior. The Iroquois' law and custom upheld freedom of expression in political and religious matters, and it forbade the unauthorized entry of homes. It provided for political participation by women, and the relatively equitable distribution of wealth."

Even more extraordinary was the design of Iroquois government. At the center of the union was the Firekeeper, an executive position comparable to our presidency. The Firekeeper shared his power with a two-part legislature divided into Elder Brothers and Younger Brothers. Mohawks and Senecas served as Elder Brothers (an organization that parallels our Senate), and Oneidas and Cayugas sat as Younger Brothers (corresponding with the House of Representatives).

The similarities are even more striking when we look at the third branch of Iroquois government. They had a judiciary designed to check and balance the other two branches. Europeans were understandably awed when they discovered political unification accomplished by the unlikely expedient of separate powers. The Iroquois' ingenious system not only worked, it had been working for hundreds of years.

In a book called *History of the Five Nations Depending on the Provence of New York in America*, the author (with the delightful name of Cadwallader Colden) compared Iroquois patriotism to that of ancient Rome. In fact, Colden said, "When Life and Liberty came in competition, indeed, I think our Indians have outdone the Romans in this particular."

Comparing the Iroquois to the Romans proved such an irresistible image that early engravings of Iroquois politicians depicted them wearing short, curly hair and togas. This comparison was important. It allowed Europeans immediately to grasp the significance of Iroquois polity, and it undoubtedly paved the way for the surprisingly wide distribution of their ideas.

Historian Felix Cohen finds evidence of Iroquois political ideas in Thomas More's *Utopia*, and in the thought of Montesquieu, Voltaire, and Rousseau. Cohen believes that "to John Locke . . . the state of . . . natural equality to which men . . . appeal in rebellion against tyranny, was set not in the remote dawn of history, but beyond the Atlantic sunset."

The influence of Iroquois thought was not only widespread, it persisted right into this century. In *The Origin of the Family, Private Property and the State*, Frederich Engels positively dotes on the fact that the Iroquois achieved an efficient union without a repressive government. Engels even went so far as to say that Iroquois society "knows no state." This thought, like a lot of things Engels suggested, went a bit far. The Iroquois did indeed have a state. At the time it was the largest, oldest, democratic government in the world, though it might not have appeared as a state to Europeans because the Iroquois had fundamentally different ideas about land ownership. But a state? Well, at one point, the colonists were told flat out by one Iroquois chief that they had better get their act together and unify like the Iroquois if they wished to survive.

In 1744, Chief Canassatego told a group of colonial officers, "Our wise forefathers established union and amity between the Five Nations. This has made us formidable. This has given us great weight and authority with our neighboring Nations. We are a powerful Confederacy and by your observing the same methods our wise forefathers have taken, you will acquire much strength and power; therefore, whatever befalls you, do no fall out with one another."

It would be a while before colonists began chanting "United we stand, divided we fall," but it's interesting to note that Chief Canassatego's advice was delivered on July 4—a full thirty-two years to the day before the official birth of the United States. Organizing the thirteen colonies into a federal union took a little time from 1744, but Canassatego's words were hardly lost on the people who heard them.

We tend to forget that, for most of the time, Native Americans and whites lived together peacefully. Even during war some whites and Native Americans were allies, and they worked and lived alongside one another. Because of this incessant exposure, colonists slowly and imperceptibly adopted Native American ways.

We are reminded by Johansen that Native American foodstuff (beginning with the famous Thanksgiving meal of turkey) eventually overwhelmed the world market. By the beginning of this century, over half the world's crops could be traced to Native American agriculture. Corn, squash, peppers, peanuts, pumpkins, pineapples, potatoes (both white and sweet), tomatoes, cacao to make chocolate, chicle to make chewing gum, cotton, rubber, quinine, many types of beans, and about seventy other useful plants all number among products brought to us by Native Americans. We also have canoes, parkas, moccasins, dog sleds, hammocks, and pipes because they invented them. One scholar described the colonists as being "Americanized" by the natives.

In addition to the impressive list of inventions and foods was something far more important, the spirit of a democratic government. A late eighteenth-century English account of American colonists reveals how even liberty itself was regarded as a Native American idea: "The darling passion of the American is liberty, and that is its fullest intent; nor is it the original natives only to whom this passion is confined; our colonist sent thither seem to have imbibed the same principles," wrote this gentleman. It would appear (at least in mind of this author) that political liberty originated with the Iroquois Confederacy. Where else would an obedient Englishman get such an idea, anyway? While Britain's other colonies remained very much in the fold of commonwealth, the American colonies pursued a dramatically radical course—and it led to war.

The Revolutionary War was triggered when people finally realized that the interests of the American colonies and the British crown were hopelessly divided. The need to unify became even more urgent because the colonies were also growing apart from each other. It was at this crucial time that the principles of the Iroquois Confederacy may have come to the rescue. In 1751, Benjamin Franklin wrote to James Parker: "It would be a very strange thing if Six Nations of Ignorant Savages should be capable of forming a Scheme for such a Union, and be able to execute it in such a manner, as that it has subsisted Ages, and appears indissoluble, and yet a like Union should be impractible [sic] for ten or a dozen English colonies."

I don't believe Franklin thought the Iroquois were "ignorant savages." This phrase seems like it was calculated to jar the conservatives of that time out of their stagnation and prod them through the purifying flames of a liberal revolution. After all, Franklin's own militia, created to defend Philadelphia, followed the Iroquois belief that leaders should be servants. In Franklin's army the officers were elected by the men. Franklin obviously believed this was a superior system and certainly not the product of ignorant savages.

Tempting as it may be to turn the epithet "ignorant savages" around and level it at the whites (Franklin himself came dangerously close to that), it would be unjustified. The American experiment was achieved by a complex synthesis of both Iroquois and European contributions. But there was one Iroquois contribution that was so advanced it may have shocked and alarmed the founding fathers. It has certainly remained beyond the grasp of Europeans until only very recently. The Iroquois judiciary was made up entirely of women.

Clan mothers and women's councils reviewed the behavior of men they nominated to office. If any of those men erred and failed to heed three successive warnings, the women members of the judiciary swiftly and surely impeached them. Iroquois womanhood enjoyed freedoms hundreds of years ago that have still not been given to modern American women. During the era of Franklin, Jefferson, and Washington (which had only recently emerged from the age of witch-hunts), the very idea that women might direct the power of a supreme court was unthinkable—as indeed it remained in this country until only a very short time ago.

Historian Gregory Schaaf says that the prominent role of Iroquois women " . . . may explain why the founding fathers chose to keep secret the original design [of the American government]. If the founding fathers . . . disclosed the political powers of . . . Indian women, perhaps women like Abigail Adams would have assumed positions as founding mothers."

Sometimes, when it's very quiet, you can almost hear the lament of those Iroquois founding mothers and fathers who seem to say of modern America, "Maybe we made a mistake. Maybe we should not have humored them in that, wanting to stay in that kind of primitive life style. Maybe we should have said, 'No, come join us. Be citizens along with the rest of us.' "

All Quiet on the "Y" Front

THE TROUBLE WITH AMERICAN BUSINESS is that no one pays enough attention to their underwear. Underwear is the foundation of any decent sartorial suite, and the businessmen and women who ignore their underwear risk not only a sloppy appearance but failure in the marketplace. Sounds crazy, doesn't it? How could underwear contain the secrets of business acumen? Well, if you don't know the answer to that question, you might want to take a relaxing shower, slip into a pair of freshly washed briefs, and squiggle your way into your twenty-dollar designer t-shirt, because it's time you knew the history of American underwear. This history concerns men's underwear and a great American hero named Arthur Kneibler.

Before 1900, men wore union suits. Remember union suits? They were the original long johns with button flaps and button fronts. They stretched from neck to wrist to ankle and formed a second hide. We've gotten so used to indoor heating and plumbing that we forget that previous generations really needed union suits and rarely got out of them. Most men lived in them.

But after 1900, American homes began to include, slowly at first, indoor heating and plumbing. Heated homes and running water sounded the death knell of the union suit. As soon as people had the opportunity to wash more often, getting in and out of a union suit seemed like a cumbersome ordeal. Of course, nobody had noticed this difficulty when they only took it off once a week for the Saturday night bath, but when they had to get out of a union suit every day, it seemed like a minor wrestling match with a very skinny guy. So people started experimenting with new suits of underclothing that would be more suitable to the new home improvements. The first change wasn't much of a change. It was called a nainsook and was really just a union suit with four amputated limbs. The nainsook made the wrestling match a little easier but it was still a pretty big piece of clothing.

Now enter our hero, Arthur Kneibler, sometime in the year 1934, in the little town of Kenosha, Wisconsin. At this point of his ascendancy to businesses brilliance, Kneibler was working for Coopers Incorporated, a textile and apparel factory in Kenosha. It was during a feverish effort to improve the nainsook that the idea came to him: Kneibler invented the Y-front and Jockey shorts. Coopers, and the world, have never been the same.

Kneibler has been quoted as saying in the summer of 1934, "We were experimenting with a tank suit, and our experiment had proceeded to the point . . . where the garment—brief, like a swim garment, having no belt but rather an apron [at the waist] and suspenders from there on— was being tried out on a laboratory basis in our local pools. The absence of a constricting element at the waistline was quite a big point at the outset, so we put an elastic band there because, as one dove into the water, something had to stop the water from tearing the suit apart. . . . This is the way the [Jockey short] was born."

It's interesting to note here that the birth of this revolutionary new undergarment had been spawned in the water. As indoor plumbing allowed people to wash more frequently indoors, union suits were transformed into swimming suits. In fact, Kneibler said that some of the inspiration for his invention came from a French swimming suit designed as a bikini brief. A "fig leaf," he called it, because the French model had no sides.

A local urologist from Kenosha saw in Kneibler's experiments a useful dressing for surgery patients. The doctor's medical suggestions were incorporated into the design. As the new brief took shape—including the "Lastex" band at the waist and legs and the double rib-knit Y-front— Kneibler had another vision. Men who wore these shorts were also going to need a different type of undershirt.

The old-fashioned, long-tailed undershirts wouldn't work because they protruded through the legs of a Jockey short, so Kneibler invented the modern T-shirt. This was another stupendous innovation that has left a lasting, indeed profound, mark on human society. What would "Wayne's World" be without T-shirts? Or beer commercials, or the

American barbecue, where everyone needs a funny message printed on their chest? T-shirts are about as indigenous an American article of clothing as we could imagine. They are also worn worldwide.

Kneibler would have earned a place in the history books if he had just stopped with the Y-front brief and the T-shirt, but he didn't stop there. He contributed a few other amazing innovations. By July 2, 1935, Coopers had registered the name Jockey as a trademark. Several patents were obtained, too. Then Kneibler went off to peddle this newfangled underwear to retailers. Now here comes an interesting part.

Kneibler convinced retailers to sell Jockey shorts for the astoundingly expensive price of fifty cents. This was in an era in which two people could go to dinner for nearly that amount and when other brands of men's shorts sold for much less than fifty cents. How did he do it? Before Kneibler had come along, customers usually went into a shop and told a salesclerk what they wanted. The salesclerk had to open a drawer behind the counter and take out a selection of clothing to show the customer. Kneibler said all that was a waste of time and money. Instead, he put a few pairs of shorts on a piece of cardboard, wrapped them in cellophane, and put a pile of them, with a big sign, out on a table in the middle of the store.

This was a revolution in packaging and sales. All a customer had to do—and this was unheard of before Kneibler arrived—was go to the table and pick up the shorts himself. Not only did the store save time because the clerks didn't have to run around selling the shorts—the shorts sold themselves— but the store sold more shorts because they were packaged together. Of course, today, prepackaged clothing sitting on tables in stores is maybe the most common way of shopping.

So far, our hero of modern American business, Art Kneibler, has invented the Y-front Jockey short and the all-American T-shirt, and has revolutionized shopping practices in stores. Was this enough? No, not for a business-visionary of the magnitude of Kneibler. He made darn sure the whole world knew what he was doing.

Back in 1935, there was an affiliate of the Marshall Field company in Chicago called the Davis Store. The Davis Store had big windows right on the sidewalk in downtown Chicago. Kneibler got a model named Hugh Millen to pose in the new underwear and put a great big picture of—what looked like at the time to be—a nearly naked man right in the window. The picture nearly caused a riot. In fact, the Chicago police asked the store to move the picture to a side street because the pedestrian traffic had clogged the streets and everything had ground to a halt.

The result of the Davis Store ad was an avalanche of publicity in newspapers and clothing trade journals. So many pairs of underwear were sold that retailers sat up and took notice. You see, before Kneibler, retailers sold underwear at a loss. Nobody paid attention to it. But after Kneibler, selling underwear became a gigantic industry. On March 17, 1935, the *Milwaukee Journal* ran a banner headline: Orders Swamp Kenosha Firm.

Predictably, imitators flooded the underwear market. Brief underwear suddenly appeared with names like "Sporter Shorters," and "French Snugs," and "Jim-Lastics." Obviously the imitators didn't last long. You can still buy a pair of Jockey shorts, and to be honest with you, I had to look up those other names. Richard Keehan, an associate professor of economics at the University of Wisconsin, has a pretty good history on Art Kneibler and the rise of Coopers.

Kneibler never did stop innovating, nor did he stop drumming up electrifying publicity for his innovations. In February 1938, the Retail Clothiers and Furnishers held their convention in Chicago. Lo and behold, a young couple representing Coopers came out to model some evening clothes. They were wearing cellophane from the waist down. Clearly visible through the cellophane were the woman's knickerbockers and the man's Jockey "Midways." The cellophane couple were emblazoned across the vast tracts of pulp churned out by the newspapers and even landed on the pages of an upstart picture magazine called *Life*.

A few weeks later, Hitler's minister of propaganda, the famous spin doctor Joseph Goebbels himself, violently waved the issue of *Life* magazine containing the cellophane couple as proof that America was a nest of perversion and decadence. Kneibler could hardly have hoped for better publicity. Fortunately, Goebbels went the way of French Snugs and Shorter Sporters, but it's too bad we don't hear more about Art Kneibler.

Kneibler didn't just invent something useful, he followed through with hard work. He changed the way we live (his underwear design really is more comfortable than union suits); he changed the way we look (T-shirts are one of the more notable articles of clothing of our century); and he changed the way we shop. Try to imagine a store without table-ready, prepackaged goods.

We all complain about the state of American business, but perhaps our first remedy for that complaint might be to follow some first-class examples of business excellence. If American business ever pulls itself out of the doldrums, it will be due to people who follow examples like Art Kneibler, who not only invent new things but sell them well. American businesspeople who fail to take their underwear seriously risk winding up like that mademoiselle from Armentieres. You remember her, the one who hailed from "Saint Nazaire, she never heard of underwear"? And that's the naked truth.

CHAPTER NINE

FUTURE TECH

The Bohemian Nerd

I REMEMBER TWO VERY DIFFERENT TYPES of students from when I went to school. Science and math majors were one group and art majors were the other. Science and math majors carried slide rules stuck in leather holsters on their belts. They wore glasses. They were practical. They were nerds. Art majors were very different. Their hair was different. Their clothes were different. They also had paint or clay either smeared on their cloths or imbedded in their nails. They were impractical. They were dreamers. They were Bohemians. The nerds were destined to become engineers and build practical things like homes, bridges, roads, and radios. The Bohemians were destined to create statues, and paintings, and design the interiors of homes.

I used to think there couldn't be two groups more opposite in demeanor, appearance, or in ways of thinking than math nerds and Bohemians. Well, a lot of time has passed since I was school, and these two groups have grown closer together than I ever would have dared imagine. Science and technology, and art and imagination have grown so close, in fact, that it's getting very hard to tell them apart. Children may enter kindergarten as nerds or artists, but by the time they come out the other end of a university, both types may find themselves working at the same job.

The reason, if you haven't guessed already, is that the nerds invented the computer—a contraption once described as their ultimate revenge. Today, many artists use computers; tomorrow, most will. The math nerds didn't begin by inventing computers. The first thing they invented was the electronic calculator. Calculators are not computers, but the little chip inside calculators evolved into the monster thinking-machines we can buy today.

Back in the 1960s, a hand calculator was the size of a television's remote control unit. It cost about four hundred dollars and could do little more than add, subtract, multiply, and divide. About 1970, a

Japanese calculator company went to Fairchild Semiconductor (the ancestor of today's Intel Corporation) and placed an order for twelve different calculating chips to power twelve new types of calculators they planned to bring out the next year. Fairchild took the order.

Then, one of the engineers had a brainstorm. Instead of tooling up to make twelve different chips, they could save a considerable sum of money if they only made one chip that could be programmed to do twelve different jobs. They called it a general purpose calculating chip and gave it a number; they called it the 4004. In 1972, an expanded version came out called the 8008. By 1974 the chip had become the 8080. This was the first chip that could be used for true computing. It would support a keyboard and a screen, but only the most dedicated electronic hobbyists were using the chips that way. Then came the famous 8088 [eighty-eighty-eight]. The 8088 powered the original IBM PC. The original IBM PC was slow; it had very little memory and no hard disk for mass storage. But it was a real computer.

Also about this time, a teenager in California named Steven Jobs was working for the Atari game company. Jobs and a technical pal, Steve Wozniak, came across handfuls of Motorola processing chips for free. Motorola, a latecomer to the industry, planned to seed the community with their chips to see what would happen. More gear was "borrowed" from the Atari assembly line. As a joke, Jobs and Wozniak made a machine. As a joke, they called it an apple. But it was no joke when Computerland bought one hundred Apples. Suddenly, gigantic IBM had a serious business challenge from a couple of teenagers working in a garage in California. It was the dawn of the computer era.

In addition to performing astounding feats of calculation, early PCs also ran programs to make writing easier. Writers could write, delete, and write again. They could move blocks of text backward and forward, run other programs to check spelling, and print out any number of copies of what they wrote without typing. Machines began to affect creative artists. In fact, some people noticed that poets were particularly fond of word processors because poets change what they write more than any other type of writers do.

As the years rolled by, computers received more powerful processors (processors are the chips that do all the organizing). Computers also got more memory to manipulate data, and they got larger mass-storage devices, like hard drives, to play back long strings of data. When machines crossed this threshold, they began to influence another type of artist, the musician. Suddenly, musicians were using computers with the same zeal as writers.

Computers could synchronize a musical score with action in a film. Before this trick was possible, conductors had to watch the film with a whole symphony orchestra and give the downbeat in time with what was happening in the film. Today, a musical score can be synchronized with cinema action with uncanny precision by using a computer and a digitized recording of the score. Studio musicians frequently perfect a part at home by recording it into their computer. When the piece is ready they mail a disk to the producer who does the mixing, more often than not, at home.

Computerized synthesizers have become so accurate in reproducing sounds that few people can tell the difference between natural sounds and those made by a machine. Some music producers will, frighteningly, prefer to employ machines rather than people. One rock-and-roll producer I know says he never hires drummers anymore. The computers are always on time, they never drink on the job, and they never bust up his studio with wild parties. As you may imagine, computers are causing big problems with unions.

Now, in the 1990s, computers are becoming powerful enough to take on graphic arts. Compared to writing or music, arts like painting, photography, and drawing deal with vastly greater amounts of data and require computers of exceptional processing power as well as enormous amounts of storage space in which to put all that information. These kinds of machines and the clever art programs that run on them are now becoming cheap enough so that small design companies and even individuals are buying and using them. But is it art?

This perennial question may never have been a more provocative question than it is today. There is a natural resistance to computers because they are new and require some effort to learn. Computers also do bad things, like bill people incorrectly for lots of money, or forget to pay other people at all; computers also snoop and spy on people. Like anything powerful, computers are both wonderful and dangerous. But is the wonder of a beautiful image spit out by a machine really art? Can just anyone knock out stunning works of art by merely pushing a button? Or are machines just tools that still require the skill of an artist to produce art?

Graphic design professor Michael Manwaring at the California College of Arts and Crafts, a world-famous art school, has resisted buying a computer. Manwaring told *Print* magazine, "The computer is a profound tool; one might compare it to the lever and fulcrum. And like the lever, it can be used to elevate either good works or garbage." It's also true, he says, that a medium-size graphics station will set a designer back anywhere from $5,000 to $40,000. That's some tool. But designers are buying such machines in droves. The ancient 4004 calculator chip became the 8008, then the 8080, then the 8088, then the 80286 [eighty-two-eighty-six], or 286 for short, then the 386, and then the 486. Now we have the new Pentiums. The original PC ran at 6 megahertz; the new Pentiums run at 150 megahertz. (Pentium was the first in this series to suffer a design flaw, but this is probably a minor glitch in the march of cybernetic progress.) Soon, Intel will bring out the awesome P6. And as each new chip hits the market, the older chips become cheaper. Each new advance makes graphic abilities easier and more practical.

Graphics computers store vast libraries of type fonts, relieving designers of the tedium of calligraphy. Pictures needn't be drawn anymore. Designers can scan existing art into their computer. Images from one picture can be picked up and placed seamlessly into other images. Pictures can be overlaid, made transparent, and exquisitely retouched within a matter of minutes. Three-dimensional programs allow designers to wrap flat patterns around any shape.

The ease with which designers can knock out pictures is itself a problem for traditional artists. Manwaring points out that it's so easy to produce vast amounts of artistic-looking work that "the term 'graphic designer' has been lifted from obscurity to the degree that high school counselors now recommend it as a career option, sometimes for students who had never shown any interest whatsoever in art." He says that many of today's designers "are either under- or unschooled in art and design." Despite these reasonable cautions, Manwaring says, "I do not have a computer—yet." As they become more powerful, more useful, and more affordable, computers will become necessary for all artists.

We don't have to accept machines in art merely because they are inevitable. We can accept them because they are wonderful. There is every reason to demand as fine art from machine operators as we have in the past from people who operated sable brushes or pens or rapidiographs or airbrushes. Those tools required technical expertise to utilize, too, even though we think of them today as "traditional" media. Every one of those traditional media have produced their share of truly wretched works, just as some truly wretched stuff is coming from computers.

The odd thing about this debate is that we seem to live in a new world where artists program machines and scientists play with artistic possibilities. We have math nerds discussing the nuances of "true color" images and Bohemians talking excitedly about the RISC-designed Power PC and Intel's future 786 multiprocessor CPU, which will run at several hundred megahertz, have four separate CPUs, with four megabytes of onboard cache RAM. I ask you: is the world really ready for the Bohemian Nerd?

Digital Figuring

THE HIGH-TECH CROWD may crow about their digital computers, but people have computed with digital technology for many thousands of years. In Latin, the word *digitus* means finger, and surely ice-age people counted things like bison and dogs and rabbits by sticking up one, two, or more fingers. They recorded the number of fingers, or bison, with simple scores on the wall. One finger became a vertical scratch mark carved into stone.

Ice-age people probably did not have abstract notions about counting. They just knew that this finger right here accounted for that dead bison lying over there. They knew that two fingers waved in a threatening manner at a pugnacious hunting companion meant that he'd better hand over both of those dead rabbits or risk a stone lance between the ribs. Numbers were only adjectives.

The other simple thing about numbers in the ice age was that two-fisted hunters had ten digits with which to tally the hunt. Ten fingers determined our modern decimal system, a system based on ten. Let's say that an ice-age hunter named Zork wanted to account for the day's hunt. After Zork peeled off five fingers on one hand and the five fingers on his other hand, he'd have reached ten. If he went beyond that, ten would then repeat. If Zork still had a few game hens and some squirrels left over, he'd start over with the first finger and add the new sequence to the base of ten. Zork would count "one over ten" and "two over ten."

In ancient Teutonic they would have said *ein-lifon*. *Lifon* means over in Old Teutonic, and *ein* means one. And *ein-lifon* became the English word eleven. The word twelve is the same thing. *Twe* is two in Teutonic, and *lif* is a contraction of lifon. *Twelif* became twelve, or "two over," meaning "two over ten." Twenty is *twe-tig*, or "two tens," and thirty is *thri-tig* for "three tens," and so on.

The Teutons used numbers as simple adjectives: three clubs, two young'uns, one dead bear, things like that. They did not think of numbers the way we do, as belonging to a graduating scale of abstract ideas. For us, a number is not just an adjective, it is also a very real idea. If I refer to the number three, you know what I'm talking about, even though I don't specify three-what.

That leap into the abstract was no simple feat. It also didn't happen overnight. A subtle association developed between numbers as adjectives and the marks made on stone walls used to represent the numbers themselves. Long before writing developed to represent words, graphic marks were used to record numbers. If our ice-age friend, Zork, was counting out shanks of woolly mammoth, all he would have had to do was to make a line on the wall with his stone blade. Indeed, many such marks that date well before the discovery of agriculture have been found on cave walls.

Roman numerals were merely extensions of the cave dweller's wall scratchings. A one in Roman numerals looks like a capital I. But that's not really what it came from. That I probably developed from a single upright finger. Two fingers, which were represented on prehistoric cave walls by two vertical scratches, became, in Rome, two capital Is—and three capital Is became the Roman numeral three (and four for the number four, at least in its earliest representation). The Roman numeral five looks like a capital V, because a capital V is a picture of all five fingers of the human hand. The V emphasizes the web of the thumb.

Eventually someone stumbled on the idea that the position of a character could signify a number. Instead of making four strokes to write the number four, a single stroke followed by a V indicated one-less-than-five. So, too, with Roman numeral nine, which was once written as a V followed by four Is. Position eventually allowed ten characters to represent any number. But before the zero allowed that to happen, the Romans tried out many different characters. The Roman numeral for one hundred, for example, was originally written the way we write a modern bracket: a short horizontal stroke on top, a perpendicular line descending along the left-hand side, and then another short horizontal line at the bottom. Over time, this angular, bracket shape became more cursive and soon looked just like a capital C. But the Roman numeral for one hundred did not begin as a letter C; it probably began as a bracket, because a bracket is easy to chisel into stone. The number fifty, which today we know as the letter L, wasn't really an L at all—it was just a bracket without the top stroke.

Obviously, the big problem inherent in these Roman digital calculations was that they had no character with which to represent zero. There was no way to represent an "emptiness" of fingers. The world is indebted to Hindu mathematicians for creating a representation for emptiness. Surely, everyone knows by now that our so-called Arabic numerals are not Arabic at all; they are Indian numerals that were transmitted to Europe by Arabs. Modern numbers, and especially the idea of zero, came from India.

The English word *cipher* (which means zero) comes from the Arabic word *sifir*, which in turn was an approximation of the Sanskrit word *sunya*. *Sunya* means empty or void. The Italians translated *sifir* as *zepiro*, which passed into English as, you guessed it, zero.

One of the more interesting and fruitful potentials with the introduction of nothing is that we only need to pair the zero with the number one in order to represent all other numbers. The entire digital revolution has been made possible because of binary math—in other words, a numeral system founded on a base of two, not ten. Binary counting uses a zero and a one, and that's all. There is a something, and there is a nothing.

Obviously, the binary system is uniquely suited to computers because computers are made up of simple electronic switches, and a switch can do only two things: it can be on or it can be off. A switch in any other position is assumed to be broken. This is pretty much what our ice-age friend Mr. Zork did with his fingers. A finger is either counting or it isn't counting. Of course, if Zork weren't using his finger to count, he wouldn't understand it as a zero; he would just ignore it. But the principle of a finger being either up or down is the same as a switch being on or off.

Computer terminology recognizes the condition of a switch as a special type of finger called a binary digit. A single switch in a computer is called a bit, and the word bit is a contraction of two words: binary and digit. But here, with the bit—the computer finger—we are as different from an individual like Zork as Zork was different from one of his intestinal bacteria. One difference is that computer fingers provide us with many more fingers to count on. Zork could not have laid his hands on so many fingers, even if he could have tweaked all the fingers and all the toes of all the people he had ever seen in his entire, little troglodytic life. You may wonder, why? Why do any of us need so much computational power? Some people claim they are satisfied by counting two squirrels, one dead bear, and a couple of strangled game hens. This may be all the computing power you think you need. But chances are that you also use a telephone or watch television or listen to the radio. Vast computing power will enhance all of these media and will actually create whole new ways of communicating that, as yet, no one has even dreamed of.

More powerful computer chips will enhance television so that hard news and dramatic art will appear much sharper and provide a wealth of detail previously available only with fine photography. More powerful computer chips will make voice recognition common. Notes, diaries, books, and other thoughts can be, and will be, dictated to machines as if to living beings. Disabled people will acquire new abilities. The environment could be saved. The possibilities seem endless, and so, too, do the promises for this new technology.

Vast computational power holds the promise to return our planet to a simple, clean garden. We might one day be able to leave the filth and confusion of urban sprawl behind us and return to pristine forests and woody glens. Our foods, we are told, will be improved natural grains and meats, unsullied by antibiotics, pesticides, or other unpredictable chemicals. And there, in a new home, perhaps under a magnificent rock outcropping, I think I'll score a mark on the wall—a vertical line representing an upraised finger to remember that this day is the first day of digital heaven.

Interactive Television and the Illustrated Story

HIGH-TECH COMPANIES are rushing into a brave new technology called interactive TV. A full-length feature film, say about seventy-two minutes' worth, can now be placed onto a five-inch compact disc. Merely playing a movie and watching it would be one thing, but this new technology goes beyond the capabilities of simple playback. Stories in the future will be told in ways that permit the audience to determine the outcome. For thousands of years the storyteller has determined how a story unfolds, but soon we will see a radical change in the way books, movies, and musical performances are presented. The audience is moving onstage.

Movies undoubtedly will come with multiple endings. Many movies are made with multiple endings anyway but are released to the public with only one ending. Compact disc technology and computer power will allow you, the viewer, to decide if the girl gets the guy or if the guy gets the girl or if the bad guy wins or loses.

But interactive technology implies much more than just substituting one ending of a movie for another. The characters in the film could, theoretically, be replaced with other figures. It is not impossible to imagine that you could load three photographs of yourself into the computer system: two profiles and a head shot. The computer could use these images to replace the head of Humphrey Bogart with your head, in, let's say, *Casablanca*. And there you are, looking deep into the languid eyes of Ingrid Bergman. Conversely, depending on your gender, or proclivities, you might rather replace the head of Ingrid Bergman with your own and see yourself looking deep into the eyes of Humphrey Bogart. That, too, could be arranged.

The face of any movie character could be potentially remapped with faces of friends or foes or relatives or coworkers or famous political figures or your favorite athlete—anyone. You could replace the head of Arnold Schwarzenegger in the original *Terminator* with the head of your boss and watch power and authority disintegrate into mineral rubbish on your very own television set.

It should be a relatively easy task, technically speaking, to replace voices, too. A brief clip of your boss's voice, purloined perhaps from an answering machine tape, might allow his mellifluous tones to be overlaid onto Schwarzenegger's booming Germanic burr. The Terminator's memorable line, "I'll be back!" could resound in your living room as never before, a robotic death machine wrapped in the familiar admonitions you hear at work. The triumph felt at the end of the movie when the Terminator is destroyed would be profound and cathartic.

Indeed, why stop at mere entertainment? It's not too extreme to imagine that films of the future could evolve into a uniquely fluid medium with few specifics and an infinite potential—a proto-story that lets the audience play at being everyone: the writer, producer, director, and even actor. The computer could provide us with an infinitely malleable story (a narrative putty) into which we, the audience, could impress our deepest thoughts and desires.

With this malleable wonder, we might replay events in our lives in order to perceive them differently. Interactivity with the emotional world would transform the movie into a valuable therapeutic tool. Films today may be regarded as anything from simple amusement to high-minded art. But in the future, movies could be understood as pivotal events—edifying moments capable of altering the course of a human life. A realistic meeting with a departed parent or spouse could allow the forlorn to resolve a relationship that was left hanging. Adults who failed as children could be re-educated to see themselves as winners and leaders. All of these psychological transformations would carry the authority of "seeing is believing"—a fundamental, indisputable truth.

Electronic designers are also forging direct links between the computer and the senses. Virtual reality melds sight, sound, and feeling into a single, integrated experience that makes an artificial reality appear to be overwhelmingly convincing. Reliving particular lessons one learned in life or learning new lessons could be tremendously effective because intuition would appear as inner illumination.

Computer technology still has a long way to go before the illustrative narrative becomes infinitely malleable, but the crucial ingredients—greater processing power, more and faster memory, and the all-important software to do it—will all arrive, given enough time.

Now if this is a view of the future of the performing narrative, it might be useful to consider its past. The fully interactive, digital-computerized, feature-length motion picture has precedents that reach far back in time. Before there were movies there were still photographs. Before still photographs there were paintings done by hand. People have used many types of graphic representation to illustrate narrative tales, and storytellers have surely been around since the time language itself began.

Professor Victor Mair of the University of Pennsylvania's Department of Oriental Studies has traced a fascinating tradition that combines painted images with song. Mair draws our attention first to a group of painted scrolls discovered in the caves of Tun-huang in the western China desert. These particular scrolls, called Pien-wen, or "transformation texts," play an important role in Chinese literature. They are, he says, the first "extended vernacular narratives in China."

Mair's study reveals that Chinese storytellers used these pictures more than a thousand years ago to help illustrate street performances. Some of these pictures contain a series of panels that unfold the narrative sequentially. Others are long scrolls, which when unrolled reveal the narrative in a continuous succession. Mair discovered that the storytellers' art used a combination of song and prose, perhaps even dance, to animate the illustrated paintings. He further discovered that this tradition has spread over an enormous area of the planet and that it had originated in India.

Ancient Indian literature makes numerous references to itinerant storytellers who made their living telling tales in front of paintings. Some mendicants wandered from door to door, carrying religious images and, for a penny, recounted the heroic deeds of their depicted divinity. Even the Buddha refers to these storytellers to provide an example of how the mind works.

The Buddha asks a group of monks if they have ever seen a picture they call a "showpiece." When the monks nod and say that they have, the Buddha goes on to explain that the illusion created by the story-teller's art and the painter's art is in reality created by the mind and not by storytellers or painters. This exchange took place half a millennium before the Christian era. Today, almost three thousand years later, and all over modern India, travelers can still find street musicians singing in front of paintings that illustrate the epic adventures of this or that god or hero.

So, too, in Indonesia, where we find the so-called shadow plays, or *wayang*. Large paintings depicting various stories are used as backdrops to illustrate performances by dolls, puppets, and cutout figures that cast shadows on a wall. Musicians provide the audio portion of these performances, and the magic happens when the audience puts painting and song and shadow together into one seamless experience.

In the streets of Iran can be found the *parda-dar*. Raconteurs sing in front of cloth murals about the martyrdom of the Islamic saint Hussein. Farther west, in Lebanon, Syria, and Israel, itinerant storytellers once wandered about with large boxes strapped to their backs. The boxes, called "wonder boxes," had six holes with magnifying glasses stuck in them. For a price, the audience would peek inside at candle-illuminated pictures of people who were either in the news of the day or who figured prominently in ancient myth.

In Italy, street musicians called *cantastorie* were once common. These famous storytellers still exist. *Cantastorie* play guitars and sing in front of cloth paintings that depict everyone from the Madonna (that is, the original one) to popular popes.

Mair chronicles this amazing development in his book *Painting and Performance*. In it, we find singers performing in front of paintings in Germany and in Japan, in Tibet and in England. These folk balladeers recount the heroic events of many protagonists. For a penny or two, they warned passersby of the torments of the afterlife and of its possible rewards.

Eventually, according to Mair, paintings and performance evolved into a particular type of folk theater. Surely the most famous is Bertolt Brecht's *Three Penny Opera*. Brecht borrowed the plot for his play from eighteenth-century wit John Gay, but he presented it in a unique and familiar package. A street singer narrates the entire play in front of still life tableaux, in which other actors stand frozen like figures in a painting. Brecht's innovation was to have these other actors come to life, step off their tableaux, and sing and speak for themselves.

Brecht's *Three Penny Opera* is an operatic elaboration and parody of the "Moritat von Mackie Messer." "Mackie Messer," or Mack the Knife, is a famous German bankelsanger, or painting performance—a performance with roots in ancient India.

For a few thousand years, stories were illustrated by paintings and animated by street singers. Then Brecht brought the paintings to life using singers. Motion pictures introduced a whole new way of animating illustrations and of telling a story. But tomorrow, computers and interactive technology will grab the audience and draw them directly onstage and put them in charge of the action.

Interactivity may seem marvelous, but despite all its bells and whistles, it will still obey a fundamental law of nature once observed by Indian wise men. The illusion that results by combining the storyteller's art and the painter's art is in reality created by the mind, not by the storyteller or painter. The computer wizard and the filmmaker will do nothing to change that.

Acknowledgments

THE COLLABORATION BETWEEN my son and me came about as something of a rescue operation. I had undertaken to do a rather lengthy weekly radio piece for ABC's radio broadcast *Perspective*, and found after a short time that (1) good ideas didn't come to me as frequently as I'd hoped, and (2) when they did come, I didn't have time to develop them properly. This resulted in some highly subjective and introspective essays produced wholly out of my head. While some of these were interesting, it didn't take long to empty my reservoir of ideas suitable for radio commentaries. After six months, the struggle had become a strain, and after a year I sought help.

There was a problem, however. I discovered that nobody could write for me. Even skilled writers could not really relieve me of the chore of making the wording mine, particularly in cases where attitude, style, personal philosophy, or feelings were involved. I found I had to rewrite their work so extensively that I was better off starting from scratch.

Then along came my son, H. R., with the almost casual suggestion that we transform our frequent at-length conversations about everything under the sun into some of these radio commentaries. He would do some of the writing and give me a breather.

We tried. Maybe it shouldn't have surprised either of us, but for the first time I had found someone whose outlook and general mode of expression was so congruent, so compatible with mine, that I could use his pieces almost without revision. They spoke from my heart, and they didn't collide with my brain. At the same time they broadened my outlook and pushed my ability to articulate a notch higher. In short, our collaborative pieces said what I felt with more clarity and courage than I could have achieved alone. This collection, *Perspectives*, is our unique collaboration.

Curiously, father and son are not alike. H. R.'s method of dealing with the world is highly subjective and individualistic. He is a gifted painter and photographer. I am color-blind. He has learned several languages. I speak English and only a few words in other tongues. Over this past decade we have grown together in technique and together have expanded and deepened our personal views of this awesome, fascinating, and even amusing cosmos. The selections in this book are representative of those views, shared and presented by Hugh M. and Hugh R. Downs.

Our thanks go out to several people who helped bring these spoken essays to book form. Our good friend Rob Sunde, who for years was the executive producer of *Perspective* at ABC News and who has provided script selection and judicious editing. Thanks also to our agent David Chalfant at TCA, who championed the manuscript. And thanks also to Kevin Mulroy and Katherine Buttler, our editors at Turner Publishing, and Craig Comstock, who gave us valuable editorial advice when the book was in its early stages.

Hugh M. Downs
New York, 1995